EMBASSY
TO THE
EASTERN COURTS

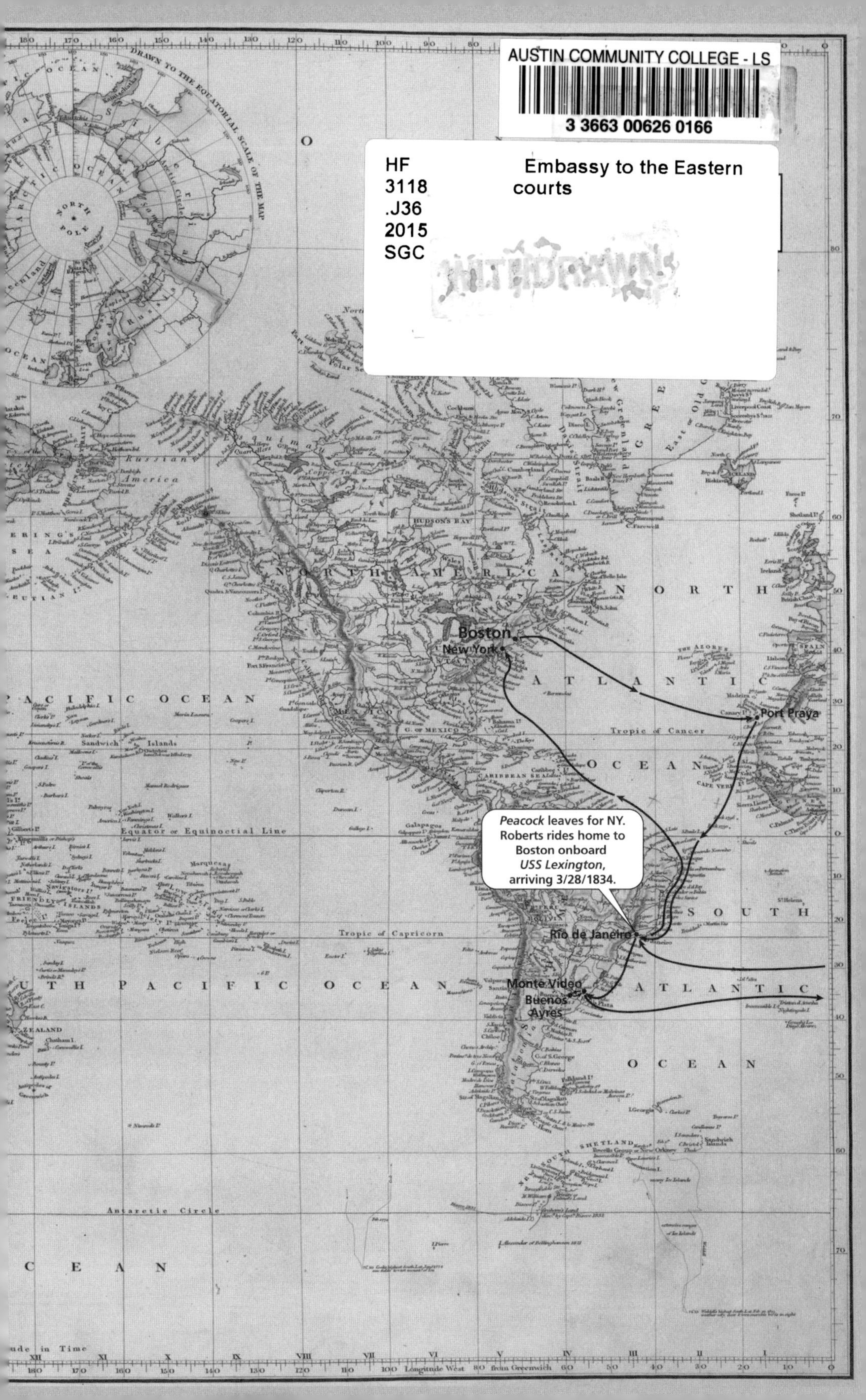
Boston
New York
Port Praya
Peacock leaves for NY. Roberts rides home to Boston onboard USS Lexington, arriving 3/28/1834.
Rio de Janeiro
Monte Video
Buenos Ayres
NORTH AMERICA
PACIFIC OCEAN
ATLANTIC OCEAN
SOUTH ATLANTIC OCEAN
SOUTH PACIFIC OCEAN
Tropic of Cancer
Tropic of Capricorn
Antarctic Circle
Equator or Equinoctial Line
Longitude West from Greenwich

EMBASSY TO THE EASTERN COURTS

AMERICA'S SECRET FIRST PIVOT TOWARD ASIA
1832–37

ANDREW C. A. JAMPOLER

NAVAL INSTITUTE PRESS
Annapolis, Maryland

Naval Institute Press
291 Wood Road
Annapolis, MD 21402

ISBN: 978-1-61251-416-1
ISBN: 978-1-61251-417-8 (eBook)

Library of Congress Cataloging-in-Publication Data is available.

♾ Print editions meet the requirements of ANSI/NISO z39.48-1992 (Permanence of Paper).
Printed in the United States of America.
23 22 21 20 19 18 17 16 15 9 8 7 6 5 4 3 2 1
First printing

Book design and composition: Alcorn Publication Design

ABOUT THE COVER

Detail from *A View of the European Factories at Canton* by William Daniell, showing the Canton waterfront on the Pearl River approaching the end of the eighteenth century.

Canton's foreign factories stood in an approximately five-acre rectangular precinct separate from the Chinese port city, isolation intended to keep their part-time residents away from the life of the city and the empire beyond. The factories' merchants—the factors and their clerks, and supercargoes off visiting ships, all men—were permitted to live there only from September through March, during the northeast monsoon; Western women (as well as "great guns and other military weapons") were prohibited in Canton anytime. The rest of the year foreigners relocated to Macao. There, in its hot-house society, they had little of substance to do but await the arrival of ships on the southwest monsoon and the start of the next trading season upriver.

The American factory, the "Factory of Wide Fountains," the sole site at which U.S. trade was permitted by China until after the First Opium War and the Treaty of Wangxia (1844), is last on the left down the long line of flag-fronted buildings in the hazy background. It stood off Old China Street, in between the Dutch, British, and Swedish factories and the unseen French, Spanish, and Danish factories at the far end of the row. None of these thirteen buildings has survived to today.

This oil painting was the second of two William Daniell did of these warehouse, office, and residence blocks. The first omitted the American factory, probably dating its reference drawing to a visit to China in 1785, rather than to a second visit in 1793–94 that was the likely basis for this work.

"A true Chinese junk is a great curiosity," Edmund Roberts wrote in his book *Embassy to the Eastern Courts*. "The model must have been taken originally from a bread-trough, being broad and square at both ends—when light, (I speak of a large one) it is fully thirty feet from the surface of the water to the . . . highest part of the poop. . . . They are generally painted white and red, perhaps blue, and the two enormous eyes of vigilance are ever to be seen on each bow. On the stern all the art of the painter is exhausted by a profusion of meretricious ornaments—an eagle, or what is intended for one, occupies the centre of the stern."

In Daniell's own explicatory notes, the big ships were described as "ill-adapted" to long voyages and "unable to contend with the tremendous gales of the Chinese seas," where 10,000 seamen were said to be lost annually. He was wrong. In the early fifteenth century, fleets of giant, nine-masted Chinese junks under the command of Admiral Zheng He sailed from Nanjing across blue water as far west as Hormuz, Jeddah, and Mombasa. Mysteriously, the seventh expedition, in 1433, was the last, after which the Chinese empire turned resolutely inward.

Daniell (1769–1837) is best known for two collections of hand-colored aquatints done together with his uncle, Thomas (1749–1840). *Oriental Scenery* was published in six volumes between 1795 and 1815 and based on nine years of travel in India. *A Picturesque Voyage to India by Way of China* was published in 1810. The Daniells prospered as a result of British fascination with the exotic and mysterious Orient, knowable then to most people only through such illustrations. Both Daniells were members of the Royal Academy of Arts and saw their works exhibited at the Royal Academy and the British Institution.

The invention of photography in 1839, and the rapid development of more or less portable equipment, meant that by midcentury Western ideas about distant and exotic places began to be informed not only by fine art, such as lithographs of scenes of Bombay like those by Goa's Jose Gonsalves or of the Levant by Scottish artist David Roberts (1796–1864) or those by Fredrick Catherwood (1799–1854) of Central America, but also by more literal images from the cameras of such pioneers of photography in the field as Captain Linnaeus Tripe (1822–1902). Tripe, an officer in the Madras Infantry, was English, as was Catherwood.

CONTENTS

ILLUSTRATIONS

Cover image: *A View of the European Factories at Canton*
End pages: The first and second cruises of the sloop of war USS *Peacock* with Edmund Roberts on board. Maps by Christopher Robinson. Base maps by J. Arrowsmith, "The World on Mercator's Projection," 1835.

FIGURES

MAPS

CHARTS

ACKNOWLEDGMENTS

The Internet might yet accomplish what the ancient library in Alexandria, Egypt, started out to do at the beginning of the third century BC—to amass the learning of mankind in a single place accessible to scholars. Two sites on today's Web, representative of many others I've used in my research, and the best of them, merit my special appreciation: those of the Hathi Trust Digital Library and the David Rumsey Historical Map Collection.

I appreciate the generous assistance of the following persons, all of whom helped me understand the story I am telling you: Nick Aretakis and Bill Reese (William Reese Company, New Haven, Connecticut), William Hubbard (Old Colony Historical Society, Taunton, Massachusetts), Kevin Brown (Geographicus Rare Antique Maps, New York City), Dean Cycon (Orange, Massachusetts), Bill Earle (editor, *Niles' Register*), Martha Elmore (Joyner Library, East Carolina University), Aya Eto (Mariners' Museum Library, Newport News, Virginia), Mike Klein (senior cartographic librarian, Library of Congress), Luis Lopes (Macao Central Library), Rebecca Livingston (Silver Spring, Maryland), Carolyn Marvin (Athenaeum, Portsmouth, New Hampshire), Abbot Daiei Matsui (Ryosenji Treasure Museum, Shimoda, Japan), Otto Mayr (Ashburn, Virginia), Mark Mollan (Navy and maritime archivist, National Archives and Records Administration), Sandra Rux (John Paul Jones House Museum, Portsmouth, New Hampshire), Terence Tai (Macao Polytechnic Institute Library), Damon Talbot (Maryland Historical Society, Baltimore), Sabina Beauchard (Massachusetts Historical Society, Boston), and Barbara Valentine Dodd (Hastings, England).

I'm especially grateful for the special assistance of several others: Ed Caylor, of Portsmouth, New Hampshire, a hero of my first book, *Adak*, was together with his wife, Janet, my host and guide to his and Edmund Roberts' hometown. Samiya Allan, who took the time in 2013 to introduce two strangers, my wife and me, to historic Portuguese Macao, resting sedately alongside the twitchy, modern city. Bill Dudley, Director of Naval History emeritus and author of half a dozen published works on maritime history, generously turned away from other things to read and comment on this story in draft, as did André Sobocinski, a historian in the Office of Medical History of the U.S. Navy's Bureau of Medicine and Surgery, Betty Jean Lofland, formerly of the University of Macao, and Mike Pestorius, a shipmate from long ago. Also Karin Kaufman, of Loveland, Colorado, who ably edited this book, as she has my others.

Finally, Suzy, now my wife of fifty years, gracefully accepted my being consumed by yet another book and prepared the digital versions of all the maps, charts, and illustrations that illuminate this story. My thanks to her for this and for everything else.

Andrew C. A. Jampoler
Leesburg, Virginia

Prologue

The 1830s

1830. In midyear, the Twenty-first Congress passes S. 102, the Indian Removal Act, easily in the Senate (28 to 19) but narrowly in the House of Representatives (101 yeas, 97 nays, and 11 abstentions). President Andrew Jackson happily signs the act into law on May 28, legalizing the eviction of five "civilized" Native American tribes (the Cherokees, Choctaws, Chickasaws, Creeks, and Seminoles) and others from what is fast becoming the Plantation South and their displacement "to an ample district west of the Mississippi" River.

1831. Charles Darwin sails in late December from Plymouth, England, on board the bark HMS *Beagle*, 6 guns, departing on a nearly five-year, around the world hydrographic survey that will coincidently provide the fodder for his theory of evolution by natural selection. *Beagle*, under the command of Lieutenant Robert Fitzroy, RN, will sail 40,000 miles during this, her historic second cruise. Darwin's profound insights about evolution and how it works deeply disturb the fundamentalist Fitzroy (1805–1865), who will in later years be credited with the invention of the weather forecast.

1832. Despite quarantines imposed the previous winter, epidemic cholera appears for the first time in the United States in early June, traveling by water, as did almost everything else in that century, and visiting diarrhea, cramps, and vomiting on its dehydrated, cyanotic victims before killing as many as half of them. President Jackson refuses to proclaim a national day of fasting and humiliation that evangelicals, and his political opponents during this election year, hope will deflect the wrath of God and relieve the scourge of a disease that after appearing first in Canada will spread in 1832–33 everywhere east of the Mississippi. Ultimately thousands of Americans will die during this first cholera eruption in North America.

1833. During nine months of 1833, the peak year for this traffic, twenty-eight transport ships sail from ports in Great Britain to the convict colonies in New South Wales and on Van Diemen's Land. The movement of these unfortunates halfway around the world has been perfected since the ten transports of the First and Second Fleets sailed in 1788–90 and saw one-quarter of their convicts die in transit and many more on disembarkation. During the same year, Parliament in London passes an act abolishing slavery in the British West Indies, Canada, and the Cape of Good Hope. It remains lawful elsewhere in the empire.

1834. Cyrus McCormick obtains a patent on his horse-drawn mechanical reaper. The invention is guaranteed capable of cutting, threshing, and bundling fifteen acres of grain per day, ten times what a team of men can do by hand, revolutionizing American agriculture and foreshadowing an era to come in the next century of plentiful foodstuffs and low farm employment. Further mechanization will powerfully stimulate farm production, but an arguably greater contribution to food stocks during this century will be guano, bird manure, a natural fertilizer hauled everywhere by ship.

1835. Alexis de Tocqueville publishes the first volume of his *Democracy in America*, based on the ten months he and a colleague spent in the United States between May 1831 and February 1832, ostensibly studying the American prison system. De Tocqueville's political and anthropological study will inform foreigners about the novel American government and nation and appear on university reading lists for decades to come.

1836. In March former sophomore at Harvard Richard Henry Dana (1815–1882) disembarks in Boston from the East Indiaman *Alert* after two years spent as a deckhand in the hide and tallow trade, mostly serving on board the brig *Pilgrim*. Dana's diary, published by Harper and Brothers in 1840 as *Two Years Before the Mast*, immediately becomes a best-selling story of life at sea. The next year the second and last of lawyer Dana's maritime books drawing on his experience, *The Seaman's Friend: A Treatise on Practical Seamanship*, is published in Boston.

1837. Martin Van Buren, Jackson's vice president, is inaugurated in March, weeks before the eruption of a financial panic and economic depression that will make his one of the few single-term presidencies in U.S. history. From his estate in New York, Van Buren will twice try unsuccessfully to regain office.

1838. USS *Vincennes*, in company with five other ships of the United States Exploring Expedition and under the command of the mercurial Lt. Charles Wilkes, USN, sails in August from the Norfolk Navy Yard, beginning a four-year voyage to the Pacific Ocean and around the world that will span 87,000 miles. Only two of the original six ships will return to home port. USS *Peacock* will be one of those lost. Sadly, the expedition's arrival in New York in mid-1842, carrying superb new charts and thousands of artifacts and specimens collected during its survey of distant waters, will be tarnished by a flurry of courts-martial.

1839. Following up on the 1835 occupation of Socotra Island, off the entrance to the Red Sea and intended for a time as the site of a coaling station, the Honourable East India Company's government in Bombay launches the seizure of Aden. By the end of this decade the British Empire will include colonies on five continents and hold commanding positions at both the east and west entrances to the Indian Ocean.

1840. The American presidential election of 1840 sees the Whig's candidate, William Henry Harrison, easily defeat Democratic incumbent Van Buren, who cannot shake the effects of the Panic of 1837 and manages to lose even his home state, New York, to the challenger. Harrison dies a month after his inauguration, leading to the lackluster administration of his former vice president, John Tyler, earlier governor of and senator from Virginia.

1

THE FIRST CRUISE, MARCH 8, 1832–MAY 31, 1834

USS *Peacock* and USS *Boxer*

1

President Jackson, Secretary Woodbury, and Mister Roberts

> The President having named you his agent for the purpose of examining in the Indian Ocean, the means of extending the commerce of the United States by commercial arrangement with the powers whose dominions border on these seas, you will embark on board of the United States sloop of war, the *Peacock*, in which vessel (for the purpose of concealing your uniform from powers whose interest might be to thwart the objects the President has in view) you will be rated as Captain's Clerk. . . . You will be furnished with a power to conclude a treaty if one can be obtained.
>
> SECRETARY OF STATE EDWARD LIVINGSTON TO EDMUND ROBERTS, JANUARY 27, 1832

1

The body of Edmund Quincy Roberts (1784–1836), of Portsmouth, New Hampshire, lies in a corner of the Honourable East India Company's Protestant and Old Church Graveyard in Macao, in the nineteenth century a tiny (barely five square mile) European outpost below the mouth of China's Pearl River, sixty-five miles downstream from Canton and some forty miles west of Hong Kong across the river's broad mouth.

The existence of a Protestant graveyard at Macao, open only from 1821 to 1858, was a concession to other foreigners by Portuguese Catholic expatriates, who had in the mid-sixteenth century established what soon grew into the sole commercial gateway to China at Canton. Until 1821 such burials had been prohibited on both sides of the wall separating peninsular Macao from the Chinese mainland, forcing at first all manner of ghoulish subterfuges to inter deceased Protestants.* It's not clear why the concession was granted, but some surmise that certain senior Portuguese officials trading in opium (among them Macao's chief magistrate, Miguel de Arriaga, in the colony from 1802

* Up the Pearl River, on Danes Island and French Island, on Lintin, Capsingmoon, and Cumsingmoon Islands, and also at Whampoa, there were no enclosed, consecrated graveyards. There the many foreign dead were interred simply in small plots, most of which have long since been forgotten and lost.

Macao's Protestant and Old Church Graveyard, now the Morrison Chapel Cemetery, and Edmund Roberts' grave. The Morrison Chapel honors the memory of Reverend Robert Morrison (1782–1834), translator of the Bible into Chinese. Sent to China by the London Missionary Society in 1807, Morrison spent the last twenty-seven years of his life there, excepting a single trip home, most as an interpreter for the East India Company. In June 1821 Morrison buried first wife, Mary, at Macao—perhaps her death and their popularity persuaded the reluctant Portuguese finally to sell a plot of land to the East India Company for a Protestant graveyard. In August 1834 Morrison joined her and their infant son, and nine years later the Morrison's adult son, John, was interred beside them. John, who'd interpreted for Edmund Roberts during the Indochina portion of his first embassy, died in

until his death in 1824), resolved big debts to the British East India Company through this favor granted in violation of local and church law.[1]

In addition to housing Edmund Roberts' remains, the graveyard at Macao is the final home of 159 other foreigners, among them the usual sprinkling of nineteenth-century traders and missionaries, their wives and children, and the officers and enlisted sailors of several navies. The dead include Ann Crockett, aged twenty-one days, the daughter of the master of Dent and Company's opium stores ship *Jane*, John Crockett, who is interred not far away from his tiny child. Another of the dead is Winston Churchill's great granduncle, at his death captain of HMS *Druid*. Yet another is Lt. Joseph Harrod Adams, USN (1817–1853), late of Commo. Matthew Perry's East Indies Squadron flagship, the steam frigate USS *Powhatan*, and the grandson of the first President Adams and nephew of the second. George Washington's godson, George Washington Biddle, lies there too, as supposedly do the grandson of another American president and the grandfather of a fourth president.[2]

1843 at age twenty-nine, soon after he was appointed Hong Kong's first colonial secretary. The four Morrisons lie not far from Roberts.

The patched stone slab on top of Roberts' grave in the site's Lower Terrace has been badly cracked for many decades. Below a text describing him as the "Special Diplomatic Agent of the United States to several Asiatic Courts," it's still possible to make out an oddly legalistic epitaph: "He devised and executed for their law under instructions from his Government treaties of amity and commerce between the Unites States and the Courts of Muscat and Siam." Credited with this achievement, Roberts enjoys posthumously the special distinction of being described as "historically the most important American buried in the cemetery" (Ride, *East India Company Cemetery*, 168).

PHOTOGRAPHS COURTESY OF PIA ALLAN, 2012

Citizens of five European countries quietly share space in the cemetery, reflecting the fact that by the early nineteenth century Western countries were well represented in Macao, where their citizens lived and died in what was for some two hundred years the vestibule of global trade with China. More than fifty, over one-third, of the dead are Americans, evidence of the large part they and their countrymen played in early Western trade with the Orient.

The British were late to come to China, spilling over to there from India, behind the Portuguese and the Dutch, but by the 1830s, largely through the vehicle of the Honourable East India Company, they had long since supplanted Portugal as the principal trader and chief foreign influence in Macao—and everywhere else along the Chinese coast where Western vessels touched in violation of Chinese law. Long before then the Dutch had quickly and easily chased the Portuguese out of much of what had been the Portuguese Estado da India and built their own fabulously prosperous Asian

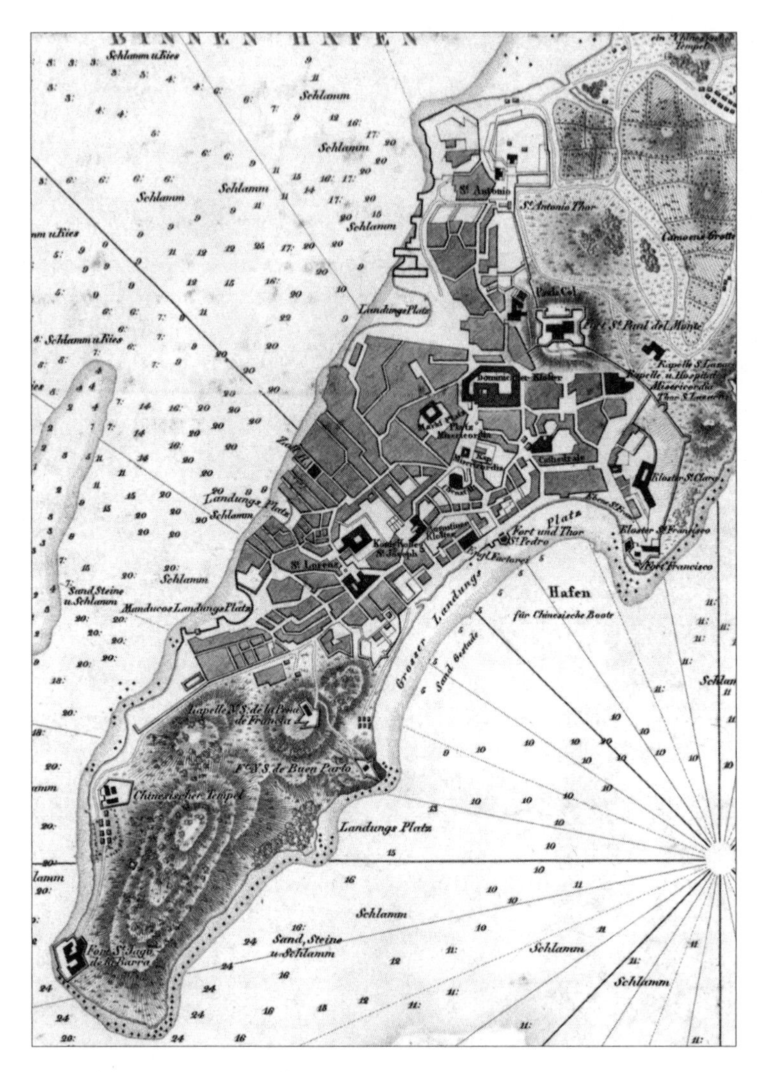

Chart 1. Detail from Macao inset from "German Coastal Chart, 1834." Macao's Protestant and Old Church Graveyard, off the southern end of Camoens Grotto, lies unmarked just west of the hilly ground above the center of this detail from the parent chart, "Die Chinesische Küste: Der Provinz Kuang-tung, zu beiden Seiten des Meridians von Macao." "Der Provinz Kuang-tung" was prepared by the eminent German geographer Heinrich Berghaus for his *Atlas von Asia* and covered the part of the southern Chinese coast that encompasses Canton, Macao, and Hong Kong. Berghaus' interest in this geography was largely academic; although there was a Royal Prussian Asiatic Company, it went out of business around the middle of the eighteenth century.

Heinrich Berghaus (1797–1884), trained as a surveyor and cartographer, is best known for his pioneering two-volume 1848 *Physikalischer Atlas* (*Physical Atlas*) of worldwide thematic maps, which included among other things the earliest known world map of human disease distribution.

Berghaus, *Atlas von Asia*, 1834, Library of Congress G7822.P4 1834.B4.

An Unusual View of the Praya Grande Macao, ca. 1830. Oil on canvas, unknown artist. Pena Hill, surmounted by a flagpole, is at the left. On the other headlands above the great arc of the shoreline's shallows lie Forts Monte (center right, commanding practically the whole peninsula) and Guia (far right, on the highest hilltop), both originally built by the Portuguese for the seaward defense of the town and its strategic anchorage from the Dutch, powerful commercial competitors against the Portuguese through the seventeenth century.
Roberts was evidently charmed when he first saw the place after nine months at sea. "Macao presents," he wrote in the posthumously published book about his mission, "a pretty appearance from the roadstead. A spacious, semi-circular bay is encompassed with hills, crowned with forts, convents, churches, and private buildings: the houses being kept well whitewashed, it gives the town quite a neat appearance." He went on to report dryly that "it is reputed to be one of the most immoral places in the world." Near the time of Roberts visit, Macao's population was estimated at some thirty-five thousand, thirty thousand of them Chinese.
Courtesy of the Peabody Essex Museum, M9751.1

empire centered (after 1619) at Batavia and based on cloves, nutmeg, mace, and cinnamon.*

The process through which the Portuguese were supplanted by the British on the mainland had been marked approaching its end by two frustrating setbacks for London and one enormous, vile triumph. The former were diplomatic, the latter commercial. The setbacks were two fruitless attempts to negotiate commercial treaties with China. Both Lord George Macartney's 1793 mission to Peking and Lord William Amherst's follow-on mission in

* The East India Company then lost its government monopoly in April 1834, when its powers and perquisites in China were largely taken over by privately owned companies that had developed the coasting trade in opium during the years immediately prior.

1816 failed entirely to establish an embassy in the Chinese capital, to open access more generally to the mainland, or to manage trade and bilateral relations following a recognizably Western model. The success was the British domination in the nineteenth century of fabulously profitable trade with China on the basis of smuggled sales of huge amounts of Indian-grown opium in exchange for tea, silks, and Oriental "preciosities."

2

Ten years before the United States had a minister (ambassador) in China, and twenty before Commo. Matthew Perry, USN, sailed across the Pacific at the head of his squadron to pry open Japan to Western trade and influence, Roberts left the United States in USS *Peacock* on a secret mission that, through the good offices of his friend and kinsman by marriage, Secretary of the Navy Levi Woodbury, he had persuaded President Andrew Jackson and Secretary of State Edward Livingston to adopt: the formalization of American trade on a most favored nation basis with Cochin China, Siam, and "the powers of Arabia on the Red Sea."[3]

Roberts' true status on board *Peacock* was being concealed to keep the purposes of his mission secret from the British, whose pressures on distant countries to ease trade restrictions in their favor already had a long history when the U.S. Navy sloop of war carrying Roberts stood out to sea in early March 1832. "Every movement of mine," Roberts had written, sounding prideful to a daughter before he sailed, "and the office I hold, is to be kept a profound secret, at least until my return, on account of its getting to the ears of the British government, who would assuredly thwart me, if possible."

A six-week-old letter from Secretary Livingston to Roberts had made the New Hampshire merchant's mission clear. After an introduction (quoted in the chapter epigraph), Livingston detailed in long, run-on sentences what the administration expected from their newly appointed commissioner in Cochin China and also in Siam and Arabia:

> You will in your passage to this place, inform yourself minutely of the trade carried on between the kingdom and the countries—the nature of products of the country, whether natural, agricultural, or manufactured—the maritime and military strength, and the articles of merchandise of personal consumption or demanded for their own commerce with other nations of the favors granted to or exactions made upon the commerce of the various nations who trade with them.

On your arrival you will present yourself to the King with your power and the letter addressed to him. You will state that the president having heard of his fame for justice and the desire to improve advantages of commerce for the good of his people has sent you to inquire whether he is willing to admit our ships into his harbors with such articles of merchandise as will be useful to him and his people, and to receive in turn the products of their industry or of their soil. That we manufacture and can bring arms, ammunition, cloths of cotton and wool, glass, &c. (enumerating all the articles you find that they usually import), that we can furnish them cheaper than any other nation because it is against the principles of our nation to build forts or make expensive establishments in foreign countries, that we never make conquests, or ask any nations to let us establish ourselves in their countries as the English, the French, and the Dutch have done in the East Indies.

All we ask is free liberty to come and go for the purpose of buying and selling, paying obedience to the laws of the country while we are there. But that while we ask no exclusive favor, we will not carry our commerce where we are treated in any degree worse than other nations. We will pay all the duties that are required by the King's authority, but we will not submit to pay more than any other nation does, nor will we bear the exactions of any of his subordinate officers, that the President is very powerful, has many ships of war at his command, but that they are only used to protect our commerce against imposition, that the King wishes to secure the advantages of our trade, he may enter into a treaty by which the above stipulations must be secured to our merchants, that as soon as this is known, our ships will resort to his ports, enriching him by the duties he will receive, and his subjects by their commerce.

An important point is to obtain an explicit permission to trade, generally, with the inhabitants, for it is understood that at most, or all of the ports, the Mandarins or other officers, now monopolize the commerce, permitting none of the inhabitants to trade with foreigners.[4]

Although Roberts' pay came two-thirds from State Department and one-third from Navy appropriations, and the Navy alone was to be responsible for his transportation and accommodation, his guidance came exclusively from the secretary of state, at first Edward Livingston of New York and Louisiana. (Jackson had first offered Livingston the job of American minister in Paris, an obvious choice given the latter's fluent French and Secretary of State Van

Buren's strong support for the assignment, but Livingston declined. Instead he became secretary of state in May 1831, after Van Buren's abrupt departure, the second of President Jackson's four secretaries of state.)

In that office in his late sixties, by then Livingston—a well-regarded lawyer and legislator and a wartime aide-de-camp to the then-general Jackson—was something of a spent force, notwithstanding his impressive résumé.* Six months into Livingston's term as secretary of state, Jackson was already anticipating the desirability of a change when he commented to Van Buren that Livingston's "memory is somewhat failing him."[5] When Roberts sailed, Livingston had been in office less than one year; he'd remain secretary of state for little more than a year longer.

Despite its august title and broad scope, the executive department over which Livingston presided—a shared presidium, Jackson ("King Andrew" to his detractors) meddled unceasingly in the business of all his cabinet officers—was a bare-bones and curiously informal operation. It comprised only the secretary, a chief clerk (since September 1817 and for a few months beyond Livingston's term in office, that man was Daniel Carroll Brent of Virginia; Brent later was posted to Paris), and thirteen subordinate clerks. Not until 1833 under Livingston's successor, Louis McLane, did the department have a fixed structure, have eight bureaus, and adhere to posted business hours, ten in the morning to three in the afternoon daily.

Its secretary, the chief of this small band, was responsible not only for the negotiation of treaties, for official correspondence with American ministers in fifteen (soon to be twenty-one) foreign capitals and with their ambassadorial counterparts in Washington, for the management of consular posts and their approximately one hundred forty occupants, and for the provision of passports to Americans traveling abroad, but also for publishing, distributing, and archiving treaties, the resolutions and acts of Congress, and state statutes. All this together with operating "the office which issues patents for useful inventions." The secretary was also custodian of the Great Seal of the United States. Explaining this potpourri, the 1832 edition of *The American Almanac*

* The arc of Edward Livingston's political career was no less improbable by today's standards than were those of the president and the secretary of the navy. Between 1795 and 1832, Livingston (1764–1836), scion of an influential New York family and Princeton graduate, was a congressman from New York, mayor of New York City, served in the Louisiana State House, later as a congressman from Louisiana, and briefly as one of the state's U.S. senators. After two years in Jackson's cabinet, Livingston became the U.S. minister in Paris, finally taking the offer made several years earlier. He died in May 1836 at age seventy-one, a month before Roberts did.

The most interesting thing about Livingston might have been his young and beautiful second wife, Louise Moreau de Lassy (1782–1860), daughter of a wealthy Santo Domingo planter and young widow of a Jamaican landowner. In 1805 she married Livingston, then twice her age. The two had one child, a daughter.

and Repository of Useful Knowledge informed its readers that the Department of State "embraces what in some other governments are styled the Department of Foreign Affairs and the Home Department."

Secret trade missions weren't an entirely new idea in Washington in the 1830s. Neither was supporting one new to the U.S. Navy. Three years earlier President Jackson had launched such a covert mission to Istanbul, quietly sending three commissioners to the Turkish capital on ships of the Navy's European squadron to solicit the Ottoman sultan's agreement to increased bilateral trade and access to the Black Sea for merchantmen from New England. In this case the secret was being kept from not only the British but also the U.S. Congress, which had not been consulted on the appointment of Messrs. David Offley and Charles Rhind, and Capt. James Biddle, USN, for this assignment.

In the event, Sultan Mahmud II did agree, in exchange for the transfer of American shipbuilding technology to restore his fleet, shattered in October 1827 at the Battle of Navarino (the worst defeat of a Turkish navy since that at Lepanto in 1571 and the last time that ships powered exclusively by sail fought at sea). An American-Turkish treaty of navigation and commerce was duly signed in May 1830 and ratified in October 1831, a month after the two countries established diplomatic relations.*

3

Edmund Roberts wasn't seeking to open trade with Arabia and Asia in 1832; his goal was to regularize it under rules agreed to by his distinguished hosts, not an original idea but one suggested to him years before by the sultan of Oman. The core of the idea underlying both of Roberts' diplomatic missions in the 1830s grew out of the unsuccessful trading voyage to the Indian Ocean of the Portsmouth-based brig *Mary Ann* in 1827–28. Roberts was the supercargo (the on-board business manager) during that speculative voyage, one financed by the sale of seventeen five-hundred-dollar shares to sixteen of Portsmouth's leading businessmen. He knew the sixteen—bankers, merchants, and local business owners, all members of the social class Roberts

* There was a possibility that the Senate would not consent to this treaty, an expression of pique by Whig senators who objected to the appointment of negotiators without reference to the Senate. In 1834 the possibility arose again over Roberts' two treaties for the same reason. The American-Turkish treaty's secret ninth clause, like all things in Washington secret only for a short time, addressed naval technology transfer. That transfer came largely in the person of Henry Eckford, a New Yorker who'd made a brilliant reputation as a shipbuilder on the Great Lakes during the War of 1812, a reputation stout enough to merit President Jackson's personal recommendation when Eckford—seriously embarrassed by a political and financial scandal in his home state—went looking for work in spring 1831. Eckford died of cholera in 1832, not long after arriving at the shipyard in Istanbul and starting work.

hoped to rejoin—personally, and they evidently had retained confidence in him despite his fall from prosperity dating back some twenty years.

In the late 1820s, Roberts was still suffering through problems that flowed originally from losses incurred, he believed, in the economic warfare of the Napoleonic Wars more than a decade earlier. Napoleon's Berlin Decree in November 1806, announcing a paper blockade of the British Isles, had followed a British order earlier that year closing ports between Brest and the Elbe. In response, two months later a British Order in Council instituted a true blockade of the Continent. The following December Napoleon replied with his Milan Decree, making neutral shipping that honored British rules vulnerable to seizure, and the following May, in 1808, he issued the Bayonne Decree, ordering American ships in European ports seized and legitimizing an open season against neutral shipping. Great Britain's riposte was another Order in Council, this one in April 1809. In all, more than fourteen hundred American merchant ships were captured during the war.[6] Roberts described the effect of these competing decrees on his business as "bare-faced robbery."

But their result was more nuanced than that, at first because President Jefferson's ill-advised initial response to trade restrictions was the Embargo Act of December 1807, a wound inflicted on New England's merchants and shipowners by their own government, and next because the restrictions proved unsustainable by either side. By 1809–10 both combatants were winking at loopholes in their restrictive regimes and issuing licenses permitting smugglers to evade them. Two years later the restrictions were gone altogether.* Roberts' problems cannot be blamed on the war alone.

Of the eleven ships Roberts seems to have held some financial interest in, only two, the sloops *Victory* and *Bedford*, were actually taken by the combatants. Among the remaining nine, the tiny brig *Norfolk* (seventy tons) mysteriously vanished in 1817 after departing Brazil; brig *Ann* was lost off Surinam in 1818; and a larger brig, *Florida*, was wrecked off Savannah the following year. *Roberts*, *Minerva*, *Abaelino*, *Islington*, and *Frederick* were all sold, and *Rolla* was broken up, presumably no longer seaworthy. The seizure of *Victory* would later form the basis for a claim against the French.

While Roberts' merchant fleet evaporated from one cause or another, the family (Edmund and Catharine, his wife of twelve years, and their six children; a seventh was to die in infancy that September) began to feel serious financial

* On June 23, 1812, a supplement to the *London Gazette* announced that in view of evidence the Berlin and Milan Decrees had been revoked by the French government at the end of April, the prince regent, in the name of the king, now revoked "wholly and absolutely" (although not necessarily permanently) the Orders in Council of January 1807 and April 1809 that had so exasperated the Americans. The decision, trapped in the slow movement of news across the Atlantic Ocean, came too late to forestall an American declaration of war in mid-June, news of which reached London in July.

pressure. Threatened with a future as a failed businessman, Roberts turned for the first time to the possibility of government employment. On December 28, 1820, he wrote to one of New Hampshire's senators, Portsmouth-born John Parrott, seeking support of his interest in being appointed the U.S. commercial agent in Havana and belatedly joining a field of at least two other applicants for the job in Cuba. The next year he lost that competition to John Warner, from a family of grocers and merchants from Wilmington, Delaware, and then the veteran U.S. consul in San Juan, Puerto Rico.

Concluding, after some months of exchanging letters with Parrott and his other supporters, that he had no chance at "an office of some consequence" but could not remain unemployed, Roberts scaled down his aspirations. The following spring he petitioned for the consul's post in "unhealthy" Demerara on the Caribbean coast of the British—recently Dutch—dependency of Guyana. Success, of a sort, came months later, in March 1823, when President James Monroe selected him for the post and signed Roberts' commission.

A slave rebellion broke out in that colony's sugar plantations that same August, to be put down violently by planters. This turbulence might have been the reason that Roberts seems never to have actually lived and served in Demerara; in fact, however, his posting was years premature. The triumph of the Revolutionary War had a small downside: New England's merchants and seamen lost access to British ports in the West Indies, one of the nodes of a profitable trade triangle that had seen vessels from the American colonies shuttle between their home ports, the West Indies, and West Africa. Locked out of the British West Indies, the search for substitute markets and new business sent ships flying the new American flag into the Baltic Sea and to other, less familiar waters, and most significantly to pivot away from the closed ports of the Caribbean (among them Demerara) and North Atlantic and toward the less familiar ones of the South and East China Seas and the Indian Ocean.

Although some surreptitious American trade flowed through the West Indies during the decade, they were not officially reopened to Americans, nor were U.S. consuls accepted in British colonies until negotiations concluded in 1830. Only after that agreement could the post of consul at Demerara possibly have been lucrative, or even self-supporting.

Long before that reopening, and although Roberts continued to appear on State Department rosters as consul in Guyana through 1830, his attention and aspirations had turned back to Havana, where Warner had conveniently died in the meanwhile after five years' service as the U.S. agent for commerce and seamen.

May 21, 1825, Roberts wrote a letter to Associate Justice of the Supreme Court Joseph Story, soliciting Story's support of his renewed campaign for

Havana.* "I have held for some time past the Consulate for Demarara," Roberts explained to a man he didn't know about a job he'd never performed, "but have not yet entered upon the duties of the office in consequence of having been obliged to settle up all my former commercial concerns (which have been exceedingly troublesome)":

> The object I have in view, Sir, is to induce the President to appoint me to the Consulate at Havana, the emoluments of which are of very considerable consequence, instead of the office which I now hold which I may say is of almost no value. I have a large family to maintain & by misfortunes in business (principally occasioned by endorsing) I am literally stript of all property & it is absolutely necessary I should be forthwith employed in some way to support them. Therefore I am obliged to call upon the respectable part of the community who know me to use their utmost endeavours & influence with the President to grant me this appointment.

"I am fully sensible, my Dear Sir," Roberts continued, "I have no claims upon you but those of humanity and I have had strong doubts as to the propriety of addressing you upon this subject and requesting your influence and support but my friends have urged the measure so strongly that the scruples of delicacy have at length yielded to those of necessity."

Roberts' earnest solicitation went on for several pages, but whatever Story might have done in response to it, Roberts appears never to have had a chance in the contest for this selection either. The pack under consideration included the son of the sitting governor of Maryland and, among others, the ultimate prizewinner, Thomas Rodney of Delaware, then the U.S. consul at Matanzas, Cuba, whose forebears included Caesar Rodney (1728–84), a signer of the Declaration of Independence.†

Alternatives exhausted and after five years of awkward pleading with possible benefactors still without a paying government job (but with a seventh and eighth child to raise), Roberts turned back to entrepreneurship.

* Roberts' letter to Justice Story is owned by the Portsmouth Historical Society and held in the collection of the Portsmouth Athenaeum. Story (1779–1845), a lawyer and politician from Salem, Massachusetts, was appointed to Chief Justice Marshall's court in 1811 by President Madison. Because of his conservative, anti-Jackson stance, Story's endorsement might have helped Roberts during the administrations of James Monroe and John Quincy Adams but not that of Jackson.

† Havana was no less unhealthy than was Demerara. Rodney managed to survive four tours on Cuba, three as consul in Matanzas, but his successor in Havana, William Shaler of Massachusetts, died there in March 1833 during the same cholera epidemic that had so frightened Roberts' daughters in New York the summer before.

From this frustration emerged the idea to charter a vessel, *Mary Ann*, and trade with East Africa.

The *Mary Ann* venture was described in an agreement signed by the investors in March, three months before sailing: "We . . . do hereby agree to fit out a voyage to sundry ports on the Eastern Coast of Africa & to any other ports in places that may appear to us or to our Supercargo to be for our mutual interests . . . having full faith & confidence in the integrity and ability of Mr. Edmund Roberts of Portsmouth N.H., we hereby constitute and appoint him Supercargo of the said contemplated expedition and our Agent to make all necessary purchases."[7]

Roberts joined *Mary Ann* in New York before her departure on June 10, having survived a carriage accident on the way. He'd chartered the ship and crew under what would be called a "wet lease" today for $650 plus expenses per month. Loaded with goods consigned for trade (including textiles, firearms, kegs of black powder, loaf sugar, and assorted Yankee notions) and under the command of Capt. William Stevens, the brig sailed for Zanzibar, the center of trade in the western Indian Ocean. *Mary Ann* would be gone for the next eleven months, the first four at sea on the way to the distant island, where she arrived in early October. There Roberts had the good fortune to stumble across Sayyid Sa'id bin Sultan (1791–1856), the ruler of Oman and Zanzibar. Everything that followed in his life flowed from this chance encounter with the sultan.

In 1806, after the assassination of his cousin, who two years earlier had usurped the throne, Sayyid Sa'id, fifteen, became the sultan of Oman. In 1821, with the death of his brother, Salïm (described by Sayyid Sa'id's biographer as a "nonentity"), that throne became his alone. Sayyid Sa'id maneuvered brilliantly among the competing African, Arab, and European—chiefly England and France—players on the Arabian Peninsula, East Africa, and the western Indian Ocean littoral. Near the end of the 1820s, with his rule consolidated at home, Sayyid Sa'id gained control of Zanzibar and Pemba, using the larger island as a base for trade expeditions deep into East Africa seeking slaves, ivory, and other products and both islands for the cultivation of cloves. During the 1830s Sayyid Sa'id regained control over Mombasa. In 1840 he transferred his court and capital from Muscat to Stone Town, Zanzibar. The move signaled Zanzibar's status as the principal commercial center of East Africa and the western Indian Ocean. Sayyid Sa'id died at sea off the Seychelles in October 1856 at age sixty-five.

When the two met for the first time on Zanzibar in early 1828, Sultan Sayyid Sa'id had "expressed much surprise that the government of the United States has never made the attempt to enter into a commercial treaty with him," adding that "the advantages arising from [the treaty] would be wholly in favor of American trade."[8] Roberts quickly picked up the sultan's suggestion and then enlarged upon it. Complete success would have included bilateral agreements across a broad arc spanning parts of two oceans and stretching from Oman to Japan. Sadly, Roberts' actual achievements were to fall far short of that ambitious standard.

American trade with Asia already had a half-century of history when USS *Peacock* departed New York for the Indian and Pacific Oceans with Roberts on board to implement the sultan's good idea and his instructions from the secretary of state. That history had begun on February 22, 1784, scant months after the Treaty of Paris marked the negotiated end to the American Revolution, when *Empress of China* loaded 60,000 pounds of Appalachian ginseng root and sailed on her maiden voyage under Capt. John Green's command from New York for Canton on the first voyage to Asia of a merchant ship flying the American flag. She arrived August 23, spent four months anchored at Whampoa, and returned home the following May 12 carrying a valuable cargo that included black tea, cotton, silk, and spices. The round trip enriched *Empress*' owners, who split among themselves a profit of almost $38,000. (The tiny, fifty-five-ton, sloop *Harriett* had left Boston for Canton two months ahead of *Empress* but never made it much past Cape Town.) Three months behind *Empress*, a leased ship from Canton, the East Indiaman *Pallas*—with a crew of Asian deckhands, foreign exotics who caused a sensation on their arrival in the United States—entered the port of Baltimore with a load that included 880,000 pounds of tea and a handsome 302-piece Chinese porcelain dinner and tea service for George Washington.

And with that, the gold rush was on. Excited by these first examples, during the next five decades literally hundreds of American ships carried on trade with China, more than sixty each year during the 1830s. As trade matured the chief exchange was furs for tea—hundreds of thousands of skins for many millions of pounds of tea leaves. The slaughter of sea otters, seals, and beavers drove some animal populations to extinction; the greedy hunt for new rookeries to exploit was one of the propellants of nineteenth-century exploration. (Also of conflict. Sealing was done on land, not at sea like whaling. Arguments over access to the Falkland Islands' rich sealing grounds triggered the fighting that drew USS *Lexington* to those islands described later.)

4

Roberts had proposed the diplomatic initiative to President Andrew Jackson through his friend, Secretary of the Navy Levi Woodbury. Jackson (1767–1845), lean and tough as beef jerky and the polar opposite of his predecessor in office, John Quincy Adams, has increasingly come to be regarded as the most consequential president between Washington and Lincoln. Today Jackson is commonly counted by historians as standing firmly in the second tier of American presidents, among Wilson, Truman, Teddy Roosevelt, and Lyndon Johnson. (His status might not be enough to preserve his face on the U.S. twenty-dollar bill, a bit of real estate being eyed by women for one of their own sex.)

Somewhat improbably, and otherwise occupied with forcing Indians off their lands, with political competitors threatening to dismantle the fledgling union through state nullification of federal laws and with his campaign to shut down the national bank, Jackson agreed, probably to cultivate his supporters in New England, who depended on maritime trade for their region's and their own prosperity.

Andrew Jackson's life and career were remarkable. A self-educated orphan (it's astonishing how many figures in this story were orphans), by age forty-five Jackson had been Tennessee's attorney general, a representative and senator in Congress, a judge in state superior court, and a major general of volunteers in Tennessee's militia. Then came the War of 1812, and—inconveniently weeks after war's end—Jackson's brilliant triumph at the Battle of New Orleans.

That victory was celebrated at a victory anniversary ball in Washington on January 8, 1824, hosted by the Adamses, honoring General Jackson and his long-ago triumph. Honor aside, the thousand-guest gala may have been part of John Quincy Adams' campaign to persuade the general to set his sights lower, for the vice presidency, rather than the presidency that both men craved. If so, the ploy failed, but later that year Adams got the prize anyway, winning the election in the House of Representatives thanks to Henry Clay's support, despite having lost at the ballot box. Charges that the two had struck a deal—Clay's political support in exchange for appointment as secretary of state—were probably correct. Adams nearly confessed as much, conceding in his inaugural address that he enjoyed less confidence on arriving in office than had his predecessors. Whatever place Clay thought he held in line for the top job, in 1828 it was Jackson's turn.

The eight years of Andrew Jackson's presidency are not notable for evidence of the evolution of his views over time. He came to Washington in January 1829 at sixty-one, long since fully formed, and left the capital in 1837 to his successor, Martin Van Buren, much the same man as had first arrived there. In one particular, however, the departing Jackson was different from the man who had taken up office on March 4, 1829, following an inauguration ceremony famously remembered for the thirsty, ill-mannered mob that descended on the White House afterward. He began opposed to the Navy and to appropriations for capital ship construction and finished an enthusiastic proponent of American sea power. The evidence of this transformation, observed years ago by John Schroeder in *Shaping a Maritime Empire* (Greenwood Press, 1985), is in Jackson's annual state of the union addresses to the Congress, in those days delivered in writing and not read by the president.

In his first address, December 1829, Jackson counseled against the construction of large combatant ships (which in peace would "lay in the harbors" subject to "rapid decay") and recommended instead "judicious deposits in navy yards of timber and other materials" that could be quickly assembled into ships should that be necessary. In his last address, December 1836, he instead urged upon Congress "attention to the necessity of further appropriations to increase the number of ships afloat and to enlarge generally the capacity and force of the Navy." Ships afloat, no longer a strategic reserve of live oak lumber.

Levi Woodbury, Jackson's secretary of the navy between May 1831 and June 1834, was no slacker either. The span of his career in public service is no less unimaginable today, a trifecta encompassing all three branches of government and service as a trustee for his alma mater, Dartmouth. Beginning in 1823, Woodbury, then in his mid-thirties, was successively governor of New Hampshire, speaker of the state's lower house, twice a United States senator from his home state, a cabinet officer for two presidents (Jackson's secretary of the navy and his and Van Buren's secretary of the treasury after the Senate refused its consent to the appointment of Roger Taney in 1834), and from September 1845 until his death at sixty-two in September 1851 an associate justice of the Supreme Court. In 1844 and again in 1848, Woodbury tried but failed to become the Democrat's candidate for president, losing first to James Polk in 1844 and four years later to Lewis Cass.

Woodbury, who came from a state with important maritime interests and had served on the Senate's Committee on Naval Affairs in the late 1820s, was an obvious choice for navy secretary. A choice that would have been congenial to Asa Clapp, an enormously wealthy shipowner from Maine and only coincidently Woodbury's father-in-law. Following the president's early lead, among Woodbury's chief achievements as navy secretary during an era when hardwood stands were a strategic resource, was the substantial expansion of the Navy's Live Oak Reservation to 150,000 acres. Live oak, believed to be five times as durable as common white oak and good for fifty years at sea, was until the 1860s essential to the construction of combatant ships and sea power. Another action emblematic of the times was Woodbury's decision to offer a small cash payment to sailors in lieu of their daily grog ration, an incentive to be abstemious on board ship.

Woodbury became navy secretary in early 1831—after first declining the post of American minister (ambassador) in Madrid, offered him by Van Buren—following an upheaval in the administration that saw all but one of Jackson's cabinet officers leave office practically at once. The sudden departures were the culmination of tensions that tore official Washington and its high society apart over the humiliating ostracism of Secretary of War John Eaton's wife, Margaret. Peggy Eaton was widely believed to be a fallen woman and unfit to appear in polite society.*

Jackson's determined defense of her virtue and of the Eatons in general ultimately failed, and on April 19–20, 1831, first Secretary of State Van Buren and Secretary of War Eaton resigned, and then Ingham (treasury secretary), Berrien (the attorney general), and Branch (navy secretary)—all Eaton critics—were forced out. Some Washington insiders judged the two new service secretaries, Lewis Cass at the War Department and Levi Woodbury at the Navy Department, to be upgrades from their predecessors.[9] Maybe so, but Woodbury's term in office wasn't especially notable for anything he did.

Not that the post at the head of the Department of the Navy wasn't important. Even after the creation of the Board of Navy Commissioners by statute in 1815 (which until 1842 delegated to those three senior captains the construction, outfitting, and repair of ships, and the procurement of naval stores and other material), the incumbent secretary of the navy retained until after the Civil War personal control of the movement of ships and squadrons and the selection, assignment, and promotion of officers. All this with a secretariat staff of nine clerks and two messengers and an annual payroll for all twelve under $19,000, of which the secretary's comprised nearly one-third.

Being a member of Jackson's cabinet could not have been easy for anyone. King Andrew didn't look to his cabinet officers for initiative, churned them around furiously (there were four secretaries of state in the years 1829–37), and practically never met with the entire cabinet at once. It assembled in full strength on average only twice each year. An informal Kitchen Cabinet of the president's cronies had much more influence than did the several secretaries.

5

Secretary Woodbury's support of Edmund Roberts turned out to be essential, not so much to place the subject of trade treaties on Jackson's foreign policy

* Postmaster General William Barry of Kentucky was one of Margaret Eaton's very few defenders in the capital. (Another was Martin Van Buren.) Barry was the first postmaster general to sit as a member of the cabinet, some forty years before the post office became an executive department. He stayed in office into 1835. Barry died en route to Madrid, where he was to serve as U.S. minister to the Spanish court. John Eaton replaced him there.

agenda but to get Roberts the negotiator's commission over the petitioning of a much more experienced and likely claimant, John Shillaber of Danvers, Massachusetts, the American consul in distant Batavia.

Shillaber (in some places "Shellaber"), living then on Java, had been appointed in July 1824 by President Monroe, propelled into the newly vacated post by a recommendation from the wealthy New York trader, John Jacob Astor, and possibly helped by the fact that Monroe's secretary of state, John Quincy Adams, was also from Massachusetts. Shillaber was the fourth American consul at the capital and chief port of the Dutch East Indies since Thomas Hewes, the first, was appointed by President Jefferson in November 1801. He was to serve for just over ten years, until June 1835, with substantial periods during that decade away from his post and off the island of Java.

At the turn of the century, the post of consul already had a decade-long history in the United States. The first fifteen consuls were appointed by President George Washington in June 1790, a dozen to ports in Europe and the other three to ports in the West Indies. At first they were to report commercial information and military intelligence to the State Department every six months; soon their duties expanded to include the care of distressed American seamen, not to cost more than twelve cents per man per day. Approaching forty years later, the United States had one hundred additional consuls, a population spread across 115 foreign ports. Not all were American citizens, and for many decades all but very few, for example the four consuls general in the Barbary states, were unpaid by the thrifty government they served.

The defects of the American consular system through much of the nineteenth century were visible to anyone who looked. Among the thirteen American merchants in Canton who in 1807 petitioned the president for "a more efficient consular establishment," there was the chief of Perkins and Company, the company established a few years earlier by Samuel Shaw, *Empress*'s supercargo. Shaw experienced the problems personally; he was the first American consul in Canton, having assumed the new consular post in January 1786 knowing he did so "without being entitled to receive any salary, fees, or emoluments whatsoever."

Later President Jackson and Secretary Livingston also saw the flaws and spoke out about them, Jackson in memoranda to Congress in 1831 and 1833, the second forwarding and endorsing Secretary Livingston's plan for replacing "the worst consular system in the world" with a paid corps of professionals.*

* A modest attempt at improvement and standardization of foreign service practice came in 1834, when Secretary of State Louis McLane arranged to have Jonathan Elliot's book *The American Diplomatic Code* distributed free to U.S. diplomats and principal consuls as a reference and handbook. Elliot's two volumes (published in Washington that same year) encompassed, in the words of a subtitle that could have served as their table of contents, *A Collection of Treaties and Conventions between the United States*

Nothing came of either man's initiative, a lapse that almost certainly prompted the publication in New York of an anonymous short pamphlet, *Outline of a Consular Establishment for the United States of America in Eastern Asia* (E. French, 1838) that reiterated the administration's general critique and specifically recommended the establishment of a cluster of six American consulates in Southeast Asia centered on a consulate general in Canton with subordinate offices at Manila, Borneo City, Batavia, Singapore, Bangkok, and Hué.

"Our government has," *Outline of a Consular Establishment*'s admiring and also anonymous reviewer wrote in October that year in the *North American Review*, "in commercial affairs, been singularly remiss, in the proper maintenance of its official representation abroad. . . . Instead of its being the legitimate offspring of the government itself . . . it has been but the mere product of accident." Compared to his counterparts, "the well-pensioned functionaries of the European powers," an American consul was

> a mere merchant, or mayhap a petty shopkeeper, having his official dignity engrafted upon his private and more substantial business. In these circumstances, he is either pinched in his means of support, and thus tempted to extortion in his transactions with those who require his protection; or, reveling in wealth, and wholly absorbed in the affairs of an immense counting house, he looks upon the duties of his office as trifles beneath his attention. . . .
>
> He, therefore, unless better rewarded by his government, cannot be expected to devote his whole time and talents to the interests of his country. . . . It is not the fault of the officer, but of the system, which, if bound by necessity to its demands, he is rather the victim than the perpetrator.[10]

Until 1856, the vast majority of consuls subsisted in part on the duties and fees they were permitted to charge passing mariners for services, but largely on

and Foreign Powers from 1778 to 1834 with an Abstract of Important Judicial Decisions on Points Connected with Our Foreign Relations, Also a Concise Diplomatic Manual Containing a Summary of the Law of Nations from the Works of [Six Authorities] and Other Diplomatic Writings on Questions of International Law Useful for Public Ministers and Consuls and for All Others Having Official or Commercial Intercourse with Foreign Nations. Roberts had a copy of Elliott's book in his personal library, together with books on East India, China, Java, Sumatra, and Ceylon as well as John Crawfurd's *Mission to Siam and Cochin China*.

McLane, from Delaware and Livingston's successor as secretary of state, was a former U.S. senator, minister in London, and treasury secretary when he took the job at the State Department. He managed to stay there only one year, from May 1833 to June 1834. Beginning in the mid-1830s, squadron commodores sailed to their stations with a copy of *The American Diplomatic Code* and the "Red Book" (officially *Rules of the Navy Department Regulating the Civil Administration of the Navy of the United States*), first published in 1832 by Secretary Woodbury to formalize financial and other management practices in the service.

income from private enterprise, with the predictable distractions and abuses arising from conflicts of interest.

Joseph Balestier, the American consul in Singapore through the 1830s and 1840s, is a representative example of the economics of consular office in distant places.* In 1849 he told the secretary of state that his yearly income from fees amounted to only one hundred dollars, while entertainment and other costs of his office amounted to three thousand dollars per year. Like counterparts elsewhere in the tropics, Balestier made his living as a shipping agent and—in his case unsuccessfully—as a sugar planter.[11]

Reform was very slow to come. In March 1853, when Commodore Perry's East India Squadron called for coal and mail at Point de Galle, Ceylon, on its way to Japan, "the Commodore and his officers were not a little mortified, as well as somewhat embarrassed, by finding at their arrival . . . the United States commercial agent, a native of Scotland, confined to his premises under an execution for debt." Perry's conclusion: "Our country had no right to expect our consuls and commercial agents, many of whom were unfitted in every respect for their stations, either to represent or sustain the commercial interests of the nation so long as the system then existing was followed. The fees at many of the places where our consular agents were accredited, it was notorious would scarce suffice to clothe them, and, accordingly, to eke out a scanty living, they were often obliged to resort to some sort of business, often not of the most dignified character."[12]

Finally, after 1856—three years after Shillaber's death and four after Balestier left Singapore—consuls were granted a salary, but even then many (those paid under a penurious "Schedule C") were allowed to continue private trading. Where merchant traffic and the associated fees and duties collected were high, a consular post could be a profitable sinecure, especially when coupled to successful local, private trading.

Shillaber's timing was poor, even though after five years at Batavia he should have known better. By the 1820s international trade had centered on Batavia for fully two centuries. Henrik Brouwer, a Dutch East India Company captain, blew there early in the seventeenth century, riding the Roaring Forties on the fastest route across the Indian Ocean. In time, what had been a village on the far side of the Sunda Strait became the eastern terminal of a busy sea lane from Amsterdam via Cape Town, as well as the central node of an intra-Asian trading network that connected the Spice Islands and stretched north

* Consul Balestier was married to Maria Revere (1785–1847), one of American patriot Paul Revere's fifteen children. In 1843, a few years before her death, she presented a bell cast at her father's foundry in Boston to the Church of St. Andrew in Singapore, where it remained until 1889, ringing every evening at eight o'clock. The bell, long since cracked, is a part of the collection of Singapore's National Museum.

to Japan. But American trade with the Dutch East Indies peaked during the first half of the 1820s, and then steadily declined, a consequence of restrictive Dutch commercial policy cramping trade and especially of competition posed by the port of now-British Singapore, commanding the narrows on the preferred route between the Pacific and Indian Oceans—the Strait of Malacca and the Great Channel out of the Andaman Sea.[13]

By the early 1830s Batavia was a backwater. "There are but few places so large as Batavia," Roberts wrote in his *Embassy to the Eastern Courts*, "in the present day, which show less signs of an active commerce, less bustle on the quays, or exhibit a greater degree of dullness, and want of bustle in the streets. This is owing, in part," he explained,

> to the belligerent attitude of Holland and Belgium; the alarming war with the Sumatrans; the establishment of a free port [Singapore] by the British; but more particularly, to the narrow-contracted views of the government in regard to commerce. The Dutch government wish to drive all foreign commerce from their ports in Netherland's India with the exception of native traders of the Indian isles; and to extend, if possible, their unjust and iniquitous system of monopolies, and of forced cultivation, upon the natives.

Moreover, life in the Dutch colonial capital threatened more than a foreign merchant's bottom line. It also threatened his vitality. The Daniells, uncle Thomas and nephew William, traveling together on Java during an extended sketching trip through the Orient, thought "the place suggests the melancholy idea of a garden blooming on a grave; the earth teems with delicate fruits, but the air is loaded with pestilential vapours, and vegetation seems to flourish at the expense of human life." Less poetically, Roberts described "choked canals covered with slime, and green stagnant pools, a resort of frogs, snakes, and other reptiles . . . miserable palm-leaf hovels encumbering the space" once ornamented by "splendid habitations."

Peacock's surgeon, Benajah Ticknor, agreed; the once–Queen of the East had been reduced to something much less grand. "This, you know," he wrote from Batavia to a friend in Ohio in July 1833 after a month at anchor, "has been considered one of the most unhealthy ports in the East, and indeed the whole world. . . . It is said that Batavia is much more healthy than it formerly was, and there is undoubtedly less sickness & mortality; but this is owing, in the first place, to the removal & death of a large proportion of those who were liable to the diseases of the climate, and in the second place, to a change in the habits & mode of living of those who remain."

The changed mode of living had seen Europeans move out of downtown Batavia, "situated immediately on the bay & in the neighbourhood of extensive marshes" and to its suburbs in the country, "2 to 5 miles back from the bay and in great measure beyond the reach of marsh effluvia." The town, Ticknor continued, "is still enveloped by an atmosphere as pestilential as it ever was, and it is now considered about as fatal to pass a night there as it was during the period of greatest mortality. No foreigner ever spends a night in the town, without being soon afterwards attacked with fever."[14] The source of Batavia's deadly problem, however, wasn't the usual suspect, "marsh effluvia." It most probably was female *Anopheles* mosquitoes ("moschetoes" to Roberts) buzzing happily during the rainy season above the fishponds along the bay. They carried the tiny *Plasmodium falciparum* parasite, whose life cycle produced a lethal strain of malaria, a connection between disease and vector that wouldn't be made until the end of the century.

Disappointed by slow business or pursued by hungry mosquitoes, fairly early in his unpaid government employment Consul Shillaber determined to spend as little time actually at his post as possible. After 1827 he was there only part time. Shillaber spent some of 1829 and all of 1830 on furlough in New York, not returning to Batavia until midsummer the next year.* In 1835 the again absent consul (by then living in Canton) was finally replaced.

Absences aside, Consul Shillaber claimed a special perspective on the challenges and opportunities East and Southeast Asia offered to ambitious Americans and the expertise to play a key role in trade improvement. Between February 1826 and April 1832, from Batavia and New York, Shillaber wrote the State Department a dozen times to suggest trade treaties with the states of the region and volunteer himself for the negotiation mission.

The first letter was in February 1826, when he wrote Secretary of State Martin Van Buren that he'd be "highly honoured & gratified if the Govt. of the U. States would authorize me to make commercial arrangements with some of the Native independent sovereigns, of these eastern regions, for American trade," and added, seemingly offhandedly, that "the appearance of one of our national ships in this part of the globe would have a good effect." One year later he reminded the department of his suggestions. He did so again, on October 29, 1829, while on leave in New York, and yet again on December 10, 1830, reminding Van Buren that during his years in Java he had gained "knowledge of the . . . many peculiarities & commerce of these people."

* The late 1820s were good years to be absent from Batavia. During the Java War of 1825–30, fought in Central and East Java and generally along the island's north coast by the Dutch and their Indonesian mercenaries against native troops led by Javanese royalty, some 215,000 died (mostly Javanese) and vast tracts of cultivated land were damaged. The inevitable Dutch victory saw the "Culture System," an oppressive export crop—instead of rice—economy, imposed on the entire island.

In 1831, after six years in Batavia of the just over ten he nominally served there, Shillaber received a December 13, 1830, letter from Washington that revealed someone had been paying attention. "I am directed" wrote Secretary of State Van Buren's chief clerk, Daniel Brent, "by the Secretary to inform you . . . that the suggestions contained in your Letter with regard to the practicability of establishing Commercial Regulations or Treaties between the United States and the Independent Sovereigns of Siam and Cochin China, and to the advantage to be derived from such measures, will receive our attention":

> It is desirable, however, that you should make a more formal communication to this Department upon the subjects referred to, describing, in more detail, the inconvenience to which the Trade of the United States is now exposed from existing regulations, or the want of suitable regulations in the Countries in question, and the advantages of which that intercourse is, in your judgment susceptible from the formation of the Commercial Regulations recommended. A more precise knowledge of the nature and character of the Government in question will also be required.
>
> If the President upon the view of the whole subject, should hereafter determine upon making the attempt to place our commerce with those Countries upon such a footing, I am directed by the Secretary to state that in that case a Commission and instructions will in due season be forwarded to you for entering upon the necessary negotiations to that end.[15]

That apparent promise to Shillaber was never redeemed, and in the end Roberts got the job Shillaber had campaigned for at such length. Roberts' New Hampshire connection, and the turnover of administrations from Monroe to Jackson (and the departure of a secretary of state from Massachusetts), proved to be decisive. Surely disappointed, Shillaber remained nominally the consul in Batavia until he officially resigned in June 1835, apparently piqued at losing the post of American consul in Canton to Peter Snow (1788–1843), son of a former consul there and himself a sadly unsuccessful player in the China trade.*

* Snow, then in his teens, first went to China with his father, Samuel, in 1803. In and out of China in the four decades that followed, Peter Snow failed in private business, as his father had, while his wife and all but one of their children died at home in Rhode Island. In January 1832, Shillaber, now living in Macao, where he and a sister had relocated, perhaps to escape his debts after the failure of his private business in Batavia, applied to Jardine, Matheson and Company for financial backing to begin trading in rice in Angier.

2

The Frigate USS *Potomac* at Kuala Batee

While this little force stood thus under arms on the beach, before receiving orders to advance, what an interesting spectacle must they have presented to the American eye! Who could behold, without feelings of the deepest interest, so small a body of men, thus paraded on a foreign and hostile shore, armed, and eager to march wheresoever led, in the stern demand for justice, on account of wrongs suffered by their unoffending and unprotected countrymen! Rough, hardy sailors, as most of them were, they presented a picture that was by no means deficient in those exquisite touches which constitute the "moral sublime."

REYNOLDS, *VOYAGE OF THE UNITED STATES FRIGATE POTOMAC*

6

President Jackson's December 1832 message to Congress included brief mention of an act of "atrocious piracy" committed early in the year against an American merchant ship, the Salem-based *Friendship*, "by inhabitants of a settlement on the west coast of Sumatra." The previous February *Friendship*, 366 tons and a crew of seventeen, had been forcibly boarded in the Sumatran pepper port of Kuala Batee (sometimes "Quallah Battoo" or "Kwala Batu"), Charles Knight, her first officer, and two members of the crew killed and three others wounded and the ship looted of money (specie), cargo, navigation instruments, and her furniture by the raiders.* Days later her master, Capt. Charles Endicott, managed to recapture his ship, helped first by Po Adam, rajah of nearby Pulo Kio, and later by some Americans off three ships in port nearby at Muckie: *James Monroe*, *Governor Endicott*, and *Palmer*.

Friendship then limped to Massachusetts, arriving at her home port in late summer to spread word of this attack on the business interests of Salem's important community of traders and outrage against the American flag. Safely

* Such violence wasn't uncommon. A few months earlier Knight's brother, Enoch, had been one of two crewmembers bludgeoned to death when a shore party off *Glide*, also out of Salem and then trading in sea cucumbers—a delicacy—with China, was set upon on Ovalau Island by native Fijians.

back, Endicott claimed he'd lost more than $41,000 in the assault, including some $12,500 in coins and $8,800 in opium, eight 140-pound chests' worth.

Friendship's close escape from piracy got special traction at home. Built in 1815 in Portland, Maine, she'd been owned since 1827 by a partnership of three influential Salem merchants: Nathaniel Silsbee, Dudley Pickman, and Robert Stone. Silsbee (1773–1850), captain of *Benjamin* on the way to India at twenty and later founder of the Salem East India Marine Society, was also former president of the Massachusetts Senate. In 1832 he was U.S. senator from Massachusetts and chairman of the Senate's Committee on Commerce. A powerful reprisal against the Malay pirates neatly comingled his personal and the public's interest and prompted a letter to the president urging action. The always-feisty Jackson didn't need the cue.

On August 19, 1831, the Navy dispatched the frigate USS *Potomac*—"with orders," President Jackson reported to Congress—"to demand satisfaction for the injury if those who committed it should be found to be members of a regular government, capable of maintaining the usual relations with foreign nations; but if, as it was supposed and as they proved to be, they were a band of lawless pirates, to inflict such chastisement that would deter them and others from like aggressions." She sailed on August 24 with 502 officers and men on board. (Meanwhile *Friendship*, now seventeen years old and tired by hard use, drifted out of the spotlight and was sold by her owners to whalers in Fairhaven, Massachusetts.)

That first departure from port for the U.S. Navy's newest combatant ship had been a very long time coming: *Potomac*'s keel had been laid at the Washington Navy Yard in August 1819 and she was launched in March 1822, but nearly a decade more had to pass before *Potomac* was finally made ready for sea.

Until August 9 the frigate had been preparing for her maiden voyage, an otherwise routine deployment to join the sloop of war USS *Falmouth* and the schooner USS *Dolphin* on station as the Pacific Squadron's new flagship. En route to round South Africa, *Potomac*'s first port was to have been in England, dropping Martin Van Buren there to take up new duties as the U.S. minister after spending the previous two years as secretary of state. But on August 9 orders from Secretary Woodbury to Commodore Downes assigned his ship to "new duties of a character highly delicate and important."

"A most wanton outrage was committed on the lives and property of certain American citizens at Quallah-Battoo, a place on the western side of the Island of Sumatra, on the 7th of February last," the secretary wrote to Downes:

> You are therefore directed to repair at once to Sumatra, by the way of the Cape of Good Hope, touching on the voyage thither only at such

places as the convenience and necessity of your vessel may render proper. . . . The President of the United States, in order that prompt redress may be obtained for these wrongs, or the guilty perpetrators be made to feel that the flag of the United States is not to be insulted with impunity . . . directs that you proceed to demand . . . restitution of the property plundered . . . as well as for injury done to the vessel; satisfaction for any other depredations . . . and the immediate punishment of those concerned in the murder of the American citizens. . . .

If a compliance . . . be delayed . . . you are authorized . . . to vindicate our wrongs . . . cut off all opportunity of escape . . . seize the actual murderers . . . retake such part of the stolen property as can there be found . . . destroy the boats and vessels of any kind engaged in the piracy, and the forts and dwellings near the scene of aggression, used for shelter or defence; and to give public information to the population there collected, that if full restitution is not speedily made, and forbearance exercised hereafter from like piracies and murders upon American citizens, other ships-of-war will soon be dispatched thither to inflict more ample punishment.[1]

Uncertain about what *Potomac* might face on arrival in Sumatra six months after dispatch, and eager to ensure her new mission's success, Navy Secretary Woodbury prudently backed up the frigate by ordering USS *Peacock* and USS *Boxer* to pause there at the start of their diplomatic mission, to ascertain if the 50-gun *Potomac* required reinforcement.

On February 5, two months out of Rio de Janeiro and roughly a year after the raid on *Friendship*, USS *Potomac* anchored off Kuala Batee in eighteen to twenty fathoms of water over a mud bottom (except for occasional lumps where rock ballast had been jettisoned earlier by ships at anchor). The amphibious assault that followed the next morning was later described and celebrated in the "Battle of the Potomac with the Malays," a poem "written by one of the crew" and published in 1832 as a broadsheet by the Hunt Brothers of Faneuil Hall Market, Boston. "As the sun was retiring behind the high mountains," wrote the anonymous poet, "The forts of our enemy full in our view; / The frigate Potomac, John Downes our commander, / Rode proudly at anchor off Quallah Batoo." Perhaps not so proudly: main deck guns run in, gun ports closed, and every second gun-port door painted over to conceal the true size of *Potomac*'s broadside battery, on arrival the American frigate successfully passed herself off as an innocent East Indiaman "of great burden and capacity" under the Danish flag.

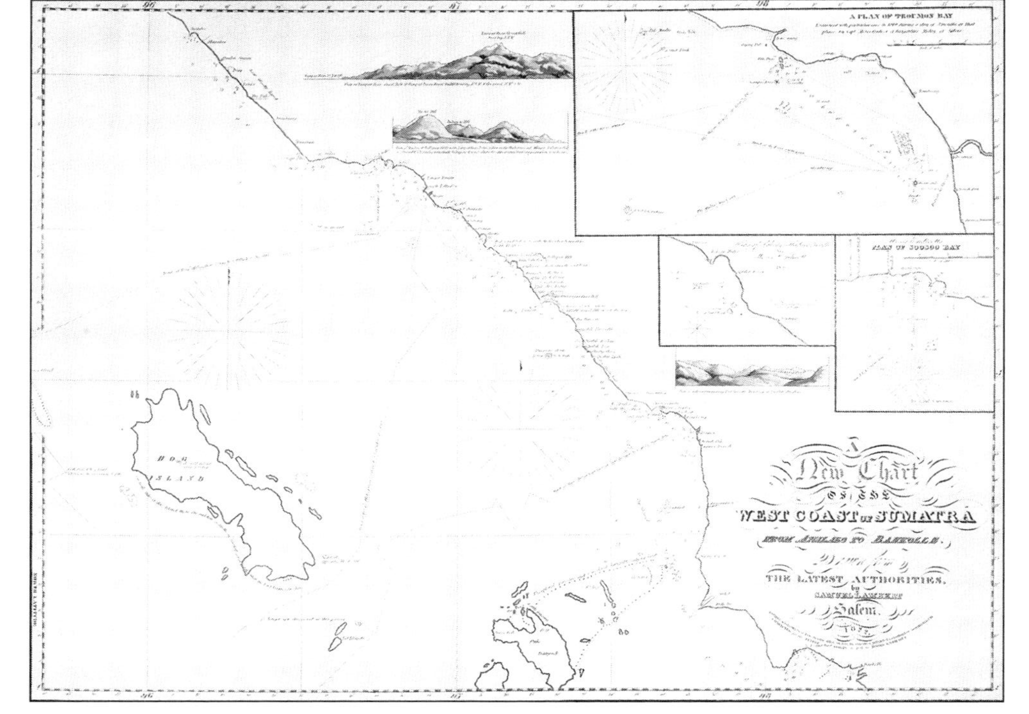

Chart 2. "A New Chart of the West Coast of Sumatra from Analabo to Bankolle Drawn from the Latest Authority." By the 1830s, and after circumventing the Dutch who got there first, Salem's traders had for three decades successfully monopolized America's pepper trade with Sumatra through Kuala Batee and three other ports—Muckie, Soosoo, and Pulo Kio (all part of today's Aceh Province of Indonesia). Until finally edged aside by those from Boston, Salem's merchants and sailors managed to dominate this rich spice trade for another fifteen years.

All four principal pepper ports appear on this 1822 chart of western Sumatra by Samuel Lambert, updated to 1827 by Moses Ellicott. Lambert (1768–1832), scion of an old Salem family, was a member of the local East India Marine Society, a mariner, and a publisher of navigation charts.

James R. Buffum, Salem, 1827, Collection of the Massachusetts Historical Society.

Downes' civilian secretary (Jeremiah Reynolds, in 1835 the author of one of two books about *Potomac*'s cruise but not yet on board during this excitement) later thought that Downes had arrived from Cape Town with his mind made up to shoot first. At dawn the next morning, Commodore Downes put ashore a 282-man landing party of armed sailors and Marines. The poem continued: "At the dead hour of night, when all nature was silent, / The Boatswain's pipe called each man to his post; / Our hearts armed with justice, our minds fully bent, / To attack and destroy that piratical host." And a few stanzas later:

> Our boats were all ready and we were prepared,
> To fight or to die for our cause it was just;
> Our muskets were loaded and our bosoms were bared,
> To the strife or the storm, for in God was our trust. . . .
> To their force, to their arms, to their strength we were strangers,
> But bravely advanced to the forts of our foe;
> We thought of no trouble, we thought of no dangers,
> Determined, unless we in death were laid low,
> To revenge the sad wrongs that our friends and our nation;
> So oft have sustained from these demons of hell;
> Our work we commenced, and the bright conflagration,
> Left but few of our foes the sad story to tell.

Once on shore the Americans swiftly reduced the port's several forts to smoking rubble, shelling one of them with "Betsey Baker," a 6-pounder the assault party had managed to wrestle ashore in one of the ship's boats:

> Exposed to their fires, the Potomacs advanced,
> Beneath their rude ramparts stood firmly and brave;
> Resolved that the stripes and the stars of Columbia,
> E'er long on their ramparts triumphant should wave.
> Their firing soon ceased, and our brave pioneers
> Then open'd a path and we entered their gates;
> We pass'd but a moment, gave three hearty cheers,
> Then hoisted the flag that is worn by the States.*

* That moment, the American flag newly flying over one of the defeated forts at Kuala Batee and above four exhausted and one dead handsomely uniformed Marines, as imagined by artist Donald Dickson, decorated the cover of the *Leatherneck* magazine of October 1930, published just months before the raid's centennial anniversary. A lone sailor is partly visible in the background. In fact, sailors outnumbered Marines six to one in the assault. In a long cover story by Frank Hunt Renfrow, decorated by imagined dialogue and other colorful touches of pure fiction, the mythmaking continued inside the

The dead included Kuala Batee's chief and perhaps as many as 150 of its residents, including a number of women, some of whom were combatants. In exchange, *Potomac*'s crew suffered two killed and eleven wounded.

"The Potomac victorious, once more under weigh," exulted the poet,

Floats proudly along the smooth Eastern waters;
Columbia! Columbia! The deeds of that day,
Shall be told by thy sons and sung by thy daughters. . . .
May success then attend us, wherever we roam,
And nothing our cause, or our progress impede;
May the Potomac with honor and glory come home,
And her name ne're be stained with an unworthy deed.[2]

Poetry aside, *Potomac* remained twelve days off Kuala Batee, while her surgeons dealt with a sick list that grew to fifty-seven names, before sailing for Java in the middle of the month. (Astonishingly, Daniel Cole, a Marine shot through his right lung during the assault, survived his "supposedly mortal" wounding.)

Notwithstanding the secretary's instructions to Commodore Downes, the devastating raid had not been preceded by any attempt to sort out the circumstances of *Friendship*'s boarding or to assign responsibility for the depredations. "No demand of satisfaction was made previous to my attack," Downes ingeniously explained, "because I was satisfied, from what knowledge I had already of the character of the people, that no such demand would be answered except by refusal." The only ship's property he'd managed to recover, the commodore reported in a letter to the secretary on February 17, was *Friendship*'s medicine chest.

"Chastisement" successfully delivered, *Potomac*, again proudly flying the flag of the arriving Pacific squadron commander, sailed the next day for Batavia, and later Macao and Canton. There Downes had been instructed to provide American merchants with "any temporary relief or aid . . . without involving this country in any hostilities with the regular and authorized authorities of China." Departing Kuala Batee, *Potomac* remained at sea a further twenty-eight months, completing in May 1834 the first west to east circumnavigation of the globe by a U.S. Navy combatant ship.

---

magazine. But Renfrow got the essential story right: *Potomac*'s retiring shore party left behind it a verdant ruin. The man most gratified by this destruction might have been USS *Potomac*'s acting assistant sailing master, John Barry, who'd been second mate in *Friendship* when she was overrun by the Malays, who volunteered for this mission as a civilian and joined the landing party on the beach.

USS Potomac *Attacking Malay Pirates at Kuala Batu* and *U.S. Frigate* Potomac *Destroying Malay Pirate Forts at Kuala Batu Island off Sumatra, Indonesia.* Oil paintings by Louis Dodd. At daybreak on February 6, 1831, USS *Potomac* put well-armed Marines and sailors ashore at Kuala Batee in four separate "divisions," each under orders to assault one of the forts at the place. The surprise raid was quickly successful, the operation taking only two and a half hours. Later in the action, some members of *Potomac*'s landing party gathering on the beach to return to the frigate came under fire from a surviving, hidden fortification south of the river. This attack prompted Commodore Downes to sail *Potomac* deeper into the

Much too late to make any difference, it developed that Captain Endicott's story of an attack by larcenous Malays on innocent American traders might have been fiction, or at best only partly true. A certain Mr. Dana, supercargo in the ship *Israel* trading between Canton and Marblehead, Massachusetts under Capt. W. Crocker's command, told USS *Peacock*'s surgeon when they met in Whampoa during the first week of December 1832 that while on board *Friendship* soon after the attack, he'd learned of a provocation: gross fraud committed by Endicott on the natives, who had caught the ship's master using false weights to cheat them.[3] Earlier, midway through *Peacock*'s call at Manila, Ticknor had heard yet another explanation for the attack on the ship. This one claimed that *Friendship* had the bad luck to arrive at Kuala Batee first after an American and a French vessel had both sailed off without paying for the pepper they'd taken on board, "which so enraged the natives that they determined to be revenged upon the first American or French that came into the harbor."

harbor, and from there, as depicted in these paintings, she fired three broadsides. *Potomac* would have hauled down her bogus Danish flag and flown the stars and stripes when she first opened fire, but although he catches the mood perfectly, Louis Dodd has small details of that morning not quite right. Half of *Potomac's* gun ports had been painted out to make the frigate better resemble an East Indiaman, and she was alone, not escorted by a U.S. Navy schooner. Dodd (1943–2006), of Hastings, England, was a prolific British marine artist, well known for his luminous oils, painted in many coats on wooden panels.
COURTESY OF BARBARA VALENTINE DODD AND AKG-IMAGES, LONDON

Whatever the provocation, Ticknor was mortified by the American response. "However just it may have been to inflict punishment on those who had been concerned in the affair of the *Friendship*," he wrote, "and however expedient it may be considered . . . to involve in the punishment of the few guilty, a large number of those who could not have had the least participation in their crime, for the purpose of striking the natives with the greater terror of American vengeance; I cannot bring myself to believe, that the advantages which will result from this severe measure, although they may be realized to the utmost that could be expected, can possibly be such as to justify so great a sacrifice of human life." What seemed like summary execution to Ticknor discomforted others, too.

Niles' Weekly Register, looking back on July 14, commented in an item titled "A Speck of War in the East": "The rightfulness of the attack is doubted by many—the outrages committed on the ship Friendship, surely, placed the authors of them in the position of pirates—hostes humani generus [enemy of humanity]—but in such summary proceedings, care may not always be exercised to distinguish between the innocent and the guilty, and it would seem that a demand for redress should have preceded the infliction of so awful a punishment."*[4] The *National Intelligencer* newspaper sided with *Niles*, and the anti-Jacksonians by criticizing Downes' impetuous act. The *Globe* (masthead motto: "The World Is Governed Too Much"), published weekly by Jackson's worshipful friend Francis Preston Blair, sided of course with the president and with Downes against their critics.

So did a piece published in the *North American Review* a few years later that described the "high handed aggression on our undefended commerce [the attack on *Friendship*]" as having been avenged by *Potomac* "in strict accordance with established maxims of civilized intercourse with the Indies, by confounding together both the innocent and the guilty; though, in this instance at least, there was no other way left of making an example of punishment, if that was to be done."

The hubbub hadn't prompted any obvious second thoughts on the president's part. In his fourth annual address to Congress, December 4, 1832, Jackson wrote to members that "a frigate was dispatched with orders to demand satisfaction for the injury. . . . This last was done, and the effect has been increased respect for our flag in those distant seas and additional security for our commerce."

Neither did Secretary Woodbury appear to have any. The day before Jackson's message was delivered, the secretary's report for 1832 had noted with satisfaction,

> The chastisement inflicted by the frigate *Potomac* on the piratical Malays, in February last, is the sole occurrence of importance among our vessels that compose the squadron of vessels in the Pacific. . . . It has been gratifying to learn, by accounts from that quarter of the world, subsequent to the visit of *Potomac* to Sumatra, that the result of that visit has been to silence all exultation and menaces of further violence from those sea robbers: to draw from them acknowledgements of past errors, and promises of future forbearance of like offenses, and to insure, as yet, a scrupulous fulfillment of those promises. But to guard against their perfidy, orders were given that

* Hezekiah Niles (1777–1839), and later his son and two successors, published *Niles' Register* between 1811 and 1848 in Philadelphia, Baltimore, and finally Washington. Described in one subtitle, ponderously, as "containing political, historical, geographical, scientifical, statistical, economical, and biographical documents, essays and facts: together with notices of the arts and manufactures, and a record of events of the times," to the editors' credit, their sixteen-page weekly remains today a good record of those times.

> the *Potomac* should be followed by a detachment from the Brazil Squadron [*Peacock* and *Boxer*], part of which detachment has since sailed, and has instructions to touch not only at Sumatra, but such places in India, China, and on the eastern coast of Africa, as may be conducive to the security and prosperity of our important commercial interests in those regions.

Behind the scenes, however, there was official anxiety in Washington over the summer about Downes' precipitate assault on the Malays the previous autumn. On July 16, 1832, acknowledging receipt of nine letters from the commodore spanning eight months at sea, Woodbury wrote Downes, saying, "The president regrets you were not able, before attacking the Malays at Quallah-Battoo, to obtain there, or near, fuller information of the particulars of their outrage on the Friendship, and of the character and political relations of the aggressors":

> It was desirable, also, that a previous demand should have been made for restitution and indemnification; as, whether necessary or not on principles of national law, it would have furnished the most favorable opportunity for success in obtaining redress, and would have tended to remove any complaint in any quarter, on account of the nature and consequences of the attack.
>
> On every circumstance, influencing your judgment to dispense with these, he wishes the fullest information, since it may hereafter become material.[5]

Seven months later Downes replied from Callao, Peru, that intelligence he'd collected at Rio de Janeiro and Cape Town on the way to Sumatra, from officers well acquainted with cruel and treacherous Malay character, had informed his plan. *Potomac* finally returned to the United States in May 1834. Commodore Downes (1786–1854) never again served at sea.

Woodbury's annual report would soon be proved optimistic. *Potomac*'s raid and bombardment failed completely to "silence all exultation and menaces of future violence." Somehow, the murderers of ten crewmembers from the Salem whaler *Charles Doggett* on Fiji in September 1834 got a bye until 1840, when the U.S. Exploring Expedition arrived off the island, but after *Potomac*'s raid on Kuala Batee a pattern was fixed: landing parties and long guns would be the usual, albeit sometimes long delayed, American response to crimes committed against U.S. ships and crews in distant waters.

In October 1835, Capt. John Aulick, USN, commanding the 18-gun USS *Vincennes*, put an eighty-man armed party ashore at Savai'i, westernmost of the Samoan archipelago, and incinerated a village in reprisal for an assault the previous July on boat crews from the Nantucket whaler *William Penn*. The offending chief, who escaped *Vincennes*' raiders, was pursued unsuccessfully off and on during the next six years, a chase punctuated by other village burnings. Another such attack, inflicted in early January 1839 by the 44-gun frigate USS *Columbia* (like *Potomac* also on her first cruise) and 18-gun USS *John Adams*, and equally devastating, was a reprisal for the murder on August 26, 1838, of Capt. Charles Wilkins, master of the Salem-based bark *Eclipse*, and the ship's boy, and the theft of 18,000 Spanish dollars and four chests of opium from the ship by local pirates. In this incident, 320 went ashore from the two ships and soon reembarked to leave behind them "nothing . . . visible to the eye but ashes covering smoking ruins, upon which the town of Muckie and the forts once stood." The episode is remembered in history, if not in rhyme, somewhat grandly as "the Second Sumatran Expedition."

And so it went for another thirty years or so. Assaults on ships and crew members parried by attacks on villages on shore.

Seventeen thousand miles from home, at Bencoolen in Sumatra in late August 1832 (and one year after *Potomac* had sailed from Boston but months before the secretary's report), USS *Peacock*'s captain learned that Kuala Batee was in ruins and that nothing further there was required of him. The news freed Captain Geisinger and Edmund Roberts to get on with the latter's diplomatic mission.

The two ships, *Potomac* and *Peacock*, were not to meet until late morning March 25, 1834, when USS *Potomac*'s appearance, flying Commo., John Downes' broad pennant, in the harbor of Rio de Janeiro triggered a concert of gun salutes from the several combatant ships already in port, among them the flagship of the U.S. Brazilian squadron USS *Natchez* (Commodore Woolsey) and a French brig of war just in from Toulon. *Peacock* alone fired twenty-six, half for Downes and half for Woolsey.

3

Master Commandant Geisinger, Chargé d'Affaires Baylies, and Surgeon Ticknor

At 11 O'clock a.m. we weighed anchor, and with a fair wind stood out to sea. . . . To describe the feelings that are called forth for taking leave of one's family and friends for the long period of two to three years, and perhaps forever, and with the prospect too of receiving no intelligence from them during the long separation, would be impossible. It is not in the power of language to convey an adequate idea of the emotions that agitate the heart in such circumstance such as these.

Surgeon Benajah Ticknor, USN, on board USS *Peacock*, March 8, 1832

7

As described by the annual reports of its secretary, the U.S. Navy of the early 1830s confidently maintained an American presence in distant waters: in the Mediterranean, off the coast of Brazil, in the West Indies, and in the Pacific. When USS *Peacock* first sailed for Asia and Arabia in 1832, the fleet in commission and at sea numbered just nineteen men-of-war. According to Secretary Woodbury's proud reckoning, those nineteen combatants, armed with a total of 467 cannon and shorter-range carronades, made the U.S. Navy then the fifth or sixth largest in the world. The most powerful of the nineteen were four frigates, three in the Mediterranean (*United States*, *Brandywine*, and *Constellation*) and a fourth, Commodore Downes' *Potomac*, in the Pacific. The rest of the fleet on foreign stations was comprised of relatively small sloops and even smaller schooners.

Another twenty-one ships were in ordinary, meaning tied up in port, afloat with guns and ballast on board but "covered with tight roofs and side hurdles," not provisioned, and without crews assigned. A further dozen were "in the stocks," in dry storage at shipyards undergoing or awaiting heavy maintenance, and many months away from being ready for sea.[1] The fifty-two-ship fleet total included thirteen sloops, all armed and configured generally as was *Peacock:* square-rigged on all three masts with a mizzen course aft. Not all were actually pierced for the usual eighteen guns. Some, *Peacock* among them, only carried twelve.

All were, of course, propelled entirely by wind on canvas, although as early as 1816 the U.S. Navy had begun to experiment—awkwardly—with steam power. The first such experiment was in the form of a barely mobile, center-wheel catamaran, the steam battery *Fulton*. Designed for the protection of New York Harbor and half a century or more ahead of the state of the art, *Fulton* blew up in a powder room explosion in 1829. That catastrophe absorbed, Navy officers watched as the first commercial steamships began crossing the Atlantic during the next decade, following the lead of SS *Savannah*. Finally, in the early 1840s, the Navy commissioned and sent to sea its first steam-powered paddle frigates, USS *Mississippi* and the short-lived USS *Missouri*. (She was lost to a fire soon thereafter, demonstrating, not for the last time, the difficulty of safely fitting this new technology into highly flammable wooden hulls.) It took decades before engineering plant maintenance and coal resupply while deployed gave combatant ships anything like the range and endurance they enjoyed in the age of fighting sail, and screw propulsion gave back valuable midships space to gun batteries.

As they are today, the Navy's capital ships in the 1830s were very expensive to operate. As designed, the gigantic, one-of-a-kind, four-decker USS *Pennsylvania* needed eleven hundred men to sail and serve her 140 guns—equivalent to, say, the entire male, young adult population of St. Louis, Missouri, in 1830—explaining why this dinosaur went to sea only once, in 1837. But even the Navy's 74-gun ships of the line and its 44- and 36-gun frigates required relatively large crews to sail and fight—nearly 800 men in a 74 and 450 at least in a 44. *Peacock*'s entire compliment amounted to less than half that last number. For this reason the big ships were often in port, in ordinary, leaving most of the Navy's presence at sea to the more economical 24-, 18-, and 12-gun sloops and schooners. (A 24-gun sloop, the Navy estimated in 1830, cost $62,254 to operate for one year, the total including pay and subsistence for the crew, provisions, hospital stores, and wear and tear. A schooner cost less than half that, $29,120.)

The force afloat was supported by a shore establishment of seven shipyards, six on the Atlantic stretching south from Portsmouth, New Hampshire, to Norfolk, Virginia, and beyond to a yard on the Gulf Coast, at Pensacola, Florida. (Among the seven, President Jackson, who twice fought and defeated the Spanish at Pensacola and then lived in the city as Florida's first territorial governor, would have known the least of them, Pensacola, best.)

Boston and Norfolk were the largest and most capable shipyards, thanks in part to the availability of a new dry dock at each place, both finished in 1833 at great expense. The one at Norfolk was delayed by the appearance over the previous summer of "malignant cholera," which resulted in high absenteeism at the yard and "much languor and uneasiness in those who remained" loyally at work. Over several years that dry dock cost nearly $900,000 to construct and equip—some 30 percent of the Navy's annual budget. The large yard at Brooklyn, New York, was the candidate site for an eventual third dry dock.

These shipyards were also depots for the Navy's strategic reserves—ship sets of live oak frames and stocks of other lumber, and stores of metals, guns and small arms, of powder and shot, and of spare anchors and chain cables. Although inventories also showed some twenty-two hundred spare cannon and carronades, most, the Navy conceded, were "of such different forms and dimensions that they could not be used as armament for vessels." All together these stocks, including the unusable guns, represented some $5.58 million in total investment.

Through the decade the Navy was manned by roughly one thousand officers and five thousand enlisted men in all grades. (An additional thirteen hundred officers, noncommissioned officers, musicians, and privates constituted the U.S. Marine Corps of the time.) Enlisted recruiting was done at stations in Boston, New York, Philadelphia, Baltimore, and Norfolk, and apprentice training was done on board receiving vessels in the same cities. From these five, sailors were distributed to commissioned ships preparing to deploy and signed on for the length of the cruise.

Navy pay and subsistence accounts during the 1830s totaled roughly $1.5 million per year, out of a total department budget of approximately $3.6 million, which in turn represented approximately one-fifth of the federal budget during the decade—the price of keeping the world's "fifth or sixth" largest navy at sea at the end of the age of fighting sail.*

Peacock in the early 1830s was four years into her second incarnation and less than a decade away from grounding and destruction on the bar of Washington's Columbia River in the summer of 1841 while part of Lt. Charles Wilkes' famous, notorious U.S. Exploring Expedition.[2]

The first USS *Peacock* had been built in Manhattan by the Brown Brothers, Adam and Noah, in 1813. Her distinctly unwarlike name was a reminder of USS *Hornet*'s astonishingly quick victory over the brig sloop HMS *Peacock* in the late afternoon of February 24 off the mouth of the Demarara River in Guyana. The two spotted each other at 3:30 p.m.:

* In fact, *after* the end of that age. The last sea battle fought entirely by sailing vessels was at Navarino in the Ionian Sea in October 1827, between the navies of Ottoman Turkey and Great Britain, France, and Russia.

> At 5.25 pm the ship and brig exchanged broadsides, within half pistol shot [fifteen yards]. The Peacock then wore to renew the action on the other tack, the Hornet quickly bearing up, received Peacock's starboard broadside, then ran the latter close aboard the starboard quarter. The Hornet then poured in so heavy and well directed fire that at 5.50, having had her commander killed, and being with six feet of water in the hold, and cut to pieces in hull and masts, the Peacock hoisted from her fore rigging an ensign, union down as a signal of distress. Shortly afterwards her mainmast went by the board. Both Hornet and Peacock were immediately anchored. . . . And in a very few minutes after she had anchored, Peacock went down in 5 ½ fathoms.[3]

The obligatory court-martial after the loss of a Royal Navy ship revealed that her crew hadn't been exercised at *Peacock*'s guns for the prior three years, a likely explanation for the outcome between two reasonably well-matched combatants.[4]

In 1828, and then only fifteen years old, USS *Peacock* was brought into the New York Navy Yard and broken up. A few recycled old timbers and $60,722 in new construction resulted in a new ship masquerading as an old one, very nearly the same size as her vanished namesake but now measuring 559 tons, some 50 tons more than the original.

The sleight-of-hand construction was done anticipating that the new *Peacock* would be dispatched by President John Quincy Adams later that year into the Pacific on a voyage of scientific discovery and mapping. *Niles' Weekly Register* described *Peacock* to the public on November 8 (quoting the *New York American*):

> The discovery ship is already rigged and waiting only for her officers and men. . . . She bears the name of the old Peacock, repaired, but is, in reality, in every respect, a new ship, prepared expressly for the intended expedition. Her length is one hundred and eighteen feet; breadth, thirty two feet six inches, with a spar deck of seven feet, and measuring about five hundred twelve tons. The frame is very strong, and of the best seasoned live oak. Her timbers are entirely solid, bolted one into the other, and caulked, as high as the birth [berth] deck. . . .
>
> In addition to what is common in sloops of war, she is provided with a spar deck, which will afford shelter and comfort to the men in bad weather. . . . The naval architect, Mr. Samuel Hartt, has

> superintended the vessel . . . and the manner in which he has executed his task, reflects the highest credit on his professional skill.[5]

Several days later, on November 11, 1828, Master Cdt. Francis Gregory, USN, reported to Commo. Isaac Chauncey, USN, commanding naval forces at the New York station, that *Peacock* was now ready for sea. "The sloop of war Peacock has been thoroughly repaired," he wrote, sustaining the fiction that this was a repair, "and is now equal to a new ship, and is ready to receive her crew; this ship having been ordered for a particular purpose, half of the ports have been filled in, and a light spar deck built upon her, and her masts and spars have been reduced from the regulated dimensions. She mounts six 18-pounders."

When Andrew Jackson defeated Adams' reelection attempt and succeeded to the presidency in 1829, political support for the expedition evaporated, relegating the newly revitalized *Peacock* to a familiar mission, routine operations in the West Indies.

Perhaps the cancellation was all for the good. The impetus for *Peacock*'s stillborn 1828 expedition to the South Pacific had come originally from Jeremiah Reynolds, former editor of the Wilmington, Ohio, *Spectator*, and for a while after 1824 the acolyte of one of nineteenth-century America's more fascinating fringe theorists: Capt. John Cleves Symmes (1779–1829).

Symmes, "Captain" because he was a veteran of the War of 1812, earnestly believed, as his Circular No. 1 announced, that "the earth is hollow, and habitable within; containing a number of solid concentric spheres, one within the other, and that it is open at the poles 12 or 16 degrees." He sought "one hundred brave companions, well equipped, to start from Siberia in the fall season, with Reindeer and sleighs, on the ice of the frozen sea." He promised they would "find a warm and rich land, stocked with thrifty vegetables and animals if not men, on reaching one degree northward of latitude 82."*

For the next ten years, until his death in May 1829, Symmes was an enthusiastic missionary for his bizarre theory, leaving at home his large family—a wife and ten children—while he sought the men and money necessary to prove him correct. He failed in 1822 to get funding from Congress for a two-ship expedition to a pole.

Beginning in late 1825, Symmes and Reynolds headed east on a speaking tour. Arguments eventually separated them, but by then Reynolds too

* Better scientists than Symmes thought the same thing. The distinguished British astronomer Edmund Halley held beliefs very like those of Symmes, granted Halley's ideas of a hollow and perhaps peopled center of the planet predated Symmes' by more than a century. Bizarre ideas about the nature of Earth's poles were common through the end of the nineteenth century and not entirely dispelled until the start of the twentieth saw successful expeditions to both places.

SYMMES'S THEORY

OF

CONCENTRIC SPHERES;

DEMONSTRATING

THAT THE EARTH IS HOLLOW, HABITABLE WITHIN,

AND

WIDELY OPEN ABOUT THE POLES.

By a Citizen of the United States.

"There are more things in Heaven and EARTH, Horatio,
" Than are dreamt of in your philosophy!" SHAKSPEARE.

"If this man be erroneous, who appears to be so sanguine and persevering in his opinions, what withholds us but our sloth, our self-will, and distrust in the right cause, that we do not give him gentle meetings and a gentle dismission; that we debate not and examine the matter thoroughly, with liberal and frequent audience; if not for his sake, yet for our own? seeing that no man who hath tasted learning, but will confess the many ways of profiting by those, who, not content with stale receipts, are able to manage and set forth new positions to the world. And were they but as the dust and cinders of our feet, so long as in that notion, they may yet serve to polish and brighten the armory of truth; even for that respect they are not utterly to be cast away." MILTON.

CINCINNATI:

PRINTED AND PUBLISHED BY MORGAN, LODGE AND FISHER.

1826.

Title page to *Symmes's Theory of Concentric Spheres* and pencil portrait by John J. Audubon, 1820. Symmes was already a minor public figure at the time of this portrait by the still unknown Audubon; his Circular No. 1, released in 1818 and addressed breathlessly to "each notable foreign government, reigning prince, legislature, city, college, and philosophical society, quite round the earth" having been issued nearly two and a half years earlier to mixed acclaim in the West and incredulity in the East. Seven other "circulars" followed in the next year.

The theory was then laid out in detail in a 168-page, anonymously published book that made his case for a hollow earth, "habitable within, and widely open about the poles." This is the title page of that book, printed in 1826. The "good likeness" of him was sketched while Audubon (1785–1851), then a failed dry-goods merchant and recently bankrupt, was living in western Kentucky with his family. Audubon began painting his famous birds of North America later in that same decade. Prints of these life-sized paintings, first published in Edinburgh in 1826 and in publication through 1838, were an instant commercial success and account for the artist's brilliant reputation today.

Portrait courtesy of the New York Historical Society, No. 1864.4.

had become fascinated by polar exploration. In 1828 he managed to persuade President Adams' secretary of the navy, Samuel Southard, to hire him to plan what was anticipated to be a three-ship Navy expedition to the South Pacific.

Reynolds' proselytizing aside, further stimulus for the adventure came in the form of news that the British *Cherokee*-class brig, HMS *Chanticleer*, Capt. Henry Foster, RN, commanding, was sailing from England to the southern Shetland Islands, after which many suspected she'd proceed even farther south, stealing the march toward the pole from the Americans. Competition with the despised British aside, the overriding reason for forward progress toward the pole seems to have been Secretary Southard's personal interest in the project—and political pressure from New England sealers looking for a new rookery to savage now that the seals of the Shetland Islands had been harvested to extinction. For their parts, American naturalists ("scientist" would not be in use for another decade) were skeptical of the contribution to knowledge this marine mammal hunting party would actually make.

Even before Symmes' death at fifty in May 1829, *Peacock*'s planned expedition toward, and hopefully to, the South Pole (she was to be accompanied by two smaller combatants, a brig and a schooner) had attracted opposition in the Senate on more substantial grounds than doubts about Symmes' grasp on reality; instead, it was on questions about the Navy Department's legal authority to expend public funds on a project not blessed by the Senate.

Under Commo. Isaac Chauncy's supervision, *Peacock* had been built at the Brooklyn Navy Yard to a design by Naval Constructor Samuel Hartt, one that incorporated special strengthening for operations in icy waters. A brig, *Seraph*, had been conditionally purchased from her owners in Connecticut to be *Peacock*'s escort. The necessary instruments and charts were already being acquired by Lt. Charles Wilkes, USN, who was maneuvering for command of *Seraph* during her impending "voyage of exploration in the Pacific polar seas" (*Niles*' phrase). Recruiting for a civilian scientific corps was meanwhile also under way. And a captain, War of 1812 veteran Thomas ap Catesby Jones, had been selected by the secretary to command *Peacock*. All this before the Senate's Committee on Naval Affairs had signed on to the plan, much less a majority of the whole chamber.

On February 5, 1829, that committee's chairman, Senator Robert Hayne (1791–1839) of South Carolina, raised questions about how this initiative had gone so far without the Senate's acquiescence and asked for an explanation. (Members of his party, Democrats from the South, usually saw the Navy as an extravagance that benefitted only New England's interests.) Hayne—much better known for his ardent states' rights advocacy and support of nullification than his place on this committee—anticipated this as the coming of a three-year, half-million-dollar boondoggle. Secretary Southard wrote in reply eight days later that it was all scrupulously legal and would cost only $204,000, but a month after that Jackson's inauguration sent Southard back home to New Jersey, marking both the end of his nearly six years atop the navy secretariat under two presidents and the end of this program.

Jeremiah Reynolds didn't give up on a voyage toward one of the poles just because USS *Peacock* was denied to him. In late 1829 he sailed in the brig *Annawan* (one of the three ships of the failed South Sea Fur Company and Exploring Expedition) for the seal rookeries of Antarctica. Stranded in Valparaiso in 1832 after he was put ashore by her dyspeptic crew—aggrieved by poor hunting—as good fortune would have it, Reynolds was rescued that October by USS *Potomac*, passing through the Chilean port on her long way home after bombarding "Quallah-Battoo." She took the frustrated polar enthusiast home.* By curious coincidence, the same Jeremiah Reynolds would several years later become the paid editor of Edmund Roberts' journal of his first embassy to Asia, under contract to the author's son-in-law, Amasa Parker, preparing it for publication after Roberts' death.

Jackson's victory denied *Peacock*'s crew a role in what might have become a quixotic search for an entrance near the South Pole into the planet's interior and made the suddenly unemployed ship available for assignment to the West Indies Squadron. Touched by yellow fever that killed some on board, and then relieved by USS *Vincennes* on that station in late winter, *Peacock* went out of commission and into ordinary at Boston that April. At the end of 1831, Secretary Levi Woodbury reported to Congress that after reprovisioning, work on running rigging and sails, and new paint on her hull, *Peacock* could again be ready for sea.

8

The competition for command at sea among the service's captains, master commandants, and lieutenants was keen. Master Cdt. David Geisinger, USN

* Reynolds subsequently wrote a book about *Potomac*'s round-the-world cruise, *Voyage of the United States Frigate Potomac*. Unusually, a second book about *Potomac*'s cruise was published in the same year by another civilian ship rider, this one Rev. Francis Warriner, A.M. (1804–1866), on board her seeking to cure his health, a change in climate being one of the usual things that early-nineteenth-century physicians prescribed to counteract many types of enfeebling disease. His book: *Cruise of the United States Frigate Potomac*.

One of *Potomac*'s assistant surgeons, Jonathan Foltz (who would go on to a brilliant career in navy medicine), wrote an essay about the same cruise, "Medical Statistics of the Frigate Potomac During Her Voyage Around the World." Foltz was proud that during 514 days at sea, *Potomac* saw only twenty-five deaths and had just seven men invalided ashore, these totals from a crew of nearly five hundred men.

(promoted to that rank in March 1829 and so among the more junior of his thirty-six contemporaries) was flattered when early in January 1832 a letter came from Secretary of the Navy Woodbury offering him command of *Peacock*, an appointment tendered by the secretary "in justice to [his] rank and worth."

The start of Geisinger's "worth" dated back twenty-two years, to before the War of 1812, when he joined the Navy. Later, in late September 1814 as a midshipman in the sloop of war USS *Wasp*, he had been put in charge of the prize crew of the captured British merchant schooner *Atalanta*, an honor accorded him reflecting the fact that two months before he'd bravely been the first of *Wasp*'s boarding party on the deck of HM Brig *Reindeer* during a bloody, ultimately successful battle. Young Geisinger sailed his prize, loaded with wine, brandy, and silks, from off Madeira across the Atlantic to Savannah, thus surviving the disappearance of USS *Wasp*, last seen October 9 and soon thereafter mysteriously vanished with all hands. (An account of that remarkable bit of good luck constituted almost all of Geisinger's obituary in the *New York Times*, published March 10, 1860, upon his death in Philadelphia at seventy.) During the two decades after that war, Geisinger (1790–1860) served at sea in the brig USS *Firefly*, and in United States Ships *Macedonian*, *Independence*, *John Adams*, and *Constitution*, and ashore at the Philadelphia Navy Yard.

Flattered, and surprised, Geisinger hadn't expected orders back to sea, he wrote the secretary, until spring. "The time for necessary preparations is short," he continued, "but standing as I do first for a command on the list of master commandants, I am unwilling to be passed over & therefore readily accept the offer which you make me. I should however be glad to be indulged as much as possible in regard to time at home." The familiar hope of deploying sailors in every age, this wasn't to be. Secretary Woodbury's letter went on to say that *Peacock* was to sail on the first of February and would spend half of the following two years "in the India Seas." Nor did Geisinger get his second and third requests: that Lt. William McKean, USN, "an officer of great worth" and much experience, be ordered to *Peacock* as her first lieutenant (McKean soon declined to sail in a more junior position) and that a Mr. Hansley Newport be appointed captain's clerk. He did, however, manage to have the gunroom stocked with several midshipmen he'd asked for by name.

While at sea in the grade of master commandant, Geisinger would be earning $60 per month and drawing five rations per day, equal to a further $1.25. (Roberts, his nominal subordinate, would be earning about the same, $1,200 per year.) At first, Woodbury expected that *Peacock*'s route would take the sloop along the east coast of South America, around Cape Horn and then

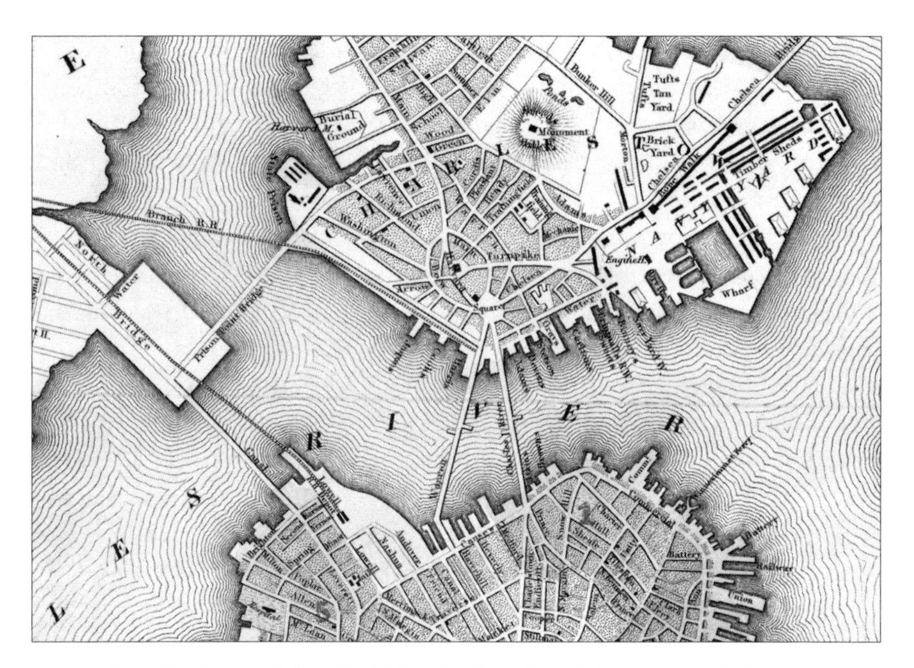

Map 1. "The Charlestown Navy Yard." In 1800 President Adams approved the recommendation of Secretary of the Navy Stoddart for the construction of navy yards at Portsmouth, Boston, New York, Philadelphia, Washington, and Norfolk. These, plus a seventh yard at Pensacola, Florida, on the Gulf of Mexico, constituted the shore establishment that in 1832 supported the Navy's commissioned ships and those stored in ordinary. By then the Charlestown Navy Yard had already launched six ships, including USS *Boxer*.

The yard's facilities when *Boxer* and *Peacock* sailed included three ship houses built atop construction ways, several wharfs, miscellaneous shops and sheds, some housing, and very near the engine house the nearly finished second of the navy's two dry docks. (A naval hospital and magazine would be built soon, off the yard's property but not far away.) Several years later Charlestown became home to the Navy's first ropewalk, a modern quarter-mile-long factory for the manufacture of cordage, shown here just east of Chelsea Street.

This map of the Charlestown Navy Yard in 1838 is a detail from engraver G. W. Boynton's map of Boston from T. G. Bradford's *An Illustrated Atlas, Geographical, Statistical, and Historical of the United States and Adjacent Countries* (Philadelphia: E. S. Grant, 1838). Boston proper lies across the two bridges over the Charles River, and a corner of Cambridge is barely visible over the Prison Point Bridge.
Courtesy Boston Public Library

into the Pacific, where Roberts would begin his delicate diplomatic mission. As it happened, she sailed the other way, around the Cape of Good Hope.

Despite Woodbury's schedule, *Peacock*'s sailors and her Marine guard detachment didn't report on board their ship at Charlestown until 10:30, the morning of February 7. Fully manned and with her captain on board, *Peacock* went into commission later the same day, her new status marked by the first hoisting of the colors since her nineteen-month West Indies cruise had ended at the yard in April nearly a year before. A few days later *Peacock*'s revitalization had proceeded to the point where her officers were now able to mess, to take their meals, on board in the wardroom, comfortably warmed by a stove. Elsewhere in the ship and about town, temperatures hovered around freezing, but it was midsummer where *Peacock* was going and that thought might have warmed anyone working in the open who could look that far ahead.

Peacock's crew then spent the next four weeks in frenzied preparations to sail, pausing briefly on the seventeenth only so all hands on deck could cheer USS *Boxer* as she put to sea for Liberia on her maiden voyage. The two were scheduled to rendezvous in Brazil and to sail together to the Indian Ocean, but that didn't happen. They would not be together again for seventeen months.

9

Like *Peacock*'s, *Boxer*'s name memorialized a U.S. Navy victory over the Royal Navy during the War of 1812. Nothing so grand as the big frigate duels that marked the American navy's coming of age, but violent nevertheless. In September 1813, His Majesty's Brig *Boxer*, 10 guns, suffered quick defeat in a fight with the 12-gun USS *Enterprise* off Portland, Maine, in an hour-long battle that saw both commanding officers die on deck. Defeated, HMS *Boxer* barely escaped sinking and was sold out of prize court into merchant service. The 1831 schooner USS *Boxer* has been counted as the second commissioned ship with that name ever since, and the two names, *Enterprise* and *Boxer*, have reappeared on the United States Navy's combatant ship register into this century.

Charlestown (now the Boston Navy Yard) was USS *Boxer*'s home yard. Her keel had been laid there in June the year before, and she'd been launched into the Charles River just five months after that. *Boxer*'s deployment preparations in port at the navy yard took the first eighteen days of February 1832 to complete, cold days during which snow squalls blew over bits of ice floating on the water while her crew finished work on their ship, loaded fifty-two hundred gallons of water on board, and stowed dry stores and spare parts below for the long cruise to come—everything from barrels of bread, beef, and pork to lamp wicks and wheel ropes.

After her launching on November 22, 1831, *Boxer*'s further construction and fitting out at the yard appear to have been hurried, despite the $30,697 spent to build her. Approaching three weeks out of home port, the crew was busy in the magazine, cautiously moving priming and cannon powder around and lining its bulkheads with sheet copper to prevent the intrusion of sparks. Problems with seawater leaks into the starboard bread room followed. And then, in Rio de Janeiro in September, the nearly new schooner needed to be careened, "heaved down," to permit her entire hull to be recaulked, sheathed, and recoppered—an enormous voyage repair that began with sending down all the spars and much of the rigging, removing the guns, and unloading the ship, and ended with reloading her. The need for extensive repairs does explain, in part, why *Boxer* remained in Brazil two and a half months, into the first week of November 1832.*

As designed by Samuel Humphreys, *Boxer* was a fraction of USS *Peacock*'s size: 194 tons instead of 512, 88 feet long rather than 118, and drawing only twelve feet or less to *Peacock*'s sixteen. (*Boxer*'s relatively shallow draft, Geisinger would point out in December to the secretary, would have made the still-absent schooner useful approaching both Hué and Bangkok. River mouth sandbars denied his deeper draft sloop direct access to Hué and Bangkok except at the highest spring tide.) Although on the coming cruise both ships carried two 8- and eight 24-pound guns, *Peacock* had the longer gun deck. She'd been originally built to carry twenty-two 32-pound carronades, not just ten.

Moreover, *Boxer*'s crew numbered half of *Peacock*'s 140 officers and men. Manned for sea, USS *Boxer* boasted a complement of only twelve officers (counting the captain's clerk as one) and fifty-eight enlisted men. The deck-hands among these fifty-eight included twenty-five seamen and ordinary sea-men but also eleven landsmen and five boys. No one of these last sixteen had been to sea before. While *Boxer* tacked toward open water with the Peacocks' cheers fading away astern, the inexperience of his crew might have concerned her veteran (and as it would turn out, interim) commanding officer, Lt. Benjamin Page Jr., USN.

"The day we left Boston was excessively cold," Acting Midn. William Reynolds wrote. "A gale of wind came on, with snow, we were covered over . . . [sea] sickness the worst kind of sickness any person can experience made me wish myself home more than once. So it continued for 4 or 5 days, nothing but squalls wind, rain, snow, and ice every one of us was sea sick, every one wish-ing himself at home, some cursing the Navy, the Schooner, the Ocean, and if they got home, they never would go to sea again."†

* The requirement for repairs in Rio cannot, however, be blamed entirely on shoddy work at Charlestown. In May, while shifting anchorages at Maranhão, Brazil, *Boxer* had been run aground (only "for a short time" on sand, her captain reported to the commodore, implying the fault lay with the pilot). A formal survey done at the end of August found injury to the parts of ship's skin and certain frame members as well as to her caulking and coppering.

† But Reynolds (1815–79) did go to sea again. After forty-two years of intermittent Navy service that began in USS *Boxer* in 1832 and included sailing as a passed midshipman with the U.S. Exploring Expedition in 1838–42, Reynolds rose to rear admiral and command of the Asiatic Station in 1875, flying his flag in USS *Tennessee*. He served on twelve Navy ships and commanded three others. Again suffering poor health after 1860, Reynolds retired in December 1877. His letters to his father, publisher of the Lancaster, Pennsylvania, *Journal*, are held in the Reynolds Family Papers collection at Franklin and Marshall College.

Boxer's small crew grew smaller still as her cruise progressed. While the months wore on, the schooner saw her crew dwindle. Five men (Cottridge, Cummings, Brady, Congdon, and Whitemarsh) stole the No. 2 cutter and deserted the week before she sailed. (Zachariah Whitemarsh, the armorer, made good his escape, but the other four were captured the next day and returned to the ship. They were flogged in mid-Atlantic a month later. For their crimes Brady got eight lashes, Cottridge ten, the two others twelve.) In mid-April at Liberia, three men (William Humphries, John Hogan, and William Bramble) were discharged from the Navy and transferred to the "destitute" schooner *Eagle* and the brig *Bethial* in port. Both American merchant vessels had insufficient hands on board to sail them home from their moorings in the river off the American Colonization Society's young settlement at Cape Mesurado because of desertions and deaths from fever. The former Navy men rounded out their crews.

After sailing from Boston in February, *Boxer* had spent eight days in early April in Liberia, showing the flag. She then crossed the mid-Atlantic westbound and moved down the Brazilian coast, first calling at Maranhão then at Pará do Belém. There, at the end of May, Acting Sailing Master William Irving, the navigator, was put ashore on a sick ticket, suffering from chronic rheumatism. At about the same time, Acting Midshipman John Underwood (one of five of these junior officers on board) deserted, successfully making his way home from Pará on one of the American brigs in port.* Next came Pernambuco and then, farther down the coast, Bahia, after which, on August 16, *Boxer* arrived in Rio de Janiero.

September 6, the day that careening began in Rio, five more men deserted: James Carr, Peter Weed, Charles Coombs, Richard May, and Thomas Harding. Caught the next day, Weed, May, and Harding were flogged for the attempt on October 20. (Despite the fact that nearly one-fifth of *Boxer*'s enlisted crew attempted desertion, the log suggests the ship had relatively few discipline problems. Only one other man, surname Cole, was flogged, he for drunkenness in December 1832.)

---

* Before deserting, Underwood, of Portsmouth, New Hampshire, had been falsely charged with the theft of a gold watch by one of the ship's lieutenants. Midshipman Reynolds, his messmate, described Underwood as "a very vulgar young man not having brought up in a gentile society also very ignorant, ill behaved &c. . . . One day he was sent ashore as officer of a boat he took his clothes in her under pretence of his going to have them washed cleared out, left the boat and that was the last we seen of him." More generously, Captain Page thought that Underwood's chief problem was not that he was common but that his parents had spoiled him.

Consul Abraham Smith reported sixteen American ships in port Pará during the first half of 1832, drawn there by the strong market for imported foodstuffs (the Amazon basin grew practically no food) and by exports of rubber, hides, dyestuff, and tapioca.

Three days later, October 23, Captain Page was relieved of command and left *Boxer* "on account of ill health." The diagnosis of a board of three surgeons convened by Commodore Cooper was that Page was suffering from "an obstinate chronic state of the stomach and bowels . . . a rheumatic nervous affection of the right side of the head and neck . . . a hernia liable to strangulation, which is aggravated by the bad state of the bowels, which produces irritation of the prostate gland and a retention of urine." All these ills, the three concluded soberly, meant that "it would not be desirable or expedient for [Page] to proceed" on deployment.

Page probably wasn't missed. "Our captn [sic] is a man who is not liked by the officers or men, he does not behave like a gentleman to either," Midshipman Reynolds had written to his father from Rio de Janeiro two months earlier. "He thinks if we go to the East Indies he will not go with us. He is afraid of his health. I hope he will not go." The departed Page was replaced by Capt. William F. Shields, USN.

Also on October 23, Irving's replacement as sailing master, Charles Poor, reported on board. The following June, Poor was promoted to acting lieutenant, opening up his place to the senior midshipman, George Hurst. Later there were other losses. Assistant Surgeon Andrew Kennedy, the ship's medical officer, "departed this life" the evening of June 14, 1833, at the hospital in Batavia, eventually replaced by Assistant Surgeon Edward Gilcrist off the *Peacock*.* A week later the body of Hugh Williams, ordinary seaman, was sent ashore (the ship's log says nothing else about his death) and two sick men were transferred to *Peacock*, presumably so they could be seen by Surgeon Ticknor.

November 3, 1832, *Boxer* finally left Rio de Janeiro for the long passage across the South Atlantic and Indian Oceans to Bencoolen, held in the Brazil Squadron by Commodore Cooper and now five months behind *Peacock*. She arrived January 21, 1833, for a nine-day port call. For the next five months *Boxer* bounced between Angier and Batavia, on Java, spending long months swinging at anchor in the steamy Dutch colonial capital during two separate visits, until 5:30 on July 22, when she finally sailed in company with *Peacock* for the Sunda Strait and Angier on the way to Muscat and the Red Sea.

* "A mortification of the Bowels was his disease," the ever-chatty Reynolds wrote his family in Lancaster, Pennsylvania, sharing with them news of "the most painful & the most melancholy occurrence which it has been my lot to witness for years." Kennedy died "in a land of strangers" after a week's illness.

10

Edmund Roberts took time during the last few days before sailing from Boston on his embassy to write his eight daughters, the eldest twenty-two, the youngest only seven, who because their mother was dead would necessarily take care of themselves and rely on the kindness of others until their father returned home. His instructions to them in that final letter from shore sound like optimistic advice to a departing collegian today: "You must live comfortably, dress well, and very nicely, make yourselves agreeable to everybody, and live prudently."

As it developed, Catharine, the eldest Roberts daughter, took care of her five youngest sisters at the family home in Portsmouth. The second and third eldest, Sarah and Harriett, were, they described, comfortably, agreeably, and respectably situated "nearly five hundred miles from our native place" in the upstate New York home of a churchman.

Ship's work almost complete, on March 1 *Peacock* was hauled out from alongside a navy yard pier into the stream of the Charles River; two days later her stores of black powder for the guns were delivered, and five days after that, March 8, 1832, last-minute preparations completed and now heavily laden, she set sail near midday for Buenos Ayres, Argentina. In a last letter from Boston to the secretary dated the same day, Geisinger reported USS *Peacock* under way with the new U.S. consul to Argentina, Francis Baylies, on board (Geisinger made no mention of Roberts); his ship "abundantly supplied with everything necessary" and propelled by a strong breeze from the northwest.

The enlisted crew, her "people," the ship's surgeon allowed soon after departure, was the healthiest and finest looking he had ever seen, the men "more quiet and orderly in their conduct, especially on Sunday, than any crew I have ever sailed with." Roberts thought so too. He was gratified to see the "men who might, otherwise, have been occupied in relating idle stories, singing immoral songs, quarrelling, or creating a mutinous spirit among their fellows" instead reading books from the ship's library, and absorbing from their selections, he believed, not only information but also a code of morals.

On departure *Peacock* drew some fifteen and a half feet of water; nicely trimmed to within a half-inch fore and aft, with fair winds and seas and a clean hull, she could cover eight or nine miles in an hour. Finally under way five weeks later than Secretary Woodbury had hoped, with her hold newly packed with all manner of stores and victuals and her tanks filled with drinking water, and carrying forty-seven hundred Spanish dollars of public funds, "which may be applied to such purposes abroad as her future service may require," USS *Peacock* joined the other Navy ships at sea. She would spend the next twenty-six months away from home, nearly fourteen of them under way, and not touch another American port until the end of May 1834.

Peacock's berthing spaces were no less congested than was her cargo hold. Most of the 170 or so crew and passengers on board were to spend the next months and years of their lives in a space not as large as the interior of several modern Conex ocean cargo containers. The *Peacock* was badly ventilated, largely unlit, often wet and cold, and always damp. When not cold, she was often insufferably hot. "A sloop-of-war is totally unfit to be employed on a long cruise in hot climates," Ticknor wrote while sailing the Arabian Sea between Mocha and Muscat. "It is impossible that a ship of that class can possess those accommodations for officers & men, which are indispensably necessary for their health & comfort, & at the same time, carry a sufficient supply of water & provisions. No vessel of a smaller rate than a frigate should ever be employed on such a cruise; for none of a smaller size can afford the requisite accommodations."

At sea *Peacock*'s steerage and her forecastle were crowded with their usual complement of midshipmen, sailors, and marines. Officers' country, comprising the captain's stateroom aft and the several officers' cabins that surrounded the wardroom, was especially congested. That's where Consul Baylies and his family would be accommodated during their transit to his new post. Baylies' high status meant that he, Elizabeth, his wife, their eight-year-old daughter, Harriet, her governess, Leonice Sampson, age twenty, and an unnamed servant would displace Captain Geisinger from his cabin during the nearly ten weeks necessary to sail to the Argentine capital.

According to her father's journal, little Harriet soon became everybody's favorite. She was showered with pets (an African linnet, the size of a wren, from the captain; a monkey from Lieutenant White; a months-old pointer puppy; and a goat kid, one of three), entertained on a swing rigged for her off the mizzen boom by Lieutenant Cunningham, and nourished with milk from the on-board herd of eight goats and with wine at the wardroom dinner table, slipped to her by Captain Geisinger under her father's indulgent observation.*

* Lt. John White, USN, who gave little Harriet her monkey, left USS *Peacock* for home on a sick ticket at Montevideo on June 25. Geisinger was very reluctant to lose White, whom he described in a letter to Secretary Woodbury as having "great experience in the Indian & China Seas," and being a very good navigator. In a formal medical report on the crew's health to Captain Geisinger written in Rio Janeiro weeks earlier (on May 10), Ticknor had described White as "laboring under an affection of the limbs and also under a good deal of constitutional disease which will totally disable him for any activity during the cruise." In his private journal Ticknor explained more candidly that the symptoms which had been described to him as "elephantiasis" were really the product of White's years of heavy drinking, intemperance already evident to the surgeon during *Peacock*'s first day at sea.

Despite Geisinger's determination to keep White on board—the captain went so far as to offer to share his and Roberts' crowded cabin with the man, "to make him as comfortable as possible"—a second assessment by Ticknor confirming that White was unable even to stand and that there was

Surprisingly, Roberts and Baylies seem to have written nothing describing *Peacock*, but William Ruschenberger, the Navy surgeon who was to ride in her through the next cruise would, and his observations (like Ticknor's) weren't complimentary. "She has a light spar deck," he wrote, "and in port at least, affords the officers a sheltered walk in very hot or rainy weather, besides a more ample space for the hammocks of the men. In other respects the ship has no commendable quality. She is an indifferent sailer, very wet, and both for officers and crew the accommodations are very limited." Geisinger agreed. He described *Peacock* to the secretary as "not remarkable for sailing."

Four years later, in a letter to then-secretary of the navy Mahlon Dickerson, who replaced Woodbury in July 1834, Geisinger complained about "the very great deprivation of the usual comforts & conveniences of a naval commander in taking out Mr. Baylies & his family to Buenos Ayres, and being thrown out of my cabin for 3 months & having to sleep on the Gun Deck."[6] Not really three months, more like ten weeks (actually sixty-eight days under way) because slow progress down a direct course for Argentina soon persuaded Geisinger that he would need to stop on the way for fresh water. The diversion would also put *Peacock* in a place where she could ride the northeast trade winds and more easily skirt Cape St. Roque, at the northeastern point of South America.

Peacock's new route took her to Buenos Ayres via a bank shot off out-of-the-way St. Jago (Santiago today), largest of the Cape Verde Islands—seventy-six hundred miles all together. After a month at sea, the ship arrived April 9 to spend four days taking on water and replenishing at anchor in parched Porto Praya (Praia), where almost two years of drought had inflicted great suffering on the islands' mostly black inhabitants. To ease their misery, Geisinger sent ashore a barrel of beef, two of pork, one of beans, and another of rice.

On April 13 *Peacock* weighed anchor for South America, joining the familiar track from Portugal through Maderia and the Cape Verde Islands, across the equator, then past Pernambuco at the great bulge of the continent and Bahia, into Rio Janeiro, eventually on to Monte Video, and finally to drop anchor at Buenos Ayres, on the southwestern shore of the Rio de la Plata. This crossing of the equator was Captain Geisinger's first, very late in the career of an officer who'd served in uniform since 1809. By the 1830s a decades-long parade of Portuguese ships heading to their huge colony had worn that track into a groove, one followed during the centuries since the

no prospect of recovery on board forced Geisinger's hand. White's departure came not ten days after Stocker, the boatswain, and Redding, the carpenter, also left *Peacock* to go home, after voluntarily turning in their acting appointments. Stocker, Geisinger explained to the squadron commander, had lost the confidence of the officers and respect of the men because of his intemperance and misconduct; Redding he described as "totally inefficient."

Treaty of Tordesellias had divided the unknown New World between Iberia's two Catholic kingdoms.

The stop at Porto Praya had given Roberts an opportunity to write his first detailed descriptions of people and places and compile trade statistics. These slowly grew into the heart of a memoir that Harper and Brothers published in 1837, well after the author went back to sea on a voyage he wouldn't survive. For his part, during the cruise Ticknor made an entry in his journal every few days or even more often. (An annotated edition was published in 1991.)[7] Between Boston and Porto Praya, for example, he recorded a whale sighting. The event, Ticknor noted, was "highly satisfactory to any body capable of experiencing any delight in viewing the stupendous works of the creator; but it is peculiarly satisfactory to him who believes the Bible, to behold one of that species that was employed as an agent for manifesting the miraculous interposition of divine power, in preserving the life of a disobedient prophet, while endeavouring to evade the commands of his God." (Ticknor's reference was to Jonah, who sailed for Tarshish instead of going to evangelize in Nineveh, as commanded by God, and for his disobedience and instruction was swallowed by a whale during a great storm at sea.)

Peacock stayed in Rio de Janeiro for most of May. In a letter to his daughters three weeks after departure, Roberts described Rio as intended by nature "to be the first commercial city south of the equator," thanks to "its fine geographical situation, for ships passing into the Pacific & Indian Oceans, the easy access, the boldness, the depth and extent of its harbor, the great abundance and cheapness of the necessities of life in wood, water & provisions, the great salubrity of its climate, it being free of the ordinary tropical distempers." The port call was marred only by the ubiquity of slaves, "poor, friendless creatures draped in filthy scanty rags, covered with loathsome diseases, badly fed and worse lodged," whom he estimated constituted some two-thirds of the population.

11

If Surgeon Benajah Ticknor's journals, hundreds of neatly handwritten pages drafted while he was on board and now held in Yale's Sterling Library, are believed, USS *Peacock* was a miserably unhappy ship during the many months it took her to sail some 42,000 miles from Boston to Canton and back to New York under Captain Geisinger's command. That judgment needs to be tempered by the knowledge that Ticknor, forty-three when he sailed in *Peacock* following a tour of shore duty at the Navy's hospital in Baltimore, was a practiced critic and complainer. He probably should have quit the sea years earlier. On

November 9, 1818, months after embarking in his first ship, the 38-gun frigate USS *Macedonian*, in Boston for a passage around Cape Horn to a deployment off the Pacific coast of South America, Ticknor recorded in his journal,*

> I have, every day that I have been aboard the ship, seen more reason to be dissatisfied with my situation and felt a greater reluctance to remaining in it. The conduct of those among whom [meaning the officers of *Macedonian*'s wardroom] it was my misfortune to be obliged to live, the more I become acquainted with it, exhibited in a more odious light, the vile deformity of their hearts, and if it could have been left to my choice to spend these years in the purgatory of Roman-Catholics or in this society, I should certainly have chosen the former.

Fifteen years later, then on board USS *Peacock* at Batavia, he wrote to a friend (Congressman Elisha Whittlesey of Ohio), "A naval life is becoming more & more irksome to me every day, and until there is a radical change in the Navy, no man of regular habits can find any satisfaction in it." Why Ticknor chose to become a Navy surgeon is unknown; why he stayed one until 1854 (in the meanwhile rising to be fleet surgeon first in USS *Ohio* and again in USS *Columbus*, then flagships of the Mediterranean and East Indies Squadrons, respectively) is a mystery.

But disaffection wasn't uncommon among the ranks of Navy surgeons in the nineteenth century. Doctor William Wood, USN, surgeon on board the steam frigate USS *San Jacinto*, flagship of the East Indies Squadron in the 1850s, and by then a twenty-five-year veteran in the service, was no less unhappy with life at sea and with the Navy than had been Ticknor a generation earlier. Scarcely a dozen pages into his book about *San Jacinto*'s Pacific cruise in midcentury, Wood—we'll meet him again later—described her as "a clumsy, black-looking vessel, with a smoke stack protruding from the deck, and guns projecting from her sides," and then writes about boarding for the coming deployment, "It was once more a shivering plunge into the ceremonies, the restrictions, the petty formalities and mole hill–mountain jealousies

* USS *Macedonian*, ex-HMS *Macedonian*, was captured by the 44-gun USS *United States* off the Canary Islands in October 1812. Her cruise seven years later off Chile and Peru under command of Capt. John Downes, USN, was to protect American flag shipping from getting embroiled in Chile's and Peru's wars of independence against Spain.

Ticknor's three years in the frigate *Macedonian* (1818–21) were an opportunity for him to comment critically on the nasty habits and debased morals of civilians and shipmates alike, including Downes, whom he judged incompetent and selfish. In 1832 the same John Downes, now a commodore in command of the Pacific Squadron, flew his flag in USS *Potomac*.

and privileges—to say nothing of the physical privations—of man-of-war life. Permission to go and orders to come given by strange men younger than myself, whom I never saw before."

While Ticknor had found the Navy to be godless, Wood thought it undemocratic, and not "in harmony with the national character." But what Wood was really brooding about in the confines of his stateroom ("dark, cramped and dreary; six feet square, broken upon by crooked ship knees and heavy beams," very like the other four officers' cabins on *San Jacinto*'s port side, aft) was his status. Surgeons, like pursers, engineers, and other staff officers on board, were second-class citizens in the wardrooms of the nineteenth-century Navy. Only line officers, those eligible for command at sea, enjoyed first-class status, and well into the twentieth century this sharp caste distinction rankled those lower down in the social order.

But nineteenth-century physicians and surgeons worried about their rank and status in civil society too. Hobbled by an almost complete ignorance of the origins of disease, the 1800s saw a flowering of rival approaches to medical practice that espoused all manner of cures, including in the case of homeopathy "medicines" that had no active ingredients at all and, in the case of Christian Science, cures that abjured the idea of medicine entirely. Hydropaths believed in the healing power of water, osteopaths in massage, naturopaths in botanicals, chiropractics in spinal manipulation, allopaths in what became mainstream medicine . . . and so on. The lusty scramble for patients and fees among all these rival practitioners, and the absence of education and licensing requirements for any of them, lent nothing to and took much from doctors' dignity.

The oldest child of eight in a poor Vermont farming family, without formal education and orphaned in his teens after the death of his father, Benajah Ticknor (1788–1858) was apprenticed at twenty to a local doctor, then the usual route into the profession. In 1818 Ticknor was in his fourth year of private practice in Canfield, Ohio, when he learned that his application to become a surgeon's mate in the Navy had been finally accepted. Ticknor left for Boston and USS *Macedonian* immediately, for what was to be the first of his six tours of sea duty and the first-ever Navy deployment into the Pacific. During *Macedonian*'s peacetime cruise, she lost twenty-six of her crew of four hundred, of whom nineteen sickened and died, four others were lost overboard, two were killed in a minor fracas with the Spanish navy, and one was the loser in a duel.

During Ticknor's early years of service at sea, Navy medicine became more professional and its practitioners' status slowly improved from equivalent to tradesmen carrying a surgical toolkit to one more nearly approaching that of line officers. Impelled by Secretary of the Navy Samuel Southard, in office from September 1823 to March 1829, the Navy switched to a formal examination system for both the initial commissioning of surgeons and their subsequent promotion, established a medical course in Philadelphia for the further training of surgeon's mates, and sought (for a long time unsuccessfully) to increase pay to match that of U.S. Army surgeons. In 1823 Ticknor, then assigned to the frigate USS *Congress* at Norfolk, was one of the first surgeon's mates to take the new course in Philadelphia after the school opened and one of its first graduates. In June 1824 he stood for a promotion exam and was rated first among applicants. The next month Ticknor was promoted to surgeon. (In 1828 the rank of surgeon's mate was retitled "assistant surgeon" to lend incumbents more status.) Despite his humble beginning, by the start of the 1830s and measured against contemporary standards, Ticknor was a well-trained, experienced ship's surgeon.

His status and expertise was recognized in 1836, when Yale awarded Ticknor an honorary MD. It's not clear why the college granted him this distinction, but the practice had an old history there. The first MD degree awarded by Yale, in 1723, was an honorary one, as were many in the years that followed. It's likely Ticknor sought the degree as part of his campaign for promotion in the Navy, a campaign was ultimately successful. In 1852 he left the post of chief surgeon at the Boston Navy Yard and retired from the Navy.

His journals in USS *Peacock* reveal Ticknor to have also been a cramped and humorless man, one who fell easily to criticizing those who failed to practice the Protestant religion, to meet his standards of personal sanitation, or even to observe Western dress codes, but there's no reason to doubt his charges that the ship's first lieutenant, Robert Cunningham, was a prickly martinet whose management style must have made life in *Peacock*'s wardroom hellish for her seven more junior officers or that *Peacock*'s captain, David Geisinger, was a foul-mouthed, choleric intemperate often incapacitated by drink. (The Navy evidently held a higher opinion of Geisinger than did Ticknor: in October 1847 then-captain Geisinger was ordered back to Asia to take command of the East Indies Squadron, flying his flag in the nearly new sloop of war USS *Plymouth*, no more suitable frigate being available.)

Although Ticknor writes nothing about it, under this leadership life in steerage for the embarked midshipmen, or on the gun deck for the enlisted crew, could have been no better. Ticknor mentions the midshipmen hardly at all and names individual enlisted crewmen only to report their deaths from cholera while and immediately after *Peacock* was at Manila in October 1832.*

* The disease was endemic in South and Southeast Asia but had not been seen elsewhere before the late 1810s, the start of the first global cholera epidemic. In the summer of 1832, Sarah and Harriett

Far away in New York state, Roberts' daughters were imagining a far more gracious life for their seafaring father than this prickly reality. "One thing in particular, I am sure we cannot be too thankful for, and that is you enjoy every worldly comfort and convenience in your present situation which you can possibly desire," one wrote. "Oh how different from that long, comfortless, suffering voyage which you before took to Africa [the reference is to *Mary Ann* and Zanzibar]—when you were on a little vessel with no convenience or luxury and part of the time suffering from the want of the common necessities of life. Now you are in a noble frigate, with every luxury for the body and every means of improvement for the soul."

Ticknor, who found in the "noble frigate" *Peacock* nothing for the improvement of his soul and everything for its debasement, wouldn't have recognized Harriett's description of Navy life at sea. Nor, probably, would have her father, who spent the months afloat during his first mission in uncomfortable condominium with *Peacock*'s abrasive and hard-drinking captain.

Other Navy ships might have been little different from *Peacock*. Only wardrooms often hot from friction between officers would explain Secretary Woodbury's instruction in leadership to departing squadron commanders and ship captains. When frigate *Potomac* put to sea in 1831, for example, the boilerplate in the secretary's instructions included explicit reminders that the commodore should exercise constant watch over "the moral conduct and professional acquirements of junior officers" and enjoin "all grades of officers that they are not to speak reproachfully or contemptuously of each other, disrespectfully of their superiors." Officers were to be reminded "never on any account to comment on each other in the public papers."

Commanding officers were further to guard against "partiality or prejudice in the treatment of inferiors. Every officer is entitled to, and must enjoy, all the privileges of rank and station." Moreover, Woodbury hoped that proper discipline while deployed on distant stations could be maintained without placing officers under arrest and sending them home to await court-martial after the return of their ships to home port.

Roberts, both teens living and working in tiny Delhi, New York (population six hundred), apart from their eldest sister and the rest of their siblings, watched the appearance of the disease in New York City and Albany and its approach with increasing anxiety. "All the large towns and cities in the eastern and middle states have exerted themselves as far as possible to make their streets clean, having every part purified with lime," Harriett wrote her father on July 4. "The papers are full of 'prescriptions' and 'preventatives' all of which are said to be the very best, so that the mind hardly knows which to choose."

Cholera was, Harriett believed, as did many others in this faithful era, evidence of divine wrath. "Oh! Is it not a dreadful judgment, dear father, sent by the righteous hand of our Heavenly Parent, to remind us—his erring children, of His power and our frailty," she told him. That common belief prompted appeals to the president from churchmen for a national day of prayer, fasting and humiliation. Jackson rejected their petitions, leaving it to his political rival, Henry Clay, to endorse them.

12

Francis Baylies, of Taunton, Massachusetts, was appointed chargé on January 3, 1832, to replace his predecessor, John Forbes, who after six years at his post had died in Buenos Ayres the summer before. The appointment followed by a few weeks President Jackson's third annual message to Congress, in which he'd written to members,

> In the course of the present year one of our vessels, engaged in the pursuit of a trade which we have always enjoyed without molestation, has been captured by a band acting, as they pretend, under the authority of the government of Buenos Ayres. I have therefore given orders for the dispatch of an armed vessel to join our squadron in those seas and aid in affording all lawful protection to our trade which shall be necessary, and shall without delay send a minister to inquire into the nature and the circumstances and also of the claim, if any, that is set up by that government to those islands.

Baylies was that minister. The fact that he was unemployed, thus available and willing to go, seems to have been Baylies' principal qualification for a post certain to require exceptional diplomatic skills. His mission, which also included authority to negotiate a trade agreement, turned out to be a short and frustrating one. The new American consul ended up spending less time on the ground at Buenos Ayres—a little more than three months—than he'd spend in round-trip transportation from home.

Forbes' sudden death left Consul George Washington Slacum, from Alexandria (then a part of the District of Columbia), as acting head of the legation for a year until the new chargé arrived on post. Slacum (d. 1861) was no neophyte—his nomination as American consul at Buenos Ayres had originally gone from President Monroe to the Senate for confirmation in mid-April 1824—but he seemingly found himself in 1832 over his head in the nasty fisheries dispute to which President Jackson had alluded. (Nasty and remarkably durable. It echoed through diplomatic correspondence well into the mid-1880s and President Cleveland's first administration.) Agitated local press coverage in the Spanish-language *La Gaceta Mercantil* and *El Lucero* and the English-language *British Packet and Argentine News* helped to keep the pot stirred.

What simmered during the first half of 1831 as a legalistic dispute over sovereignty of the Falkland Islands and access to nearby whaling and sealing grounds escalated to a crisis in July with the armed seizure by the Argentine commander of the islands, Luis Vernet, of the first of three American sealers, the schooner *Harriet*, followed in August by schooners *Breakwater* and *Superior*, the confiscation of their catch, and the arrest of their crews. (Vernet, born in Hamburg but with French Huguenot roots, had been appointed chief of the new "Political Military Commandery of the Malvinas Islands" two years earlier.) The crew of a fourth American sealer, *Belville*, wrecked on the Patagonia coast, was reportedly also collected and confined. Those impoundments prompted Consul Slacum to call on the 18-gun sloop of war USS *Lexington* for help.* In response, *Lexington*, commanded by Capt. Silas Duncan, USN, and then assigned to the Brazil Station, sailed on December 9, 1831, for the islands, arriving at Berkeley Sounds on Solidad, the easternmost of the Falklands, the last day of the year.

Captain Duncan's appearance offshore and his subsequent confiscations, arrests, and evacuation of the population challenged the Argentines' claim to the islands based on their belief—intact today—that as once part of the Spanish Viceroyalty of Rio de la Plata, they'd been inherited from the metropole upon independence.

Duncan's after-action report was sent to Secretary Woodbury on February 3, 1832, from Monte Video, coincidently during the same week that USS *Potomac*, on the opposite side of the world, was busy firing on the town and forts of Kuala Batee. "I investigated the matters in question," Duncan wrote to the secretary, describing the excitement colorfully but not entirely accurately,

> and finding them to be of the most iniquitous and illegal character,—I determined to break up and disperse *this band of pirates, many of whom had been sent from the prisons of Buenos Ayres and Monte Video, and were thus let loose to prey upon a peaceable and industrious part of our community*. . . .
>
> I have confined the individuals engaged in these transactions, who could be identified, and *have besides brought off the whole of the population consisting of about forty persons*, . . . principally Germans [who] appear to be industrious and well disposed persons.
>
> I have now on board as prisoners seven individuals who are charged with illegally capturing and plundering the Schooner Harriet.

* The same USS *Lexington* that between Saturday, March 1 and Thursday, April 24, 1834, with Master Cdt. Isaac McKeever, USN, then in command and at the end of her deployment, would carry Roberts the 6,948 miles logged from Rio Janeiro back to Boston at the end of his first diplomatic mission. *Lexington* then continued on to New York, arriving there on May 25.

Prudently, Duncan sailed with his prisoners not to Buenos Ayres but to Monte Video in Uruguay, from where, after the seven were put ashore, he went on to Rio Janeiro near mid-February to resume his station.

By then the exasperated Argentine foreign relations ministry was no longer willing to deal with Slacum. A week later his hosts withdrew the consul's exequatur, converting him into a private citizen and in effect unilaterally suspending diplomatic relations with the United States. *Peacock*'s arrival in port Buenos Ayres on June 5 put Baylies on the ground in the middle of this thicket when his family left the ship five days later, sent ashore with a fifteen-gun salute while the crew decoratively manned the yards. (The family's departure after three months on board freed Geisinger's cabin, into which the captain and Roberts now promptly moved. In time the two men's heated arguments, heard through the bulkheads of the cabin, became part of the soundtrack of the remaining long months at sea.)

Before Baylies and company disembarked, Captain Duncan came on board from *Lexington* to call on the new consul, to give him, Baylies wrote home to brother William, "in detail an account of the people amongst whom the U.S. Government, in its bounty, have sent me to reside for four years, which, if true, could render a residence amongst any well regulated tribe of Indians preferable."[8]

His own prejudices reinforced even before leaving the ship, Consul Baylies was skeptical of success from the very beginning. "The success of this mission is doubtful . . . ," he wrote, conceding that "with such a people semi-barbarous it is almost impossible to predict with any certainty the ultimate fate of the mission."

Baylies and his party stepped into a city that Roberts had first visited decades earlier as a young man working for his uncle, and knew well. Orphaned at sixteen, Roberts was placed with his uncle, Capt. Joshua Roberts, who had a shipping and mercantile business in the Argentine capital. Thinking, in 1804, that on the ground in Argentina he'd "enjoy every earthly blessing that we poor mortals can wish," Roberts was soon disappointed. "As I approached its shores I began to experience the mortification of disappointment. . . . This city . . . disintegrated into a mere plain over which the inhabitants were scattered without order and without one incentive to allure the traveller to enter."

Nothing there impressed young Roberts. "Instead of lofty forests 'whose heads touch heaven,'" he recorded in his *Journal of an Intended Voyage from the Rio de la Plata to London*, "I saw scattered here and there a few trees barely sufficient to repel the rigors of a winter's cold, and in the valleys just enough fruit to support the existence of those wretched beings who labored for its production. Instead of the brave, noble, honorable, disinterested Castellaneos,

I found a cowardly, dishonorable, selfish, avaricious, bigoted & superstitious set of people, caught up in pride, indolence, & misery." His uncle's death in 1808 prompted Roberts to return home to New Hampshire with his inheritance. Baylies' assessment to come of his new hosts was to be no more generous.

Slacum must have been really happy to move aside for the new man on June 15, when Baylies formally presented his credentials in the capital and undertook his mission to "obtain a disavowal of the acts of Vernet, but to make known to the Government of Buenos-Ayres the amicable disposition of the Government of the United States." Once on the ground, Baylies soon concluded that dealing with the Argentine government and its *caudillo*, Juan Manuel de Rosas, on fisheries issues or any other matter was also impossible.

Personal relations were fraught too. "With respect to myself personally the Govt had had neither the liberality or magnanimity to separate my private from my public character, and because I had offended them in my official capacity by refusing to lay at their feet the humiliating apologies which they chose to require from the United States, they adopted a system of petty insults and vexations indicating a spirit alike mean and malignant."

And so on August 18, only two months after disembarking from *Peacock*, Baylies asked Argentine foreign minister Manuel Vincente de Maza for his and his family's passports back. The explanation to Washington was that "the Government having positively refused to treat or to discuss any question until reparation was made to Louis Vernet—his band of pirates and the Argentine Republic no course was left for me but to demand my passports."*

Several weeks later, September 8, Baylies attempted to arrange passage home from Buenos Ayres either in USS *Warren* or in USS *Lexington*, one or the other to be sent off the Brazil Station early for this express purpose. Baylies' only other way home was via England in a British packet scheduled to leave Monte Video soon, a route that necessarily entailed an extra month at sea.

Writing to Master Cdt. Benjamin Cooper, USN, commanding the 20-gun sloop USS *Warren* and the senior officer present in port, Baylies asserted, "If the Government thought it expedient to direct me to take passage in a national ship on my outbound voyage it is equally expedient that my homeward passage should be made in the same manner, and there are some circumstances, which, in my opinion will go some way to change the expediency of this course into a necessity."

One such circumstance was the vulnerability of the legation archive. Because "the common usages and laws of civilized nations are not regarded here," Baylies informed Cooper, "it therefore becomes my imperative duty

* This second breach in diplomatic relations lasted until August 1844, when William Brent Jr. was finally appointed to succeed the long-gone Baylies.

to cause the documents and records of the American legation to be transported to the United States as safely and securely as possible." Another was the impending session of Congress, before which Baylies wished to appear, to "give some important explanations touching the state of affairs here."

Buttressing what might have sounded to a Navy officer as an unconvincing case for detaching a man-of-war from her station, Consul Baylies went on to remind Cooper that when in office, he'd "had power under certain contingencies to direct the movement of the whole squadron, and that Commodore Geo. Rodgers was required to take my orders, and that in cases of urgency I should not have hesitated to have required either a sloop or a schooner to carry despatches to the U. States."

On the strength of that authority, then, Baylies thought this request now was not "unreasonable or presumptuous." His clincher: "Perhaps you are not aware of the extreme urgency of this case. The negotiations having failed *War* will be the result, but this result cannot take place until the meeting of Congress. If any vessel on this station should reach home before, nothing would be lost, for she could return immediately with the squadron which will certainly be sent to these seas" to fight the war Baylies foresaw.

Two days later Cooper replied, declining politely to thin the squadron under his command, "particularly in the present unsettled state of political negotiations with Buenos Ayres," but offering to take Baylies to any port in the Brazil station and to protect the legations records on board. With that, the former consul settled reluctantly for what he could get. On September 25 Baylies left Buenos Ayres in *Warren*, not to but toward home.

The next day, under way in the Rio de la Plata and now heading for Rio de Janeiro, Baylies wrote his Despatch No. 10 to the secretary of state, explaining the quick collapse and failure of what was to have been a four-year mission, and concluding, "Under all the circumstances there is but one course left for the United States. They will certainly be justified by the whole world if they now make their power known in the chastisement of this insolent government . . . they must be *compelled* to respect our rights—there is no alternative." In Rio de Janeiro, Baylies, his family, and Slacum, now traveling as Baylies' private secretary, boarded ship *Jane* for Baltimore, where they arrived in the middle of December.[9] Baylies never managed a return to Washington. After serving a single term in the Massachusetts House of Representatives that began in 1835, he quietly disappeared from public life.

Geisinger, his command on September 26, 1832, now nearing Manila in the Philippine Islands on the way to Canton, had given up his cabin to Baylies and his party in exchange for very little of benefit to the United States. For less than nothing, if one adopted the judgment of former president John

Quincy Adams, who loathed Andrew Jackson, his chief rival in the election of 1824 and successor in 1828, and everything Jackson (and his political strategist from New York, Martin Van Buren) shaped.

"Baylies," John Quincy Adams wrote in the memoir edited by his son,

> in 1825, had, as a member of Congress, voted for Jackson as President, libeled me in the newspapers, and lost his election [in 1827 to the House of Representatives from Massachusetts' Bristol District, with less than ten percent of the vote] in consequence. He thought Jackson undervalued him, by the offer of the Collectorship of New Bedford, and Jackson, to appease him, gave him as a second sop the office of Chargé d'Affairs in Buenos Ayres. Stayed there not 3 months—just long enough to embroil his country in a senseless and wicked quarrel with the Government; and, without waiting for orders from his Government, demanded his passports and came home. Nothing but the imbecility of that South American abortion of a state saved him from indelible disgrace and this country from humiliation in that concern.[10]

Adams' sense of betrayal must have been especially acute: Baylies had supported Jackson, a rustic from Tennessee, over a fellow countryman from Massachusetts.

4

Monte Video to Manila

I have often had occasion to observe with sorrow, the exceeding deficiency of Navy officers in mental resources, and their great aversion to those studies, from which a reasonable reflecting man might suppose to derive any satisfaction; but I have never met with an instance where those faults were more apparent, than in that now under consideration. . . . It is surely the duty of every man, and especially of one occupying the important situation of commander of a ship of war, to do all in his power to remedy the natural defects of his mind and not by a misapplication of the powers which he does possess, to make his deficiencies still more apparent, and more productive of bad consequences.

Surgeon Benajah Ticknor, USN, September 1832

13

The commercial port of Uruguay's capital city, Monte Video, today looks like a long-abandoned set for a 1930s Hollywood gangster movie. Low-lying, largely vacant industrial buildings, fragments of miscellaneous stuff blowing up empty streets, everything in tones of gray. When I was there several years ago, soon after Christmas, peddlers crouched at street corners, selling each other scraps of gift wrapping paper and cheap plastic toys. No one else was afoot. All the glitter was pooled at chic Punta del Este, a resort on the Atlantic Coast around the corner to the north of the capital.

Benajah Ticknor estimated Monte Video's population in 1832 at fewer than 10,000. It was drab then too, victim of a siege at the far margins of the Napoleonic Wars that had somehow segued into intermittent fighting through the century's teens and twenties. "Formerly there was considerable trade at this place," Ticknor described, "and business was active and prosperous; but now the trade is much diminished, and there is consequently but little business done, and everything exhibits an appearance of poverty and decay." Roberts, too, was ready to sail on. He left Monte Video "better satisfied to wander ten thousand miles over a trackless and stormy ocean than to remain in a city whose former inhabitants were spread in dust amid its ruins."

Geisinger had expected the 10-gun USS *Boxer* to join *Peacock* in South America, but the small schooner never appeared during the weeks *Peacock* shuttled between Rio Janeiro, Monte Video, Buenos Ayres, and back to Monte Video. So it was that at the end of June *Peacock* sailed alone from Uruguay for Bencoolen (now Bengkulu), a Dutch-owned pepper trading port in southwestern Sumatra, ninety-two hundred miles and two months away, where the purser hoped to reprovision before passing through the Sunda Strait and entering the South China Sea.

Peacock's second departure from Monte Video on June 25 (her first had been the shuttle across the river to Buenos Ayres) was apparently welcome to the crew, despite the two-ocean crossing to come, a passage that was punctuated on July 19 by rounding the Cape of Good Hope, unusually without stopping at Cape Town. July 23, about when *Peacock* was bobbing practically becalmed a few days east of the Cape halfway to her next port of call, Secretary of State Livingston wrote Roberts to amplify his six-month-old instructions. "It is now understood," Livingston wrote, "that Peacock will proceed by the way of the Cape of Good Hope, instead of Cape Horn, as I at first supposed. This will change the order of your proceeding and bring you first in relation to the powers of Arabia on the Red Sea and the coast between that and the Persian Gulf." The secretary was still wrong about "the order of [Roberts'] proceeding" in the guidance that followed:*

> It is left to your discretion, guided by the information you shall receive, whether you will attempt to make any commercial arrangement with the Birman Empire.*The distance between the seat of government and Rangoon, their first commercial city [since 1824 the royal court sat at Ava, some five hundred miles up the Irrawaddy River from Rangoon], and their habitual procrastinating mode of doing business, may, perhaps, consume more than can be spared for this object, yet if you see a reasonable prospect of success, it ought not to be neglected, unless you find that our commerce already enjoys all the advantages

* "So wretched looking a town of its size I have nowhere seen," Howard Malcom dismissively wrote of Rangoon in 1839, after a several-years-long inspection tour of Southeast Asia in the late 1830s for the American Baptist Missionary Society. "The city is spread upon part of a vast meadow, but little above high tides, and at this season [spring] resembles a neglected swamp. . . . There is no other seaport in the empire but Bassein, which has little trade, and [Rangoon] stands next in importance to Ava, yet there is literally nothing in it that can interest a traveler." Malcom went on to describe commerce at Rangoon as "crippled by enormous port charges" and by prohibitions against the export of rice. These, and an absence of either a wharf or quay on the riverfront, forcing vessels to lie in the stream and use lighters to unload and load, further constrained trade. Perhaps influenced by Livingston's lukewarm mention, Roberts passed up the opportunity to open talks with the Birman Empire, where the United States had not had consular representation since 1820.

we could hope for from a treaty. After this Siam and Cochin-China will claim your attention.

Obviously thinking about *Friendship*'s rude treatment in 1831, Livingston then mused, "Perhaps a treaty with the King of Acheen [Sultan Mahomed Shab, then nominal sovereign of the pepper coast of western Sumatra] would give greater security to our trade with the different rajahs of Sumatra and tend to protect us in those seas from the depredations of the piratical Malays." Then again, perhaps not, so he went on, "Take it, however, as a general instruction, not to go to the expense of a treaty with any of these independent rajahs or persons who have not the power to carry their stipulations into effect."

Finally, the secretary added almost offhandedly what could have become a portentous afterthought, had anything come of it, a first step in the creation of an American naval base on the opposite side of the world. "Having no national colonial establishment and our public relations with the European powers who have them in the Indian Ocean being continuously liable to change," Livingston wrote, "it would be of great importance to secure one or more forts in that quarter into which by treaty with the native powers our ships might always be received and protected. You will, therefore, pay particular attention to this point, and secure such an asylum if possible." Livingston's letter to Roberts, who was literally half the world away, now started to pursue its addressee.

While overland mails were reasonably well developed by the 1830s (the U.S. postal system, with sixty-five hundred offices and more than 100,000 miles of mail routes in 1830 was by far the federal government's largest employer), mail and freight moved across oceans through a much less structured system and, by modern standards, at a glacial pace. In the mid-1830s, for example, letters from USS *Peacock* at Bombay, Colombo, Batavia, and Callao took twenty-one, eighteen, twenty-six, and sixteen weeks, respectively, to arrive in Washington. On October 30, 1837, notification that *Peacock* had arrived in Portsmouth, Virginia, at the end of her around-the-world cruise three days earlier reached the secretary of the navy's office at the same time as did a letter announcing her departure from Rio de Janeiro August 28. Delivery of mail flowing the other way, from Washington to a ship somewhere at sea, was as slow and occasionally turned into a tail-chase, with the letter never catching up.

With such time lines, anything remotely like modern command and control was impossible. Instead, once their ships left home port, captains and commanders had enormous latitude in how they performed their sailing instructions. Sometimes they did so brilliantly, but occasionally, invariably in the case of some officers, the result was embarrassing—or worse.

Secretary Livingston's July letter to Roberts joined a stream of other government and family correspondence and some official cargo shipments already pursuing the novice diplomat via what amounted to opportune lift provided by vessels with other business in the ports where *Peacock* was expected to touch on her mission or whose route might permit them to "fall in" with either *Peacock* or *Boxer* at sea. Through the summer and autumn of 1832, the brig *New York*, the schooner *Columbia*, and the ships *Roman* and *Cabot*, among others, sailed carrying freight and letters from the State Department for Roberts. (*New York* caught up with USS *Boxer* in port Rio de Janeiro on October 31, when she transferred her twenty-four boxes consigned to Roberts to the schooner. Those boxes were finally put ashore at Batavia the following June for delivery to *Peacock*.)

The most important of this wandering stuff was the official gifts that Roberts was to distribute, to lubricate his introductions to and negotiations with foreign potentates. At first Livingston had been reluctant to dispatch his envoy with any presents for his hosts, but the secretary reconsidered and agreed to a mixed bag of gifts, including two hundred rifles and muskets, a hundred sets of "infantry accoutrements," several ceremonial swords, lamps, statues, and yards of carpeting, a proof set of American coinage, a steam engine, and even a model railroad "12 feet in diameter which can be screwed to the floor of the room." Livingston's late approval meant that none of this was loaded on board *Peacock*. Twenty-four boxes were sent on board USS *Boxer*. The rifles and muskets went in a merchantman, *Eliza*. Nothing made it to Roberts in time to be presented at his first port of call in China.

In Canton Roberts bought some thirty-two hundred dollars of presents on credit through Olyphant and Company, the New York trading house of the marvelously named David Washington Cincinnatus Olyphant. Roberts' unwillingness to arrive empty-handed at foreign courts was well intentioned, but his substitute gifts lacked the appeal of American-sourced ones. They were rejected outright by the Cochin Chinese. Worse yet, during the pause in the United States between his first and second embassies, a miserly Congress failed to agree to reimburse him for this debt.

14

Just before noon, August 28, 1832, *Peacock* anchored in eleven fathoms near Rat Island, offshore Bencoolen on southwestern Sumatra. The crossing of the Indian Ocean had been easy, marred only by the loss of the captain's gig, battered to pieces during a two-day storm, and by the abrupt failure of what had been until then the best of the ship's two navigation chronometers, forcing reliance on the other, known to be fast. (Days later and midway across the South China Sea, between Java and the Philippines, thanks to her "useless" chronometers *Peacock*'s dead reckoning position was discovered to be nearly half a day's sailing in error.) On the way from South America she'd averaged just under 150 nautical miles per day, equivalent to almost six knots while under way, and on one especially good day she logged 259 miles, averaging better than ten miles an hour.

The place was Dutch now, but for 140 years it had been British, an East India Company pepper trading post first established in 1683 and soon graced by three small forts notorious for their miserable quality of life.* Bencoolen was a chronic disappointment to the English, never profitable, malarial, and seemingly a magnet for apprentice or journeymen alcoholics on the company's payroll. (That small establishment once proved itself capable in a single month of drinking up more in claret, ale, beer, Madeira, arrack, and toddy than the total value of the year's exports of pepper from western Sumatra.) Such business as was conducted was occasionally interrupted by bloody native uprisings. It would prove no less disappointing to the Dutch.

When *Peacock* anchored offshore, the largest of Bencoolen's forts (Fort Marlborough, an imposing rectangle with steeply sloped brick walls) contained the home and office of the Dutch resident, the district governor and senior member of a small, all-male community of white expatriates. The original purpose of what turned out to be a four-day port call was an anticipated rendezvous with USS *Boxer* and an opportunity to rewater and resupply. In this the stop was a disappointment, despite the gracious hospitality offered to *Peacock*'s officers by Johannes Knoerle, the Dutch resident. *Boxer* wasn't at Bencoolen (and not even on the way; delayed first by repairs to her hull and later by Captain Cooper's orders, she didn't sail from Rio de Janeiro for the Far East for another nine weeks), and available provisions were scant, but the visit wasn't entirely misspent time.

On arrival, Knoerle informed Geisinger that USS *Potomac* had destroyed Kuala Batee, thus relieving *Peacock* from diverting to take on that mission. Moreover, when *Peacock* sailed from Bencoolen for Krakatau Island late on August 31, several caribou stood uneasily on her deck. One or two were

* The first was Fort York. The Dutch took over the government and exploitation of Sumatra from the British in 1824, in exchange for confirming British rights to the Malay Peninsula and Singapore in the Treaty of London, an agreement that resolved local territorial issues open since the end of the Napoleonic Wars. The treaty was one of several among European states that parted out South and Southeast Asia to rival foreign powers, leaving only Siam free. This high-handed distribution of colonies stood more or less intact until World War II.

presents to Geisinger from the Dutchman; the others had been purchased by the purser for general consumption. The dumb beasts now went to sea for their first and last time. They would soon be slaughtered to provide a welcome change to the usual shipboard ration. Not long thereafter, events took a very bad turn for Knoerle, too. Less than a year after the Americans sailed away, he also was butchered.

As Captain Endicott, master of *Friendship*, had found out in 1831, Bencoolen could be a very hard school for foreigners. Knoerle wasn't the first resident to die horribly there. In December 1807 a British predecessor, Thomas Parr, had been beheaded in front of his wife and children by some of his Malay subjects, gruesome punishment, it was later believed, for his zeal to improve the profitability of the residency by forcing the cultivation of coffee for export. (Parr's wife and infant son survived that attack, but both were soon lost at sea when their ship went down sailing to England from India, sad victims of another of the risks of colonial enterprise.)

It's not clear exactly why Knoerle was murdered on the road to Palembang on July 28, 1833, but Roberts and Ticknor both believed—almost certainly from the same source—that his death was revenge for taking "improper liberties" with the wives and daughters of local rajahs. "His body was cut in pieces," Roberts wrote in his *Embassy to the Eastern Courts*, "and then burnt with great exultation by the perpetrators and their friends. . . . Mr. Knoerle, imprudently injured the happiness of many families by his unrestrained passions, and thereby sealed his horrid fate." But with the collapse of pepper prices and the Sumatran economy at the end of the 1820s, and increasingly greater Dutch pressure on natives in Sumatra (and in Java too, where warfare soon broke out) to produce more for export, tensions usually ran high in Bencoolen District's villages. Knoerle's murderers had ample political and economic motives to revenge their lost honor and the rape of their women.

Krakatau (now usually spelled "Krakatoa") lay eight days by sail southeast of Bencoolen in the entrance to the Sunda Strait. The "extensive and highly beautiful submarine garden over which the boat was smoothly and slowly gliding"—on arrival at the Krakatoa archipelago Roberts compared the corals passing beneath *Peacock* to sunflowers, mushrooms, cabbages, and roses—made attempts to go ashore over reefs in *Peacock*'s boats dangerous. After a full day at anchor on the north side of the volcano (unknowingly afloat inside an ancient caldera, bounded to the north by Forsaken and Long Islands) while her boats unsuccessfully sought safe landings and fresh water, *Peacock* got under way for a brief stop in Angier, a fishing village on the tip of Java.*

* Fifty-one years later, early morning on Monday, August 27, 1883, Krakatoa erupted, a blast that's believed to be one of the largest such events in geologic history. Five days later, A. P. Cameron, the

The Watering Place at Anjer Point in the Island of Java. Oil painting by William Daniell. At Angier *Peacock* quickly took on 12,000 gallons of fresh water from a creek conveniently close to shore, an opportunity that explained the presence of a Dutch outpost guarding a fishing village of no apparent commercial significance. Dutch flags fly from the pole on the right and a small boat on the left, identifying the ownership of this busy crossroads.

Citing customs house reports, Roberts noted that in the prior twelve months, eighty-two American vessels had touched at Angier, of which roughly a third went on to Batavia, the rest sailing for Canton, Manila, or other ports in Asia. Here reprovisioning also augmented temporarily *Peacock*'s on-deck livestock count, adding goats and chickens to the surviving bullocks busily fouling the ship. The ships anchored in the Sunda Strait in the background are East Indiamen, bound for home in company with HMS *Lion*. In the foreground a ship's boat loads water barrels on board. Daniells' painting, done in 1794, was exhibited at the Royal Academy in 1836.

Ticknor is the only explicit source for what the surgeon describes as an "angry dialogue" between the captain of USS *Peacock* and his titular clerk at the end of nineteen days at sea out of Java for Luzon. The two men, Geisinger, forty-two, and Roberts, forty-eight, strangers before they met in Boston, had been cabin mates in a very small space since Chargé Baylies and his family left *Peacock* the prior June in Buenos Ayres. Usually a captain's clerk wouldn't be berthed in the after cabin; Roberts' unusual accommodation reflected his

British consul in Batavia when Krakatoa blew, wrote the foreign secretary in London that geography at the east end of Java had been suddenly rearranged: "It is now reported that part of Krakatau island, the island of Poeloe Temposa and other small islands in the Sunda Straits have disappeared. . . . An island at the northern entrance to the Straits, is reported split into five pieces, while numerous small islands are said to have been raised which had no existence previously." In fact, Krakatoa had disappeared into dust, taking with it more than 36,000 lives. The ensuing atmospheric ash colored sunsets for months.

special status, but on the back side of the world from Washington it wasn't special enough to alter the chain of command at sea. (In 1835 captain's clerks would be renamed "yeomen," completing their incorporation into the ship's enlisted crew.) Finally, many months of friction between the two men reportedly flashed over when their ship anchored off the light at Manila.

Roberts' memoir says nothing about anything that might have happened during the nineteen-hundred-mile passage between Java and Luzon beyond noting that "diarrhoea prevailed among the crew" and imaginatively diagnosing that it was "probably occasioned by a change of climate from cold to extreme heat, from rainy weather, excess in fruit, and frequent change in diet, but most particularly from the compulsory substitution of yams for bread." In a letter written to the secretary of state on July 3, 1834, between his two cruises in *Peacock*, however, Roberts substantiates Ticknor's account. He asks the secretary that the captain he was to sail with next, to Cochin China, China, and Japan, be "a gentleman in the strictest sense of the word—a sober—discrete & moral man—of a good disposition . . . nor a Drunkard nor a quarrelsome man."

"The Agent or Envoy should have his rights defined," Roberts added, much wiser now than when he'd left Boston sixteen months earlier, "settled and acknowledg'd by the Commander before leaving the U. States.— He should be unquestionably entitled to use of one-half the Cabin. . . . It is quite time this point was clearly & distinctly & unequivocally settled—for the Agent is frequently & in the most insulting manner told he is admitted there by sufferance."

Geisinger too said nothing about any friction in his journal, although he would later petition for additional pay in compensation for having had to share his cabin for two years, this after the indignity of sleeping on the gun deck while the several Baylies displaced him during the first long leg of the cruise. But Ticknor, with nothing to lose, was remarkably candid. He'd had a low opinion of the captain at least since Buenos Ayres, where he implied that Geisinger escaped drinking himself to death on the River Plate only because the port call was too short to be fatal: two weeks and not two months.

15

Peacock, riding the southwest monsoon, approached Luzon just a few years after Spain first granted foreign flag vessels full access to the port of Manilla (now Manila). The city, capital of the Spanish East Indies since 1579, was opened by authorities to foreign ships in 1789, but because Spain wanted no competition for its own exports, only those vessels carrying cargo from the Orient were initially admitted to trade in Manila. For further protection, for another forty years (until 1830) foreign trade in Western goods with the Philippines was required to be conducted entirely through Spain or Spanish colonies in the Americas. Foreigners, moreover, were forbidden residence on Luzon. But such protectionist restrictions on trade and settlement were enforced unenthusiastically if at all, as demonstrated by Manila's seven thousand Chinese (Roberts' estimate).

Americans, too, had been trading in Manila long before USS *Peacock* arrived, and even some years before *Astrea*, the first U.S. merchant ship in direct trade with the port, spent ten weeks there during autumn 1796. *Astrea*'s round-trip, pioneering voyage from Salem—she was at sea from March 1796 to May 1798—appears to have been an imaginative but not especially successful experiment in business development. Her owner, the wonderfully wealthy Salem merchant Elias Hasket Derby, was, after more than ten years' effort, disappointed by Canton: the cost of doing business there was high, and thanks to a supply glut aggravated by the closure of European ports to American shipping during the Revolutionary War, the price of tea collapsed in New England in the 1790s. Manila, a familiar waypoint on all routes to and from China, must have looked to Derby like a possibility for trade worth exploring. He sent *Astrea* there twice to test the waters.

Astrea's supercargo during her first voyage to the East Indies was twenty-three-year-old Nathaniel Bowditch, also of Salem, then on the first of three cruises he made in the vessel between March 1796 and September 1800.* The cargo included hats, wine and spirits, and two kinds of compasses, all of which Bowditch hoped to sell, presumably to the islands' European community and to the crews of ships calling at Manila while *Astrea* was there.

Astrea finally sold out and sailed for Salem in early December 1797 (when Bowditch recorded in his journal, "Thus to our great satisfaction we have lost sight of Manilla"), carrying home 750,000 pounds of sugar, 63,695 pounds of pepper, 29,767 pounds of indigo, fifteen hundred hides, and a little asafran spice. After 163 days under way via the Cape of Good Hope, she anchored in Salem Harbor on May 22, 1797, the crew having spent the last three months of the cruise at her pumps, successfully working to keep their ship afloat, if not entirely dry.

---

* *Astrea* has an interesting history. In 1789 she sailed for Batavia and Canton, remaining in China for several months. Her supercargo on that cruise, Thomas Perkins, is credited with the observation of great Chinese demand for sea otter, seal, and beaver skins in trade.

Astrea's second cruise to the East Indies (August 1799–September 1800) was to Batavia (Jakarta today), but she also called at Manila, although this time for only half as long as her first port call in 1796. Bowditch's four-hundred-page manuscript account (*Journal of a Voyage from Salem to Manila in the Ship Astrea, H. Prince, Master, in the Years 1796 and 1797*) is the definitive crewmember's record of the cruise, but he's much better known as the author in 1802 of a navigation text, *The New American Practical Navigator*. Reissued in ten editions during his lifetime and many times since, Bowditch's book went on to become an institution, and he to distinction as a mathematician and astronomer.

Manila in the 1830s was the western outpost of a Spanish empire approaching the twilight of its glory days. The era of Spain's greatest vitality—vigor fed by silver mined in Peru and Mexico and coined into the world's first global currency—roughly between 1655 and 1815, overlapped the years when the Manila galleons shuttled between Acapulco and Manila, carrying specie out to the Philippines on the tropical easterlies and oriental preciosities back to Mexico on the prevailing westerlies. After first bringing prosperity and power, and then enervating inflation, New World silver finally petered out. Military and naval defeats, and agitation for independence in Spain's European possessions and its colonies in the New World, further weakened what had been for a time the first global superpower, a state whose possessions once spanned parts of Western Europe and two-thirds of the globe. Another three generations remained before a final humiliation came at the hands of the Americans.

On October 1, 1832, soon after anchoring at Manila off the mouth of the Pasig River and even before clearing quarantine and exchanging gun salutes with the fort, *Peacock* was boarded by the American consul, Alfred Edwards (newly appointed and the fourth since John Kerr, *Astrea*'s factor and the first American consul in the port), and Henry Sturgis, founder of Russell, Sturgis and Company, merchants of Boston with interests in Manila and Canton. Consul Edwards housed Geisinger and Roberts ashore in his handsome home-cum-office and warehouse during the port call—*Astrea*'s crew had likewise stayed on shore with Kerr—easing the pressure on Roberts but according to the surgeon not much improving the captain's sour mood.

The two businessmen hosted *Peacock*'s extended visit during the month—all of October; she finally sailed for Canton on November 2—the sloop lay at Manila. Merchant ships often took weeks to turn around in port after an ocean crossing, but it's not clear why *Peacock* spent so long at anchor in Manila, unless it were simply to "recruit" the crew, a word that in the nineteenth century meant to "repair by fresh supplies any thing wasted," to rest and restore strength after seven months out of home port. Even so, time at Manila must have passed slowly, especially slowly for enlisted crewmembers, who were confined on board through the weeks in port when not ashore on ship's business.

Bowditch wrote in 1796 that "October and November in Manilla are not very healthy. Shiver & fever are then very rife." The Peacocks, in port during the same season as *Astrea* but decades later, found that still to be true. The sloop's first victim of tropical disease, a sixty-three-year-old sailor named Charles Peterson, suddenly fell ill with cholera on October 14 after downing a ration of boiled pork and beans. "The evacuations became copious," Roberts wrote of Peterson's symptoms on the basis of the surgeon's description, "coldness and insensibility supervened; the pulse became scarcely perceptible; the countenance livid, ghastly, and sunken; spasms attacked the lower extremities. And the surface was covered with a cold, clammy sweat." Unmentioned was another of late stage cholera's symptoms, a distinct blue cast to skin caused by dwindling oxygen transportation by arterial blood.

Before sunrise the next day, Seaman Peterson was dead, having been treated with the usual ineffective potions and lotions—but not the rehydration that in a later age might have saved him. Before sunrise Peterson's shrouded body was unceremoniously tipped into the bay not far from the ship, because the surgeon and first lieutenant wished to conceal the presence of cholera on board. The watch officer's log entry for the period included a scant epitaph: "At 4:15 Charles Peterson (seaman) departed this life. At 5:30 buried his remains in the bay." "Departed this life" was the usual descriptive phrase used to record a death at sea in the log, in this case followed immediately by "Received on board 200 lbs. beef and 150 lbs. bread for the crew."[1] So it was days later with the remains of William Shillaber, buried in Manila Bay off the *Peacock*'s launch on the first leg of the boat's trip to shore, there to pick up sixty-two bags of bread and eighteen coils of grass rope and return.

All told, five other Peacocks died of cholera before the sloop arrived in China: Seamen Worth, Charlton, Cullen, Johnson, and Holt. Two more, Seamen John Powers and William Buker, died December 15 and 20, after *Peacock* anchored in the lee of Lintin Island. Both were buried on shore. The last, Thomas Johnson, died in port Vung Lam, Cochin China, January 16, 1833, at 4:00 p.m. Loaded into the fourth cutter, Johnson's body "was committed to the deep" half an hour later.

Cholera wasn't new or unknown to authorities in Manila in 1832. The disease had made its first appearance in the city in early October 1820, brought there, it's now thought, in the country ship *Merope*, in from Bengal with a load of Indian cottons and the bacterium *Vibrio cholerae*. ("Country" here meaning that *Merope* was trading between India and China.) That original outbreak of cholera in the Philippines, part of the first global epidemic of the disease, triggered on October 9 murderous riots by natives, who believing the fatal outbreak confirmed they were being deliberately poisoned by foreigners took terrible revenge against whites and Chinese in Manila. Among the hundred or more massacred in the street were Captain Nicholls, *Merope*'s English master, and one transient American, Midn. Thomas Wilson, USN, ashore off the frigate USS *Macedonian* (in which Benajah Ticknor was then at sea as a surgeon's mate for the first time) on a sick ticket awaiting a ride home. *Peacock*'s cholera cases twelve years later were part of the second global epidemic, spread, as were the five others later in the nineteenth and early twentieth centuries, largely by ship.

The next three cases of cholera appeared during the following week; the second (Francis Worth) and third (John Charlton), a day apart and quickly fatal, prompted a letter from Ticknor to Geisinger that ignited another confrontation between the surgeon and his commanding officer.* "With respect to the causes of this disease," Ticknor wrote Geisinger on October 22, lighting the fuse,

> my opinion is, that they exist to a considerable degree, in the atmosphere; but it is certain that there are other causes which frequently induce it in those who would be likely to escape it, and which always aggravate it. Of these, the principal are all kinds of irregularity, & excess, especially in drinking. . . .
>
> Knowing, as you do, the habits of sailors, it must be perfectly obvious to you, that there would be great danger of this disease being increased to an alarming extent, if the permission which you have given, for the men to be allowed liberty on shore, were to be acted upon. . . .
>
> I take the liberty further to recommend, Sir, then, as the cause of the Cholera exists principally in the atmosphere . . . and as the other cases of disease that have occurred on board have been gradually assuming a more severe character, we leave this port as soon as possible.

Uncharacteristically, Geisinger took good advice. Liberty was cancelled, provisions purchased and loaded, and even while other crewmen fell sick, *Peacock* urgently prepared for sea. She sailed for China in the late afternoon of November 2. (Three weeks later eighteen sailors and five Marines were permitted ashore on liberty, the only mention of shore leave for any crewmember in the ship's log of the cruise.)

Roberts, who'd been camping comfortably at Consul Edward's for weeks, was reluctant to cease his sightseeing and go back on board. "To be compelled to leave a comparatively healthy and pleasant abode on shore, for a floating hospital, tainted with a highly infectious atmosphere, was painful and dangerous," he wrote, "but such was our lot; for thirty sick-hammocks were slung on the starboard side of the gun-deck when we weighed anchor, and a panic was visible in the countenances of nearly the whole crew." Ticknor wasn't

* The first argument had been over the covert disposal of Peterson's body. Geisinger, whose instructions and preparations to bury the man on shore crossed with his burial at sea, Ticknor wrote, then "showed all the petulance of an ungoverned child when something has happened contrary to his wishes."

reluctant. His November 2 journal entry was unequivocal: "Never before did I experience greater satisfaction leaving port, than at this time; for I had never left a port before where I suffered more from anxiety and a hot suffocating climate than Manilla." Unknowingly echoing Bowditch, he concluded, "I was therefore greatly rejoiced, as were all of us on board, to turn our backs upon this miserable place, and none of us had the least desire to visit it again."

Ticknor's vague notion that cholera was somehow spread by air precluded him from trying to establish why the outbreak on his ship struck and killed these ten sailors in particular, exploring whether they shared a mess or a watch and if that community or something else suggested an explanation why they had died of cholera and others had not. Still, by the standards of the day, *Peacock*'s cruise was a remarkably healthy one: only twenty-one of the crew died during her many months out of home port.

5

China, Cochin China, and Siam

Edmund Roberts was a superb specimen of an American. Over six feet in height, elegant in his dress and manners, highly accomplished, and fairly well educated, he made an instantly good impression on the Orientals, who were impressed with his truth, honesty, humanity, and generosity.

William Griffis, *New York Times*, August 6, 1905

16

Four months into her journal's fifth handwritten volume (of an eventual total of nine), Harriett Low, a twenty-year-old "travelling spinster" from Salem, recorded USS *Peacock*'s arrival off Macao—her home for the past two years—on the early afternoon of November 9. (*Peacock*'s log followed the American calendar, and showed the date as the eighth.) The next day the sloop moved eighteen miles northeast, from Macao Roads' open and exposed anchorage to the near side of Lintin Island, lying equidistant from Macao and Hong Kong. The name means "solitary nail," a reference to the island's sharply peaked mountain. She anchored there in ten or so fathoms a mile and a half offshore, sheltered with others in the island's lee from the northeast monsoon that blew from late autumn through to early spring.

"Mr. Roberts and the first Lieut., Mr. [Robert] Cunningham, came and dined with us [on board the American bark *Lintin*]. Very pleasant and gentlemanly men," Harriett Low noted in her journal that evening. "Mr. Roberts, a fine looking man, looks like a clergyman, a statesman, or anything great you can name. They all made many pretty speeches at the pleasure of seeing ladies, meeting their country women, etc."* That dinner came early during

* Harriett Low (1809–1877), from Salem, accompanied her uncle, William Henry Low, soon to be for a few years head of Russell and Company's Canton office, and his wife Abigail to China in September 1829. Harriett remained in Macao as Abigail's companion until November 1833, writing prolifically the whole time in a journal meant for her sister in Massachusetts, when the three finally left for home. Only the women made it back. William Low died in March 1834 midway through the return voyage.

A second woman from Salem, Rebecca Kinsman, went to Macao in 1843 with her merchant husband, Nathaniel, and two of their children, he after a career at sea to represent the New York merchant house of Wetmore and Company. Before she returned home to Massachusetts in 1847, one child had died, another had been born, and she'd been widowed. Her husband is buried in the Old Protestant

The Opium Ships at Lintin in China. While legitimate traders could unload and load at Whampoa, the "inner anchorage" of Canton, opium smugglers could not so brazenly violate Chinese law prohibiting drug imports. But they could do so at Lintin, twenty-five miles below the mouth of the Pearl River. There the drug was openly warehoused in receiving ships and moved from them in fast Chinese boats under oars, past always ineffectual and often corrupt customs officials, to Canton and other distribution points on shore.

Roughly thirty vessels were anchored off the island when *Peacock* drew up on the tenth, perhaps one-third of them American, most carrying opium. The drug sold ashore, Ticknor wrote, for a low price of $4.50 per pound in chests of about 140 pounds each. Helpfully, Macao's first English-language newspaper, the biweekly *Canton Register*, published market prices for opium. During this era the drug traded freely in the United Kingdom too. Not until the Pharmacy Act of 1868 were restrictions placed on the sale of opium in the British Isles.

This oil painting by William Huggins (1781–1845) shows three ships, the center one British and the other two American, in the busy anchorage in 1824. To the right a Chinese smuggler rests at its oars, just behind feeding seagulls. Huggins sailed as crew on East India Company ships before he became a marine painter to the British court and is admired for his technically accurate depictions of ships and their rigging. He exhibited at the Royal Academy and the British Institution. This painting later appeared as a popular aquatint engraving by Edward Duncan, a superb water colorist in his own right as well as Huggins' son-in-law.

the month she stayed on board *Lintin*, the guest of the captain and his wife. Unsaid in her journal, hinted at by Ticknor, and made explicit by Roberts, *Lintin* was center node of American trade in Turkish opium with China. The bark was a floating opium warehouse, busy enough that thanks to her stocks,

Cemetery, not far from Roberts. Kinsman's diary and letters are an additional source of information on American expatriates' life in Macao during the first half of the century.

Russell and Company, her owner, stood third in the drug trade behind only the big British merchant houses dealing in Indian opium, Jardine, Matheson and Company and Dent and Company. (Excepting two American firms, Olyphant and Company and Nathan Dunn and Company, all the other foreign companies in Canton appear to have traded in opium too.)

A few years later, the squadron surgeon of the new U.S. East Indies Squadron estimated the quantity of Indian opium smuggled into China and sold there annually during the past nine shipping seasons. The low was 11,111 chests worth $10.4 million in 1827–28, and the high was 26,000 chests and $17.1 million in 1835–36, a dollar amount very close to the $17.9 million in the entire United States 1835 budget.[1]

The disease that had chased USS *Peacock* out of Manila also clouded the sloop's arrival at the Asian mainland. Saturday, November 10, Lieutenant Cunningham invited the local Americans to come on board *Peacock* to join the crew in divine services the next morning, "but as he told us they had the Cholera on board and had lost 7 men with it, we were afraid to go," Low recorded. "They got it in Manilla, they say; that Ships were laying all around them in Manilla and none had it *but* their ship. They say it was in the atmosphere, and say it is only on a particular current or draught of air, but I cannot conceive of that. They say it is not contagious, for many of the officers stood by when their men were seized with it and watched the progress of the disease, which must be *really* awful—but none of the officers ever took it."

Low's skepticism about how cholera was thought to spread was wise, but she evidently accepted reassurance. A few days later, November 16 (ironically the day that Seaman Powers' body was sent on shore for burial after his death on board the day before), she boarded *Peacock* and was "very politely received, and liked the Ship much, everything in good order and very neat." No mention now of the "really awful" disease hovering over the ship.

Peacock's arrival, of course, had been observed by the Chinese. The same day Low visited *Peacock* the imperial commissioner at Canton published a special order to the chief merchants of the port about the American ship now lying off one of the Nine Islands. As quoted in Roberts' book, the order in the emperor's name didn't bode well for the Americans' visit to China, now just one week old:

> Having ascertained that said cruiser is not a merchant ship or a convoy, and that she has on board an unusual number of seamen, cannon and weapons [the commissioner's inflated inventory listed two hundred seamen, twenty-four cannon, one hundred muskets and swords, 12,600 pounds of powder, and nine hundred cannon balls], she is

> not allowed, under any pretext, to anchor, and create disturbances. Wherefore, *let her be driven away*. And let the hong-merchants on receiving this order act in obedience thereto, and enjoin it upon the said nation's [consul] that he order and compel the said ship to depart and return home. He is not allowed to frame excuses, linger about, and create disturbances, and so involve offenses, that would be examined into and punished. Let the day be fixed for her departure and reported. Haste! Haste!

No matter. No notice was taken of the order, Roberts explained, because "so inefficient is the navy of China in the present day, that the Peacock alone could destroy the whole '*imperial fleet*,' and to have passed up to Canton and back with a *leading wind*, without receiving any material injury from the forts, as their guns are firmly embedded in stone and mortar, and they can only be fired in one direction."*

17

During the early twentieth century, the Reverend William Griffis (1843–1928) lectured and wrote prolifically with special authority about Japan. Griffis, quoted in the epigraph, is commonly accorded the distinction of being America's first "old Japan hand," reflecting his many books about the country after an initial visit there in 1870–74. (A second and last visit came decades later.) At the end of a long career, his scholarship was also recognized in Japan, by the emperor's award of the Order of the Rising Sun, third and fourth classes, two handsome decorations.

Perhaps prompted by the fact that Portsmouth, New Hampshire, Roberts' hometown, was in the late summer of 1905 host to American-sponsored peace negotiations at the end of the Russo-Japanese War, the *New York Times* published that August a short, background piece by Griffis on early Japanese-American diplomatic relations titled (literally true, but misleading) "Edmund Roberts, Our First Envoy to Japan."

On January 26, six weeks before *Peacock* sailed, Roberts received his diplomatic credentials, commissions signed by the secretary of state empowering

* Roberts wasn't boasting. In November 1816, the 44-gun HMS *Alceste* pushed past the forts guarding the river's entrance, the "Tiger's Mouth," with a single broadside and sailed to Whampoa. (Her triumph was short lived. The following February *Alceste* was lost on a reef in the Java Sea.) In January 1841 the Royal Navy again forced a passage past the forts defending the channel to Canton, but this attack included a dozen ships—including the nearly new, iron-hulled steamer HMS *Nemesis* firing guns and rockets—and fifteen hundred men. In between the two, in late 1820, USS *Congress* sailed into the Tiger's Mouth but left without firing a shot after being reluctantly resupplied for the voyage home.

him to negotiate in Muscat, Siam, and Cochin China, and letters of introduction to these rulers signed by the president and countersigned by the secretary. At the same time he got some signed, fill-in-the-blanks versions of these papers, empowering him to treat with other potentates—especially the emperor of Japan—should an opportunity to do that arise on the fly.

Not until June 6, 1832, when *Peacock* was already three months out of Boston and then in Buenos Ayres, were additional formal documents prepared addressed explicitly to President Jackson's "great and good friend," his imperial majesty, the emperor of Japan. These extended assurances to that worthy, to be delivered by Special Agent Roberts, of America's "perfect amity and good will" toward him. (These credentials finally reached Roberts, then back in Batavia, early the following summer.)

Americans had first tried to trade with Japan decades earlier, as far back as 1791. That March two small sloops, *Lady Washington* from Boston and *Lady Grace* out of New York, sailed wearily and unannounced into Kushimoto from Canton after nearly four years at sea in the Atlantic and Pacific. The sloops' pioneering port call seems to have been a complete failure; the aged sea otter hides they carried found no buyers during an eleven-day visit marked by frustration on both sides.

During the Napoleonic Wars, neutral American ships under charter to the Dutch East India Company moved cargoes occasionally between Batavia and Dejima—a tiny, artificial island off Nagasaki that between 1641 and 1853 housed a Dutch factory—Japan's only port open to any foreigner. That experience suggested broader opportunities. Broad enough to prompt Capt. David Porter, USN, on October 31, 1815—the year after he lost the badly outgunned USS *Essex* to HMS *Phoebe* off Valparaiso—to propose to President Madison a visit to Japan to negotiate a trade agreement as part of a much more ambitious "voyage of discovery to the North and South Pacific Oceans."*

"Sir," Porter wrote the president,

> The important trade of Japan has been shut to every nation but the Dutch, who by the most abject and servile means secured a monopoly. Other nations have made repeated attempts at an intercourse with that country, but from a jealousy in the government and from other

* That battle on March 28, 1814, in which *Phoebe* was assisted by the sloop HMS *Cherub*, is the climax of Patrick O'Brian's tenth novel, *The Far Side of the World*, published in 1984. *Essex*, later HMS *Essex*, was the first U.S. warship to sail in the Pacific, and O'Brian's title alludes to the fact that the three, actually four, fought in that ocean. The fourth was "*Essex Junior*," a former British whaler named *Atlantic* that Porter had captured twelve months earlier and had used as a tender since. After several years commanding the Mexican Navy, Porter (1780–1843) spent the last dozen years of his life in Istanbul, first as the chargé at the American legation and later as resident minister.

> causes (among which may be named a want of manly dignity on the part of the negociators) they have all failed. Great changes have since taken place in the world—changes which may have effected even Japan. The time may be favorable, and it would be a glory beyond that acquired by any other nation for us, a nation of only 40 years standing, to beat down their rooted prejudices, secure to ourselves a valuable trade, and make that people known to the world.

"Everything now favors the object," Porter continued, meaning the onset of peace after the War of 1812. He went on to expose another motive for his suggestion: "We have ships which require little or no additional expense: officers who soon will require employment, and who would be greatly benefitted by the experience."[2]

Tensions with Spain edged Porter's suggestion aside even as the president and the secretary of the navy considered it seriously. During the summer of 1846, Commo. James Biddle, USN, riding in USS *Columbus* and accompanied by USS *Vincennes*, sailed into the mouth of Edo Bay, where he tried unsuccessfully to "beat down their rooted prejudices" and secure for the United States this "valuable trade." Seven years later Commo. Matthew Perry, USN, at the head of a much more powerful squadron, finally achieved what Porter had envisioned and Biddle had attempted: "the opening of Japan."

But between Porter and Perry, Roberts was to have his chance. "We have it in contemplation," Secretary Livingston wrote to Roberts on October 28, he then nearly seven months down track,

> to institute a separate mission to Japan, but if you find the prospect favorable, you may fill up one of the letters of credence with the appropriate title of the Emperor and present yourself therefore for the purpose of opening up a trade. But in that case you must not go in a national vessel which cannot submit to the indignity of being disarmed as all foreign vessels are in the ports of Japan, and with which degrading custom a Russian frigate condescended to comply. The Peacock may convey you in a coasting vessel chartered for the purpose and not enter until you receive the appearance that nothing unbecoming the dignity of the country will be required.

Eight months later, on June 22, 1833, Roberts wrote the secretary from Batavia in reply, saying that "it is impossible at this time to proceed to Japan not having sufficient funds to make the usual presents given by the Dutch to the Emperor & his principal Officers." However, based on his conversations with local merchants, Roberts had no doubt,

> that by judicious management all the principal ports in Japan would be thrown open to the [American] trade—the [Americans] are the only people who can probably affect it—the Portuguese and the Spaniards are by law of the empire forever excluded—and the unprincipled conduct of Capt. F. Pellew of the Phaeton in 1808 in the harbor of Nagasaki, has caused the Japanese Gov't to reject every overture which has since that time been made to them on the part of the British—
>
> During the last European War several [American] ships were chartered here for the Dutch factory at Decima [Dejima] & met with no difficulty on account of the flag.*

Roberts' optimistic assessment left negotiations with Japan for his next mission.

How Reverend Griffis concluded that Roberts had "made an instantly good impression on the Orientals"—especially considering that neither of his missions in the 1830s ever sailed for Japan much less reached it—isn't known. Considering Roberts' reception at his first two stops in Asia, Griffis' assessment is gracious but much too generous: there's no reason to believe that Roberts "made an instantly good impression" on the East Asians he met, or any particular impression at all. No Asian had any basis to judge Roberts' truth or humanity, and the fumbled handling of official gifts to his interlocutors—the Cochin Chinese rejected the presents he gave them, all purchased hastily on credit in China—could only have reflected poorly on his government's substance, sincerity, and generosity.

Roberts might well have been a "superb specimen of an American," as described by Griffis (Harriett Low obviously thought him distinguished looking), but he was treated in China and Indochina precisely as all his foreign predecessors had been, with cool disdain and at arm's length across barriers of language and culture that translated awkwardly, if at all. Not until he reached Siam were his counterparts' greetings even lukewarm.

Roberts and Geisinger spent seven weeks on the ground in Canton, from November 10 until December 22, while *Peacock* swung patiently at anchor

---

* October 4, 1808, the 38-gun HMS *Phaeton* approached Dejima disguised as a Dutch ship, hoping to capture Dutch vessels trading there, the Dutch Republic then imperial France's reluctant ally in the Napoleonic Wars. Captain Pellew's threats forced the Japanese to resupply his frigate, which escaped a few days later before Japanese reinforcements arrived to storm her. The ploy poisoned British-Japanese relations.

View of Foreign Factories, Canton, 1825–1835, attributed to Lam Qua. The American factory stands at the center of this ca. 1830 oil painting of the foreign-trade concession area on Canton's waterfront. The British and Dutch factories off to the Americans' right, downriver, are marked by their flags. Lam Qua, a Chinese student in the 1820s of Macau's brilliant resident English painter, George Chinnery, had a studio in Canton on New China Street where he and his own students, perhaps as many as twenty of them, painted in both Western and Eastern styles. Lam Qua is best known not for land- or seascapes or portraits but for a remarkable series of more than one hundred oil paintings commissioned by a medical missionary, Peter Parker, of some eighty patients at the Canton Hospital suffering from ghastly pathological conditions.

miles downriver under Lieutenant Cunningham's temporary command. Roberts' book says nothing about his diplomatic efforts in China during these weeks or about what else he and Geisinger might have been doing in Canton for so long. But not until ten years later did the United States and China sign a "general convention of peace, amity, and commerce" that guaranteed merchants from the United States access to Canton, Shanghai, and three other mainland ports and otherwise encompassed the terms Roberts had been instructed to seek in Asia a decade earlier.*

* The agreement, the Treaty of Wangxia (the first pact between the United States and China, negotiated for the United States by Harvard lawyer and Massachusetts congressman Caleb Cushing, signed in Macao in July 1844, and ratified by the Senate the following January), was the American counterpart to the Anglo-Chinese Treaty of Nanjing. In 1842 that treaty had ended the first of two Opium Wars.

Although the Treaty of Wangxia banned American vessels from entering other Chinese ports, from "carrying on clandestine and fraudulent trade" along the coast and from trading in opium, its terms were otherwise remarkably generous—a reflection of what the British had managed to extract from the empire under Royal Navy pressure. They allowed, for example, the establishment of expatriate

In October 1838 an anonymous reviewer of Roberts' posthumously published book, writing in the *North American Review*, explained to his American readers the inability of their envoy to even begin a discussion in Canton about trade not as due to Roberts' incompetence but as a consequence of the East Asian national character, one defined by adherence to ritual and reverence for form over substance: "As the American Indian, when in his native and undisturbed state, breathes only war and revenge, and the Malay founds all his social happiness upon the facilities afforded him of violating the eighth commandment [lying], so it seems all the ambition of the Chinese races is limited to an exact adherence to formulas of prescribed etiquette."

By Christmas Eve, several days before *Peacock* sailed with Chinese-made gifts in hand from Canton for Cochin China's Turon Bay (later Tourane, now Da Nang), Harriett Low had figured out what the Americans passing through Macao were up to: "Mr. Roberts from the *Peacock* spent the evening with us. He is called the *naturalist*, but I suspect if the truth was known he is a *diplomatist*. Think I understand the whole business," she wrote, "they are going to Siam to form some treaties with the government. It seems Mr. Shillaber took a great deal of trouble to enlighten our government on the state of affairs in those quarters. And he was promised the commission if it should take place—but they have said nothing further to him." (Low knew the Shillabers, John, his sister Caroline, and a third, Sarah, well. The three had lived among expatriates in Macao since Shillaber had gone absent without leave from his post in Batavia.)*

18

Much strange had to happen for American relations with Cochin China to move from mutual unintelligibility in the nineteenth century, through hostility in the twentieth, to what passes loosely today for comprehension and accommodation between the United States and the Socialist Republic of Vietnam.

The first American to evidence a passing interest in Cochin China might have been, improbably, Benjamin Franklin. In October 1772 Franklin sent John Bartram a box of "Upland Rice, brought from Cochin China," via England, explaining that "it grows there on dry Grounds and not in Water like

American communities in the five ports with "houses, places of business, and also hospitals, churches, and cemeteries" and permitted the hire of Chinese-language tutors, laborers, and others. Further, American residents who committed a crime in China—other than opium smuggling—were subject to trial and punishment only by the U.S. consul "or other public functionary of the United States," and that according to American not Chinese law.

* In 1833 Caroline married a Scottish medical missionary in Macau, Thomas Colledge. Three of their infant sons are buried beside one another on the Lower Terrace of the Old Protestant Cemetery.

the common Sort." Franklin, a printer and not a planter, then moved on to other things, but years later the merits of Cochin Chinese rice attracted the attention of the new republic's most scientific farmer, Thomas Jefferson, the American minister in Paris.

Jefferson had read about Cochin Chinese upland rice in a 1779 travelogue written by Pierre Poivre (1719–1786), a sometime–French missionary and full-time horticulturalist, and concluded that for both commercial and public health reasons this might be a superior substitute for the wet rice then grown as a staple in Georgia and the Carolinas, a crop "requiring the whole country to be laid under water during a certain season of the year, [which] sweeps off numbers of inhabitants annually with pestilential fevers."[3] It's not clear if he was referring to malaria, yellow fever, or both.

"The dry rice of Cochin China," Jefferson wrote from Paris in the summer of 1787 to a South Carolina planter, "has the reputation of being whitest to the eye, best flavored to the taste, and most productive. It seems then to unite the good qualities of both the [other varieties] known to us. Could it supplant them, it would be a great happiness, as it would enable us to get rid of those ponds so fatal to human health and life. . . . I will endeavor to procure some to be brought from Cochin China."[4]

Ultimately Jefferson's approaches to Prince Nguyen Phuc Canh's handlers (the child crown prince of Cochin China lived in Paris through almost all of 1787, under the protection of the French missionary Pigneau de Behaine), the influential and wealthy British botanist, Joseph Banks, and several others for samples of seed were unsuccessful. Jefferson had to content himself experimenting with African red rice—which proved to grow well enough in Virginia but not in South Carolina—and after five years in Paris, becoming secretary of state, vice president, and finally president. Accordingly, the first Americans to contact the Cochin Chinese were not Carolina planters but sailors from Massachusetts.

After *Fame*'s failed venture but well before *Peacock*'s two visits to Cochin China in the early 1830s came *Franklin*'s visit, a brig from Salem whose master, John White, was a Navy lieutenant on furlough.* Other vessels from Salem

* Becket's *Fame* is not the same vessel as the East Indiaman of that name, which burned to the waterline off Bencoolen, Sumatra, the evening of February 2, 1824, with Sir Stamford Raffles (the founder of Singapore), his wife and children, and an irreplaceable collection that he described in a letter as "the cream and best of everything I had collected, learnt & attained during my residence in India" on board for a passage to England. Crew and passengers in this *Fame* escaped in night clothes into her quarter boats then pulled eighteen hours back to port; everything else was lost. That disaster was memorialized in a bad 1825 poem (but great example of period poetry) by a certain Mr. Glover, which began,

> Darkness succeeds; but soon a blaze of Light
> Darts its refulgence thro' the Shades of Night,
> For Lo! tremendous from the Vessel's frame,

Launching of the Ship Fame. 1802 oil painting by George Ropes Junior (1788–1819). In January 1803 the 363-ton ship *Fame*, Capt. Jeremiah Briggs, sailed from Salem to the Orient on her maiden voyage, hoping to return with a load of sugar. She anchored four months later in Turon Bay, left Cochin China after three weeks for Manila, and finally arrived back home the following March. *Fame* appears to have been the first American vessel to call at any Cochin Chinese port. *Fame*, shown here being launched with great excitement from Retire Becket's shipyard in 1802, was the seventeenth vessel built by Becket, the fourth and last generation of a well-known family of Salem shipwrights. At 102 feet long, with a 24-foot beam and drawing more than fourteen feet, she was Becket's largest project when she slid into the water in 1802. A finished hull in the water like *Fame*'s usually represented some 60 percent of the construction cost of a new oceangoing vessel. Masts and spars; rigging, blocks, and sails; cables, boats, pumps, anchors, and paint; plus the labor to deal with each would have consumed the balance of Becket's budget for the ship.

Four years later Ropes painted *Crowninshield's Wharf, 1806*, showing a fully rigged *Fame* with several other George Crowninshield and Sons Company ships (including the fourth *America*, *Prudent*, and *Belisarius*) tied up alongside Salem's India Wharf. The artist was one of nine children of a Salem ship captain, George Ropes Sr. During Ropes Jr.'s short life—deaf since birth, he died of tuberculosis at thirty—he was well known for handsome and technically accurate paintings of ships and other maritime subjects.
COURTESY PEABODY ESSEX MUSEUM, 199338

had tried to trade with the kingdom of the Cochin Chinese between *Fame* and *Franklin*, but none has left a published record of the experience as complete or popular as was Captain White's *History of a Voyage to the China Sea* (Wells &

Clouds of Saltpetre burst in liquid flame;
O'er the black Waves its poisonous vapours fly,
And scatter Death and Horror thro' the Sky.
and labored on like that for twenty-six pages. (British Library MSS Eur D742/8.)

Lilly, 1823), described by one anonymous reviewer the following year as "the most complete and authentic account which has been published, at least in our language, of the kingdom of Cochin China."[5]

Franklin sailed for Cochin China in early January 1819 and called that August first at Vungtau and then at Turon Bay, hoping unsuccessfully for permission to proceed to and trade at "Saigun" and Hué, respectively. A second attempt at Saigon months later, this time from Manila in company with the Boston-registered and equally frustrated ship *Marmion* (her own earlier solo appearance at Cochin China had also been fruitless) was only slightly more successful. That October the two American ships bullied their way sixty miles up the Mekong River (White called it "the Donnai") to Saigon, from where, after four months in port and the payment of extortionate measuring and export duties, they sailed for home lightly loaded with sugar and silk and feeling very badly used.

Franklin was back in Salem at the end of August 1820, after which Captain White got his revenge. White's published descriptions of his "frowzy" Asian hosts, "little removed from a state of deplorable barbarism," and their "engines of extortion" fed the prejudices of the times and were quoted enthusiastically in reviews of *History of a Voyage to the China Sea*. "It would be tedious to the reader and painful to myself," White wrote,

> to recapitulate the constant villainy and turpitude, which we experienced from these people during our residence in the country. Their total want of faith, constant eagerness to deceive and overreach us, and their pertinacity in trying to gain, by shuffling and maneuvering, what might have been better and easier gained by openness and fair dealing; the tedious forms and ceremonies in transacting all kinds of business, carried into the most trifling transactions; the uncertainty of the eventual ratification of any bargain . . . all these vexations, combined with the rapacious, faithless, despotic and anti-commercial character of the government, will, as long as these causes exist, render Cochin China the least desirable country for mercantile adventurers.[6]

And maybe it was, but such adventurers proved difficult to dissuade.

19

On Wednesday, December 26, Geisinger wrote the secretary to report *Peacock*'s readiness to depart Lintin the next morning for Cochin China, now that John Robert Morrison (borrowed from his father in Macao and traveling as Roberts' interpreter and private secretary) and the hastily purchased substitute gifts were on board.

"The Peacock," Geisinger continued, "is in perfect order and is abundantly supplied with provisions &c. Mr. Roberts thinks he will be enabled to leave Siam sometime in March, from thence we shall be obliged to touch at Singapore for a day or two on my way to Batavia, where I shall go for supplies. After leaving B. I shall proceed to Muscat and stop on the west coast of Sumatra, should our affairs there make it necessary."

Geisinger concluded by appending a political observation that was also a commercial for the Navy: "Our arrival at Manila & Canton was highly gratifying to the American Merchants at both places. It is deemed important by them that Ships of War should frequently visit both places, that there is a protecting power at hand ready to defend them in case of necessity for it has been the prevailing belief here until lately that the government of the U.S. is totally indifferent to the extensive commerce present in these seas and remains unwilling to afford even a single ship for its defense."

Thursday *Peacock* quit Lintin, having reluctantly given up on the possibility of a rendezvous there with *Boxer*. Now came nearly a week's worth of heavy seas and adverse winds and currents along the Cochin Chinese coast that first complicated and then absolutely prevented her safe entry into Turon Bay, a port just twenty leagues (sixty miles) away from the imperial capital, Hué.

At noon on January 5, 1833, nine days out of Lintin, USS *Peacock* finally dropped anchor at Vunglam, one of the three villages of Phuyen Province lining what Roberts described as "truly one of the finest harbours in the world"—a tourist destination today. She'd been blown and pushed some one hundred twenty miles farther south along the Cochin Chinese coast than Geisinger had hoped. *Peacock* spent nearly five weeks there while Roberts maneuvered unsuccessfully toward an imperial audience and the start of trade negotiations.

What the United States sought from the king of Cochin China (and from the emperor of China and, later, potentates elsewhere) was spelled out in some half a dozen articles of the draft treaty that Roberts carried with him. The first article foresaw perpetual peace between the United States and the king of Cochin China. The remaining ones addressed the substance of the agreement sought:

- Americans were to have liberty to enter foreign ports with cargoes of any kind and to sell or trade their goods for any produce or manufactured items found there. Traders were to "be free, on both sides, to buy, sell or exchange" on terms and for prices "the owners may think fit," and whenever "citizens of the United States may think fit to depart, they shall be at liberty so to do, and if any viceroy, mandarin, or officer of the customs . . . shall contravene this article, he shall be severely punished."

- Americans were to pay no greater duties than those paid by the most favored nation's traders.
- Shipwrecked Americans in the king's dominions "shall be taken care of and hospitably entertained" at the king's expense, subject to reimbursement upon their return. Moreover, "the property saved from such wreck shall be carefully preserved and delivered to the owner or to the Consul of the United States."
- Americans were to have leave to land and reside in ports of the kingdom "without having to pay any tax or imposition for such liberty other than general duties on imports or exports, which the most favored nation shall pay."
- Americans "taken by pirates, and brought into the dominions of the King . . . shall be set at liberty and property restored."

Finally, the president could appoint consuls to reside in the kingdom's principal ports, who were to be "the exclusive judges of all disputes or suits" between Americans, and to have "power to receive the property of any American citizen dying within the kingdom." They, members of their households, and their property were to be immune from arrest or confiscation.*

Writing from Batavia almost six months later, Roberts explained to Washington the reasons for his failure in Cochin China. "Immediately on our arrival," Roberts wrote, a letter was sent to "His Majesty Ming-Mang, King of Annam, informing him of our arrival and setting forth the object of our mission":

> On the 17th a deputation consisting of three Mandarins arrived . . . bringing back with them [President Jackson's February 26, 1832] letter directed to the King. They stated that they had been sent by the "Minister of Strangers" to inform me verbally that he had returned the letter unopened, in consequence of it being addressed to the *King* of Annam. The present sovereign of Cochin China who apes as far as possible his Lord and Master the Emperor of China, has taken upon himself lately the title of *Emperor*. . . . The Minister therefore requested that another letter be sent.†

* However, "should any Consul commit an offense against the laws of the Kingdom . . . the President will immediately displace him." From Entry 34, Instructions to Special Agents 1823–1906, vol. 1, 80–81, General Records of the Department of State, NARA, College Park, MD.

† Jackson's letter introducing Roberts, "a respectable citizen of the United States," to Minh Mang *was* addressed to "His Majesty the Emperor of Cochin China."

"Minh Mang, King of Cochin China (1791–1841)." The king was the second member of the Nguyen dynasty that ruled what is today Vietnam from 1802 until 1945, through a period as a Chinese tributary state and later during the decades-long French colonial era. King in Hué while Roberts twice unsuccessfully attempted to negotiate trade agreements with Cochin China, Minh Mang had good reason for his xenophobia during the early 1830s, given an ongoing war with Siam, relentless European economic and missionary pressure on his kingdom, and foreign support of local revolutionaries attempting to unseat him.

This drawing of the king is from the second volume of John Crawfurd's *Journal of an Embassy for the Governor-General of India to the Courts of Siam and Cochin China* (Henry Colburn and Richard Bentley, 1830). Crawfurd, a Scot, is better known as the second British East India Company resident in Singapore, appointed to that post immediately after this embassy and replacing there Sir Stanford Raffles' protégé, William Farquhar, a countryman. Roberts owned a copy of Crawfurd's *Journal* and took passages from it for his own manuscript.

John Crawfurd, *Journal of an Embassy for the Governor-General of India to the Courts of Sian and Cochin China* (Henry Colburn and Richard Bentley, 1830).

And now began a weeks-long dialogue of the deaf, during the first part of which the mandarins insisted that the president's letter introducing his envoy be offered in "silent awe" and with "uplifted hands" to their emperor, and otherwise employ the usual vocabulary of a subject addressing his sovereign. "This was instantly rejected," Roberts explained in his report, "& they were admonished not to repeat so insulting a demand for that the President of the United States stands on a footing of perfect equality with the highest Emperor & therefore no terms can be used which may make him appear in the light of an inferior."

Near midway through this stand-off, on January 26, *Peacock*'s reluctant hosts brought a feast on board the ship, some fifty dishes of "flesh, fish and fowl," vegetables, and fruit, Ticknor reported, prepared in "the best style of the country." A gift that turned out to be from the local chief. Practically nothing was consumed, however; the squeamish Americans put off by thoughts that the meal had been cooked "in the uncleanly vessels we had seen on shore, and had come into contact with filthy paws, dirty nails and vermin."

Sounding very much like White had, and equally frustrated, Roberts described his reluctant hosts as "without exception the most filthy people in the world. . . . All having a mangy appearance; being covered with some scorbutic disease, the itch or small-pox, and frequently with white leprous spots. . . . Their faces are nasty, their hands unwashed, and their whole persons most offensive to the sight and smell. . . . A whole village may be seen at the same time scratching from head to foot." From people such as these—who had "an utter aversion to cleanliness," leading him to conclude "that they all had a touch of the hydrophobia, from their aversion to water"—little good could have been expected:

> If I could have so far debased myself as to forget what was due to my country & her chief Magistrate as to submit to their proposals, it would not have ended there. I should have been told on my arrival at Hue that if I wished to be presented to the Emperor, it would be necessary that I should comply with the ceremonies of the court & submit to perform the Ko-tow or "knock head ceremony," and this would have been followed up by other humiliating conditions for it is in the nature of the ultra Gangetic nations to rise in their demands as they can enforce or in any way procure submission to their will. . . .
>
> If we have failed in this attempt at negociation our honour yet remains unstained, & the resistance made to their insulting proposals to degrade the high standing of the President of the United States,

> will teach them I trust in any future negociation with our government, that national honour is not a mere sound, or but an empty name, for in this sound rests the strength of Kingdoms, the safety of nations.

Retrospectively, Roberts mused that perhaps he would have been more successful if his mission had started as planned at Turon Bay, only fifty miles or so from Hué, instead of nearly two hundred miles south at Vunglam: "If we had been so fortunate, as to arrive at Turon or off the bar at Hué early in the S.W. monsoon, I believe the result would have been very different. We were too far removed from the Capital, & matters were consequently trusted too much to inferior agents."

Maybe. The elder Morrison's sixth recommendation to Roberts had read, "Carry up the ships as near the capital as practicable, and reveal as little to inferior officers as possible." Closer to Hué, Roberts would presumably have had fewer layers between him and the king, but even if the hierarchy of mandarins—each determined to preserve court etiquette and to protect himself, his superiors, and his emperor from any possible embarrassment from foreign visitors—through which he had to pass was abbreviated, Roberts' own sense of national and personal dignity (to say nothing of Minh Mang's suspicions) might well have guaranteed failure anyway.

Still, there are hints in the record that Roberts' frustrating visit to Cochin China might have come out differently had *Peacock* been able to anchor closer to the capital. Differently, although not necessarily successfully. Neither the emperor nor his mandarins ever grasped that Roberts was seeking more than just permission for American ships to show up in Cochin Chinese ports occasionally and trade.

One such hint is found in a chatty July 1834 letter from John Morrison, Roberts' teenage interpreter, addressed to him in Portsmouth in between his missions. "You will be surprised to hear that three or four months after my return [to Macao from Cochin China]," Morrison wrote his one-time boss, "calling upon some Cochin-Chinese officers . . . I found at the head of them our two commissioners with whom we had so many conversations at Veruzlain [*sic*]. I paid them several visits, but derived no information from them except that the day after our departure an answer arrived giving the ship permission to go to Turon and trade. This circumstance they were very anxious that I should communicate to you."

The second is in a March 1835 letter from the American consul resident in Singapore, Joseph Balestier, to then-secretary of state Forsythe reporting on his conversation with an unnamed missionary recently arrived from Cochin

China.* It seems generally to confirm young Morrison's letter: had communications between the two sides not been so slow, Balestier learned, Minh Mang's invitation to Roberts to call on Saigon ("Segong") would have arrived before *Peacock* sailed, with who knows what result.

20

Chastened, embittered even, by the failure of this first mission to Cochin China, Roberts must have been frustrated too by *Peacock*'s slow initial progress toward Bangkok and his next diplomatic encounter, what would become the first American government-to-government contact with the Kingdom of Siam and result in the first treaty between the United States and any country in Asia.

Adverse winds held *Peacock* in sight of Phuyen for three days after weighing anchor in the harbor. Not until February 13 did she round the southern tip of the peninsula and enter the Gulf of Siam, forced by poor charts to spend the next five days feeling her way north through the islands—and sea snakes—of the gulf. Her destination was an anchorage several miles south of the sandbar that obstructed the mouth of the Menam (literally "mother water," now the Chao Phraya), the great river flowing past the Siamese capital. Approaching a month later, on March 8, Roberts was finally in the presence of Nangklao, "His Majesty the Sovereign and Magnificent King in the City of Sia Yut'hia [Bangkok]," making his first call on Asian royalty. During the weeks before that audience, Roberts and Chaopraya Phraklang, the prime minister and governor of southern Siam, had negotiated the terms of the treaty.

The Siamese were not negotiating naïfs. They'd been through this several years earlier. Nangklao (1788–1851) ruled Siam as Rama III between 1824 and 1851. His reign marked the formal entry of this ancient kingdom into the Western world's trading system with a treaty signed with Great Britain in 1826 (called the Burney Treaty, after the British negotiator), following the end of the First Anglo-Burman War. The Burney Treaty's seven commercial articles—another seven addressed political subjects—and the six articles of an associated commercial agreement so favored the Siamese that a later British assessment described several of the terms as "repugnant." This treaty formed the template when U.S.-Siamese negotiations began. In both agreements, for example, duties were charged arriving merchant ships based on a

* Resident in Singapore but formally accredited to Rhio, a small Dutch property some forty miles away with insignificant foreign trade. Not until July 1836 was he actually appointed to Singapore. The reason for the delay was uncertainty about the legality of American trade with the island under the terms of the 1815 Convention of Commerce, which, because it predated the establishment of Singapore, didn't list it among the several ports open to American trade.

measurement of maximum beam across the main deck, not on the cargo carried; neither country was permitted to post a resident consul in Siam.

To the frustration of the Thai diplomatic establishment today, the best-known of the nineteenth century's five Siamese kings is not the long-in-service Rama III. Instead, it's Nangklao's half brother and successor, King Mongkut, who took the throne in 1851 as Rama IV and who famously in 1862 hired one Anna Leonowens to serve as governess of his many adolescent wives and children. For that well-intentioned act, this small, scholarly man who spent the early years of his life as a Buddhist monk patiently waiting to take his throne, will be forever imagined as Yul Brynner, Rama IV's bald and bare-chested avatar in Richard Rodgers and Oscar Hammerstein's musical *The King and I*.

The "I" in the title was Leonowens, played first by Deborah Kerr, but in real life the thirty-one-year-old widow of an expatriate Irish clerk in India with a complicated personal history that she reimagined into something much more respectable.[7] Leonowens (1831–1914) wrote her first two books about her five years in Siam's royal court. Decades later, in the hands of Margaret Landon, wife of a missionary in Thailand, Leonowens' *The English Governess at the Siamese Court* (Fields, Osgood, 1870) and *The Romance of the Harem* (James R. Osgood, 1873) became more than Victorian travelogues. They became Landon's *Anna and the King of Siam*. And from that 1940 book grew an evergreen Broadway musical and several Hollywood movies, including a forgettable 1999 iteration shot in Malaysia—Thailand would have nothing to do with it—that cast Jodie Foster as Anna and Hong Kong's Chow Yun Fat as the king.

As Anna Leonowens saw it, Rama III was a usurper; his younger half brother and her employer should have been on the throne through the middle decades of the century. "In 1825," she wrote in her first book, "a royal prince of Siam (his birthright wrested from him, and his life imperiled) took refuge in a Buddhist monastery and assumed the yellow garb of a priest":

> His father . . . had just died, leaving this prince, Chowfa Mongkut, at the age of twenty, lawful heir to the crown; for he was the eldest son of the acknowledged queen, and therefore by courtesy and honored custom, if not by absolute right, the legitimate successor to the throne. . . . But he had an elder half brother, who, through the intrigues of his mother, had already obtained control of the royal treasury, and now . . . proclaimed himself king. . . . He had the grace, however, to promise his plundered brother . . . to hold the reins of government only until [Mongkut] should be of years and strength and skill to manage them. But, once firmly seated on the throne, the usurper saw in his patient

but proud and astute kinsman only a hindrance and peril in the path of his own cruder and fiercer aspirations. Hence the forewarning and the flight, the cloister and the yellow robes. And so the usurper continued to reign, unchallenged by any claim from the king that should

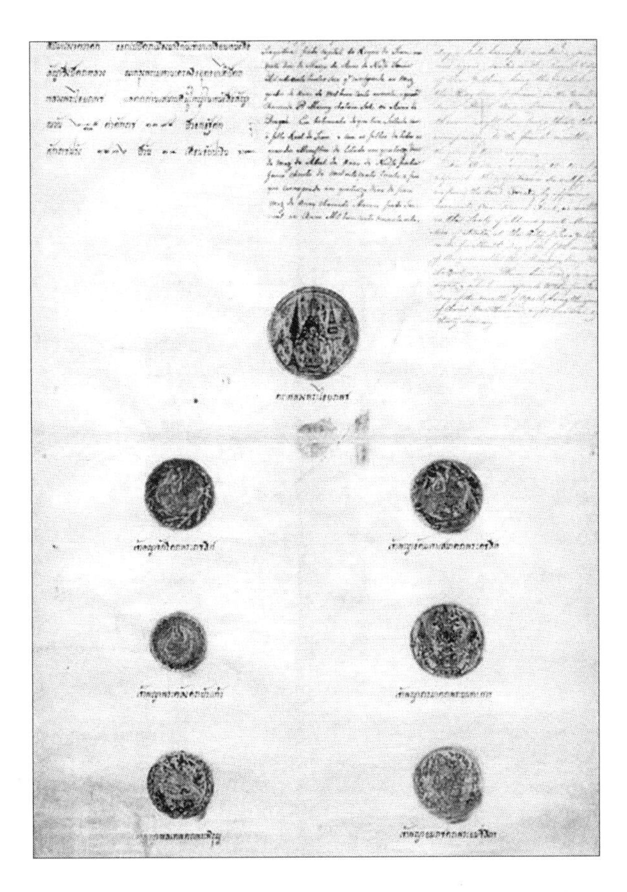

Signature portion of the more than nine-foot-long scroll of the Treaty of Sincere Friendship and Entire Good Faith Between the Two Nations. Roberts' treaty foresaw that citizens of both countries "shall with sincerity hold commercial intercourse in the ports of their respective nations as long as heaven and earth shall endure." Concluded on March 20, 1833, ratifications were finally exchanged in Bangkok on April 14, 1836, and the treaty was officially proclaimed in Washington the following June.

"As the Siamese are ignorant of English and the Americans of Siamese," the treaty preamble explained, "a Portuguese and a Chinese translation are annexed, to serve as testimony to the contents of the treaty. The writing is of the same tenor and date in all the languages aforesaid." Roberts wrote in his 1837 book, "The treaty has removed all obstacles to a lucrative and important branch of our commerce, the merchant being left free to sell or purchase where and of whom he pleases. Prior to this period, the American merchant was not allowed to sell to a private individual the cargo he imported, nor purchase a return cargo. The king claimed the exclusive right of purchase and sale in both cases."
National Archives and Records Administration

> be, until March 1851, when, a mortal illness, having overtaken him, he convoked the Grand Council of princes and nobles around his couch and proposed his favorite son as his successor. The safe asses of the court kicked the dying lion with seven words of sententious scorn,—"the crown already has its rightful owner"; whereupon [Rama III] literally cursed himself to death; for it was almost in the convulsion of his chagrin and rage that he came to his end, on the 3rd of April [1851].

This tough-minded usurper, Rama III, was the Siamese king Roberts had come halfway around the world to see. He arrived a decade into a special time in the history of the Siam and its ruling dynasty, a period of political consolidation under the royal house, of expeditionary military success, and of economic expansion (at least until rice crops failed in 1843 and 1844, and recession set in). The treaty that emerged from the negotiations would later be criticized in the United States for the "exorbitant tonnage dues" that stunted growth in trade with Siam (and stopped trade entirely after 1840), for its failure to provide for a resident consul, and for putting the lives and property of Americans at risk by not affording the protection of extraterritoriality. The last two provisions had been proposed to the prime minister during negotiations and firmly and repeatedly rejected.

Roberts' treaty with Siam was the first of his only two successes.

21

A dozen or so years later, in early May 1845, USS *Constitution*, "Old Ironsides," sailed into Turon Bay. Under the command of Capt. John Percival, USN, *Constitution* had left New York at the end of May 1844 following service in Norfolk as the receiving ship (after an aborted cruise with the home squadron) and a hasty, bargain-priced overhaul supervised by Percival, her new commanding officer. The two old salts—*Constitution* was now forty-seven, Percival was sixty-five—spent the next twenty-seven months sailing around the world, finally arriving in Boston in September 1846, worn down by 52,300 miles at sea.

Constitution's mission for that cruise—a long step down from her heroic past as the victor of thrilling duels with His Majesty's Ships *Guerrière*, *Java*, *Cyane*, and *Levant* during the War of 1812—was to show the flag and to support American trade in any way possible. Two ways were the charting of anchorage sites and the identification of coal depots (by the 1840s steam propulsion was obviously the coming thing, although big sailing barks would carry bulk freight economically for another century).

En route around the world, after almost exactly a year under way and earlier stops to drop off the new U.S. minister to Brazil and in Singapore to recruit her crew, the frigate's ninth port call was at Turon Bay. (The new American minister to Rio de Janeiro, Henry Wise, had traveled to his post at the head of a party of thirteen that included his family, their servants, and the legation's secretary. The multitude forced Captain Percival, as years earlier Baylies' presence had pressed Geisinger, to yield the captain's cabin to his distinguished guests.)

Constitution arrived in Turon Bay May 10, 1845, to bury a dead bandsman on shore and to water and repaint the ship. During sixteen days in the bay before sailing for Macao, "Mad Jack" Percival (the nickname even appears on his tombstone) managed singlehandedly to provoke what in later times would have been an explosive international incident. Somehow persuaded that Bishop Dominique Lefevre, a French Catholic missionary, needed rescue from a sentence of death—and that such a rescue was consistent with his instructions from the Navy Department to "afford every encouragement and assistance" in his power to American commerce and citizens and to nationals of friendly nations—*Constitution*'s captain sent armed parties ashore, took hostages, seized junks, and otherwise behaved badly before sailing off, leaving the missionary behind. After a few weeks of reflection, once in Whampoa, Percival wrote a nervous letter of explanation to the secretary of the navy. (Percival's rash actions prompted the fifth senior lieutenant, John Dale, to describe in his journal of the cruise his captain's "sad want of sound discretion." Thirty-four original pencil, pen, and watercolor sketches illustrate Dale's journal and provide other glimpses of Southeast Asia as it appeared to Western eyes in the mid-1840s.)

Constitution's bullying port call at Turon Bay was one reason for the failure of an American attempt five years later "to negotiate friendly intercourse" with Cochin China. Joseph Balestier, formerly the consul in Singapore and appointed a State Department commercial agent in August 1849 (during President Taylor's administration), arrived there near the end of February 1850 in USS *Plymouth* for the first stop of a mission that also included calls at Siam, Borneo, Sumatra, Brunei, and two other island sultanates.[8]

Balestier carried with him a letter of "friendship and conciliation" from President Millard Fillmore to the king of Annam "disavowing, in a formal manner, an alleged outrage committed in [the king's] dominions by Capt. John Percival whist in command of the frigate *Constitution* in the year 1845," with instructions from Secretary of State Clayton to make every possible explanation and atonement.

Constitution's "outrage" wasn't a new subject to Balestier. In early April 1847 he'd reported to Washington from Singapore that visiting Cochin Chinese mandarins had approached him "for redress of ill treatment," citing an attack by the frigate that had destroyed their port, sank junks in the harbor, and killed and wounded many, the result being, Balestier thought, that the presence of Americans in the kingdom would "be looked upon with more dread than pleasure" in the future. He understood from the mandarins that in response their king "abides the opportunity of a signal Vengeance doubtless on some of our defenseless or shipwrecked countrymen . . . the sacrifice of innocent lives under the most horrible torture as practiced on his enemies by the King of Cochin China."

President Fillmore's letter was never delivered. On arrival at Turon (Balestier called it "Tourong") Bay in February—following three months marking time at Hong Kong waiting Navy transportation; Captain Geisinger, the outgoing commander of the East Indies Squadron, refused to sail before his relief by a successor, Commo. Philip Vorhees, USN—Balestier discovered a "government wholly unwilling to enter into any negotiation whatever."* After a frustrating month, during which *Plymouth* remained at anchor and nothing was accomplished on shore, Balestier sailed empty-handed for Bangkok, *Plymouth* closely following *Peacock*'s track of seventeen years earlier. He would enjoy no success there either. But another American diplomat soon did.

22

Sunday, April 13, 1856, the second-class screw steamer USS *San Jacinto*, Capt. Henry Bell, USN, commanding and flying the flag of Commo. James Armstrong, USN, five and a half months out of New York, anchored at the bar of the Menam. She was to remain there for nearly two months while her distinguished passenger, Townsend Harris, the first U.S. consul in Japan, paused on his way to the Japanese capital, Edo, to negotiate an updated trade treaty with the king of Siam. Balestier had failed to do so in 1850, in small part because he had the bad luck to arrive off the Siamese capital during a cholera

* The phrase is from a story in the October 1, 1851, issue of the *New York Times* reporting Balestier's return to New York after two years abroad on his mission. "The first mandarin received him with polite attention and every becoming honor; but stated that his instructions from the government were positive not to listen to any propositions for commercial or friendly intercourse. . . . Having no instructions to employ force, Mr. Balestier had no alternative than to turn his course in another direction. . . . He proceeded to the Kingdom of Siam."

epidemic on shore; in large part because his "angry . . . insulting . . . threatening" approach to his hosts forced their termination of talks. The American goal was an agreement that duplicated the concessions in the year-old treaty negotiated with Siam by Sir John Bowring, British governor of Hong Kong. A new treaty, one the *New York Times* described as "formed . . . on more practicable and liberal principles" than that originally negotiated by Roberts, was the goal.

Although Bowring's treaty fell short of his description, claiming nothing less than "a total revolution of all the financial machinery of the [Siamese] Government" and conversion to the principles of free trade," it did open the Siamese market to foreigners and expand the protections afforded to resident expatriates.

Harris' face-to-face negotiations with the Siamese prime minister finally began on May 16. By May 24, when what turned out to have been "stormy" talks were finally finished and a text agreed to, Harris sounded like Baylies leaving Buenos Ayres after the collapse of that mission. "I hope this is the end of my troubles with this false, base and cowardly people," Harris wrote in his journal on Saturday, May 24, 1856. "To lie here is the rule from Kings downward. . . . I never met a people like them, and hope I may never again be sent here. The proper way to negotiate with the Siamese is to send two or three men-of-war of not more than 16 feet draft of water. Let them arrive in October and at once proceed up to Bangkok and fire their salutes. In such a case the treaty will not require more days than I have consumed weeks."

Negotiations successfully concluded and the newly designated U.S. consul in place, *San Jacinto* weighed anchor on June 1 and continued slowly toward the East China Sea and Japan.* Her always balky engines, replaced not long before this cruise after less than two years of service, had forced some voyage repairs in Penang, where she'd gone—149 days out of New York and a month late—to collect Harris. Soon came a further humiliation: a disabling propeller failure while getting under way from Hong Kong for Japan on July 10.

Unloaded and completely disarmed to reduce her draft, *San Jacinto* had to be pulled eighty miles upriver to Whampoa for repairs. (While she was towed ignobly past the second-class steam frigate HMS *Nankin*, the British band played "Hail Columbia" in sarcastic salute.) Rainy weeks passed at Whampoa in dry dock. *San Jacinto* didn't leave Hong Kong until after noon on August 12

* The new consul, appointed by Harris, was Rev. Stephen Mattoon (1816–1889), a Presbyterian missionary from New York living in Siam since 1847 who'd served during the negotiations as Harris' interpreter and before then as King Mongkut's during Governor Bowring's embassy. Matoon's wife, Mary Lourie, was one of the three missionary wives who took turns instructing Mongkut's household in English and other subjects until all three were replaced by governess Anna Leonowens.

and didn't arrive in Japan to deliver Harris at Shimoda, Japan, until late on August 21, 1856.*

A New York merchant with six years' experience trading in the East, Harris had lobbied President Franklin Pierce and his secretary of state, William Marcy, furiously for the new post in Japan, a position established in the same treaty that obtained coaling rights for American ships at Hakodate and Shimoda in 1854. Harris' campaign succeeded on August 4, when the acting secretary of state signed his commission as consul-general for Japan. One month later the secretary of state wrote Harris to add a stop in Bangkok en route to his post, explained a few days after that in a letter from the president granting him "Full Powers" to conclude a commercial treaty with Siam.

On July 29, 1858, after nearly two years in Japan, Harris signed a treaty of amity and commerce with the shōgun, opening five Japanese ports to American vessels and to resident expatriates. His success and good diplomatic service at Edo was celebrated first in a hundred-year-old play by Japanese playwright Kido Okamoto (reviewed, sort of, by Griffis in the *New York Times* of December 28, 1919, who took credit for the publication of Harris' journal, on which the play was allegedly based) and much later in a 1958 Hollywood movie, *The Barbarian and the Geisha*. The film starred John Wayne as Harris and one Eiko Ando as Okichi-san, a largely invented love interest.

* USS *San Jacinto* is better known for her role in the Civil War's notorious Trent Affair, the unlawful seizure of Confederate diplomats James Mason and John Slidell, who were traveling to Europe in the steam packet RMS *Trent* on November 8, 1861. *San Jacinto* was then under the command of the erratic Capt. Charles Wilkes, USN (the same Wilkes who'd commanded the U.S. Exploring Expedition when USS *Peacock* was lost on the Columbia River bar on July 18, 1841). Wilkes' kidnapping of the two off *Trent* in the Bahama Channel nearly provoked a Union war with Great Britain.

6

Oman, Mozambique, Cape Town, Rio de Janeiro, and New York

At the period of Mr. Roberts' voyage to the courts of Siam and Maskat, American commerce was placed on a most precarious footing, subject to every species of imposition which avarice might think it proper to inflict, at the price of an uncertain protection. Nor was it to pecuniary extortions alone that the uncontrolled hand of power extended. The person of the American citizen, in common with that of other foreigners, was subject to the penalties of law which gave the creditor an absolute power over the life, equally with the property, of the debtor.

RUSCHENBERGER, *NARRATIVE OF A VOYAGE ROUND THE WORLD*

23

On April 4, 1833, USS *Peacock* weighed anchor from Siam Roads and sailed, very indirectly, for distant Muscat and Roberts' trade negotiation with the sultan of Oman. Her first leg took the sloop slowly through the Gulf of Siam—less than one hundred miles a day, progress down track slowed by light and adverse winds—on the way to Singapore. There *Peacock* rested at anchor for the first ten days of May. That's when young Morrison was discharged from his duties as secretary and interpreter, paid, and sent home to Macao. Out of Singapore at midnight on May 11, she then sailed south-southeast (spending a week at anchor off Banca Island, pinned there by unfavorable winds and currents), through the Gaspar Strait into the Java Sea, and then due south past the Thousand Islands to Batavia Roads. Here, on June 5 and after nearly seventeen months apart, *Peacock* finally joined up with the schooner *Boxer*. (The two remained together, *Boxer* being the better sailer, until separated for ten days in late November out of Mozambique by a powerful squall. They joined up again at Cape Town for the return crossing to Rio.)

Peacock's port call at Batavia was an inexplicable seven weeks long, during which time Roberts stayed on shore at "Fancy Farm," the country estate of an American merchant "of the first respectability" named Forrestice. Between arrival on the fifth and departure for Angier on July 22, Roberts' sole official activity seems to have been arranging for the return to the secretary of state of most of the errant crates of diplomatic presents that had finally reached him via *Boxer*, much too late to be used. A few days before *Peacock* sailed from Batavia, Roberts wrote to Thompson, Roberts and Company, local merchants and freight forwarders, "The eighteen packages of merchandise remaining in entrepôt, being part of the shipment per U.S.S. Boxer consigned to me. . . . Please reship them back to the United States by the first American vessel bound there. . . . They can be shipped to any port on the Chesapeake, or any port north of it as far eastward as Portsmouth." The decision to ship all this essential diplomatic stuff back home signaled that the possibility of extending Roberts' embassy to Japan was no longer under consideration.

Out of Angier very early on July 29, through the Sunda Strait and soon past Java Head off to larboard, then on course for a quick, very wet, five-week westbound crossing of the Indian Ocean—pushed along first by trade winds and then running ahead of the southwest monsoon, *Peacock* and her escort made good some 170 miles each day—toward an overnight out-of-the-way reprovisioning stop in the former Royal Sultanate of Mocha, the first of their two port calls on the Arabian Peninsula. The only excitement came on August 20, off Cape Guardafui (at the tip of the Horn of Africa, six hundred miles from Mocha), when under full sail *Peacock*'s wheel ropes suddenly parted. Before the relieving tackle in the wardroom could be manned, restoring control of the helm, the ship nearly broached, briefly threatening the ship with dismasting.

Mocha, the crews discovered on arrival after nearly four thousand miles at sea, had become a minor theater in the contest between the Ottoman Empire and its nominal but insubordinate vassal in Egypt, Mohammed Ali. "The town has a very beautiful appearance from the roads," Midn. William Reynolds wrote about Mocha on September 10, by then eight days out of Muscat, to his father, John.[1] "The houses are white interspersed with several mosques, whose domes show to great advantage. But when you find yourself in town the scene is changed. The houses are small, old, dirty, and tenanted by miserable looking ½ starved beings who importune you for money; the streets narrow and muddy & the heat of the Sun almost insufferable, so that you would scarcely be inside the walls, before you wished yourself aboard your ship again."

On March 16, 1833, Mocha had fallen to Turkie ben al Mas, who'd earlier struck out from Cairo at the head of an armed rabble to improve his career prospects. Now the master of Jeddah, Mocha, and the coast of Yemen in between these two ports, ben al Mas was awaiting instructions from the "sultan of Stamboul," Mahmud II, the Ottoman emperor, when *Peacock* and *Boxer* appeared offshore. The new chief of the place treated

Muscat Cove, Arabia. Watercolor by R. McKenzie. "Muscat is the most sultry place in the world," the *Edinburgh Review* told its readers in October 1838. "Situated at the base of a range of naked cliffs, which reflect the rays of the sun, and screened from refreshing sea breezes by an island and high promontories, in front, it glows like an oven," the *Review*'s unnamed author continued, perhaps on the basis of personal knowledge: "No European can long endure its stifling heat, and even the Arabs suffer from it. . . . The bold character of the heights surrounding Muscat; the forts with red flags crowning all the commanding positions; the white houses of the town contrasted with the sun-burnt precipices behind them . . . all combine to make a lively and agreeable impression on the mind of the stranger not yet acquainted with the climate of the place." In his autobiographical *Seven Pillars of Wisdom*, T. E. Lawrence, better known as Lawrence of Arabia, described the enervating heat of the land breeze blowing out to sea better than did the *Review*'s author. "The heat of Arabia," Lawrence wrote in the 1920s, reliving his wartime experience during the Arab revolt against the Turks, "came out like a drawn sword and struck us speechless." Little is known about McKenzie, an officer in the Indian Navy who in 1826 painted this view of the approach to Muscat.
Courtesy of the Victoria and Albert Museum

his unexpected Western visitors generously, exchanging a fifteen-gun salute; hosting Geisinger and Roberts at an audience in his seedy "palace"; sending a gift of bullocks (Ticknor: "so lean as to be scarcely fit to eat"), sheep, and vegetables out to the men-of-war at anchor in the harbor; and promising to reduce duties and anchorage fees paid by American vessels to the lower levels enjoyed by British ships.

In exchange, ben al Mas visited *Peacock*, buffed up and holy-stoned clean for the occasion, for breakfast in the wardroom. The Turk's visit on board gave Ticknor an opportunity to carp about Captain Geisinger's practice of having the wardroom officers host and entertain official visitors to the ship, a responsibility and cost a ship's captain was traditionally expected to bear. "This may seem too trifling a matter to deserve any notice," Ticknor wrote in *The Voyage of the Peacock*, "but it serves to show certain traits of character, & therefore I mention it."

Mocha's fortifications soon again proved insufficient. Before the end of the year, not many months after *Peacock* and *Boxer* sailed away on Sunday, September 1, Ali's Bedouins wrested the port town from ben al Mas' minions and sacked it themselves, reestablishing their control of Yemen's coast on the Red Sea, and of this port whose name was and is synonymous with "coffee."

On September 18, after an uneventful crossing delayed by very light winds, the two men-of-war dropped anchor in Muscat Cove, in front of the walled town and its two protecting hilltop castles. The next day, at one o'clock, a seventeen-gun salute was exchanged between *Peacock* and the forts. "The reverberation," Ticknor wrote, "was like the loudest thunder . . . as the sound struck against different parts of the immense mountain of rock." Three hours later, Roberts, Geisinger, and *Boxer*'s captain went ashore to meet the sultan. The trade treaty's principal articles were agreed at that brief, first visit, and all the details were defined during exchanges over the following days, before *Peacock* and *Boxer* left on October 7 for Cape Town on the long way home, after having hosted the sultan and his entourage on board the sloop of war, now freshly repainted to impress the visitors.

24

Compared to his prior negotiations—one never joined and one apparently successful—Roberts' call on the sultan of Muscat was a triumph. Not surprisingly. The sultan, "his highness, the heaven-protected, the elevated in dignity, the Seid Sa'id, son of the Seid Sultan, defender of Maskat and its dependencies," the father with his concubines of at least twelve princelings (ten, perhaps more, living) and presumably many uncounted daughters, had been the original inspiration behind Roberts' mission when the two had first met in Zanzibar in 1828. Roberts had good reason to expect that a treaty "for the sake of intercourse, and amity, and the promotion of trade" would emerge from his call at Muscat on the sultan protected by heaven.*

* And it did, in a form very close to the draft text Roberts had brought with him from Washington. The commercial terms were generous: previously, Americans had paid 7.5 percent on all imports and exports; hereafter, American vessels would pay 5 percent, that only on merchandise landed, and were excused from all pilot and anchoring fees. Humanitarian aid to American ships and mariners in distress would be provided free of charge, consistent, the sultan pointed out, with the traditions of Arab hospitality, "which have ever been practiced among them."

"Glowing like an oven," Muscat impressed none of the Americans. "The more we saw of it," groused Ticknor after walking through the town toward a tour of the sultan's stables, "the more we were disgusted with it." The largely unseen Omani navy was evidently much more impressive. Roberts reported that its seventy or eighty ships (twelve carrying a dozen guns or more, and the largest, *Liverpool*, built in Bombay, boasting seventy-four) were sufficient to give Sayyid Sa'id "entire control over all the ports in East Africa, the Red Sea, the coast of Abyssinia, and the Persian Gulf."

Sayyid Sa'id appeared to be no less pleased with the treaty than was Roberts. He said so in a florid letter to "the most high and mighty Andrew Jackson, president of the United States of America, whose name shines with so much splendor throughout the world," describing himself as Jackson's "most beloved friend." The letter, written October 7, 1833 (while Jackson was focused not on trade but on shutting down America's central bank), and carried in translation to the United States by *Peacock*, went beyond gracious all the way to effusive:

> On a most fortunate day and at a happy hour, I had the honor to receive your highness' letter, every word of which is as clear and distinct as the sun at noonday, and every letter shone forth as brilliantly as the stars in the heavens. Your highness' letter was received by your faithful and highly honorable representative and ambassador, Edmund Roberts, who made me supremely happy in explaining the object of his mission, and I have complied in every respect with the wishes of your honorable ambassador, in concluding a treaty of friendship and commerce between our respective countries, which shall be faithfully observed by myself and my successors, so long as the world endures. And his highness may depend that all American vessels resorting to the ports within my dominions, shall know no difference, in point of good treatment, between my country and that of his own most fortunate and happy country, where felicity ever dwells. I most firmly hope that his highness the president may ever consider me as his firm and true friend, and that I will ever hold the president of the United States very near and dear to my heart and my friendship shall never know any diminution, but shall continue to increase until time is no more.

"I offer most sincerely and truly to his highness the president," the sultan concluded, "my entire and devoted services, to execute any wishes the president may have within my dominions, or within any ports or places wherein

I posses the slightest influence."[2] The sultan's letter in hand, later that same day *Peacock* sailed for Mozambique on the way to Brazil and home. Behind her echoed the guns of the departing salutes from ship and shore. "The effect produced by the echo, among the serrated and cavernous rocks and mountains about the cove of Muscat, and the neighboring hills," Roberts recorded about the exchange of twenty-one guns, "was surpassingly fine; loud, distinct and repeated charges were heard, apparently, for the space of several minutes, until the reverberations died away, in faint echoes, among the distant hills in the southeast, west, and northwestern quarters."

Roberts' first diplomatic mission was now finished. It remained only to sail home, signed trade treaties with Siam and Muscat in hand.

25

On October 21, three weeks out of Muscat with *Peacock* sailing south-southwest near Socotra and still more than two weeks from Mozambique Island, Midn. Lewis Roumfort, USN, one of ten midshipmen on board, died. Ticknor, who presided at the burial service in Geisinger's stead, noted later that for some months before Roumfort's unexpected death, the young officer had suffered from mental depression so profound that at sea he'd spent much of his time below "in a state of inaction." Moreover, when in port Muscat, Roumfort had often remained a long time in the water, exposed to the sun. These unhealthy habits and his practice of smoking "segars . . . more or less every day" were, Ticknor believed, "among the causes" of the fever that killed him, the first of the ship's officers to die at sea.

A short-lived plan to stop first at Zanzibar on the way home was set aside, and midafternoon November 7, *Peacock* and *Boxer* anchored off Fort Santo Sebastiano, the nearly three-hundred-year-old citadel of Mozambique, Portuguese since 1498 and the island capital of Portuguese East Africa for nearly four hundred years. What had once been an important part of Portugal's African possessions was now, since trade in slaves was outlawed in 1807, a backwater, manned by reluctant expatriates who feared that Lisbon had forgotten them.

Earlier that same morning *Peacock*'s watch had confused a small fort on Quintagone Island, five islets to the north, with the much larger Santo Sebastiano on Mozambique, and almost ran the sloop hard aground. "We ran in with a fresh breeze," Ticknor wrote, describing the near-disaster, "& under full sail until we were in less than 4 fathoms water & within a half cable length [one hundred yards] of a rocky shoal, on which the water was but 12 feet deep. . . . On discovering the mistake, the ship was rounded too, the topsails were backed, and an anchor was let go, which fortunately stopped our farther progress toward the rocky shoal. By these prompt & judicious movements the loss of the ship was prevented, there is every reason to believe, for in one minute more, if we had stood on, she would have struck upon the rocks in 12 feet of water, where it would have been impossible, in all probability, to get her off." That scare and the following six anxious hours, during which *Peacock* was "warped" (pulled) to windward out of the shallows and to safety, could have been avoided entirely had *Boxer*, sent ahead to reconnoiter, clearly signaled the danger as she stood back out to sea.

Although the port call complied with instructions from Washington to show the flag here, both ships needed water. Because tiny Mozambique Island, atop a coral reef and dry over less than half a square mile, had no ponds or springs, both crews got their water from an old two-hundred-gallon cistern that trapped rain from rooftops in the fort.

The stop for water turned into a five-day pause in the homeward-bound voyage, during which parties of ships' officers toured the fort, its neighboring town, and the shore of the African mainland a few miles off to the west. According to Ticknor, *Peacock*'s visit ended in an explosive argument between Geisinger, Roberts, and Shields (off *Boxer*) that began over the seashells collected during the past few days and revealed the tensions between them.

2

THE SECOND CRUISE, APRIL 25, 1835–NOVEMBER 2, 1837

USS *Peacock* and USS *Enterprise*

7

Commodore Kennedy, Captain Stribling, Lieutenant Commanding Campbell, and Surgeon Ruschenberger

The U.S. sloop of war *Peacock*, Capt. Kennedy, has sailed for the eastern seas, having on board E. Roberts, Esq. diplomatic agent, who is the bearer of the ratified commercial treaty between this country and Siam, and also between this country and the sultan of Muscat.

Niles' Weekly Register, May 2, 1835

26

After her long first cruise to Asia, USS *Peacock* returned home in May 1834 (several weeks behind USS *Lexington*, with Roberts on board) via Brazil, then spent the following nine months in Brooklyn at the navy yard. During part of that time, the sloop underwent substantial repairs, including, yet again, the recoppering of her hull. Some fifty years of experience with it had proved that copper prevented marine weeds fouling the hull and was proof against boring shipworms, *Teredo navalis*.

Peacock began preparations to return to Asia on March 19, 1835, when 18 officers and the first 125 men of her new crew first stepped on board. Another dozen sailors came over from the receiving ship a few days later, and later still more came to round out her complement of 201 officers, seamen, landsmen, boys, and Marines. On March 23 Capt. Edmund P. Kennedy, USN, the new squadron's new commodore, came on board. His arrival was signaled with a gun salute, and henceforth his presence was marked by the broad, blue pennant fluttering overhead.

During the following five weeks, the necessary materiel and foodstuffs were taken on and stowed below. This steady flow from shore to ship was reversed only twice, once when 210 pounds of fresh beef was sent back on shore by the purser, condemned as "unfit for use, being nothing but necks, chins, and bones," and later when three men from *Peacock*'s boat crews deserted.

On departure the sloop's load included spare masts and spars; powder and shot for her guns and muskets and cutlasses for the men; canvas sails and awnings; barrels of beef, pork, and bread; more barrels, these filled with port, sherry, and whiskey; navigation instruments and spare line and chain; hospital stores for the surgeon's use; brooms and barometers; a seamen's library of 202 books; and everything else necessary to sustain the ship and crew during the months to come. Her baggage included eight strongboxes of money—gold doubloons, Spanish dollars being available only on payment of a premium—to cover early expenses.

Peacock's burden also included fully fifty-six crates, barrels, and packages containing rich gifts from the Department of State for potentates. Diplomatic gifts, either as demonstrations of American sophistication and industry, as inducements to negotiate, or as expressions of appreciation for agreements already reached, were a frequent subject in the correspondence between the department and Roberts. Upright federal officials in Washington were uncomfortable with the tradition, which resembled bribery to Westerners, could easily be confused with tribute by Easterners, and to proud democrats anywhere always seemed to entail some bizarre Asian court ritual centered on repeated bowing and scraping—or even worse, abasement. In a government with very few sources of revenue and a tight budget, the expense of gift giving was resented too. For this second embassy, Secretary of State John Forsyth reluctantly agreed that five thousand dollars might be spent on presents to open negotiations with Cochin China and Japan, half to each. Roberts was also authorized to offer both emperors additional gifts to lubricate a future exchange of ratifications, their generosity "proportioned in some measure according to the liberality of the provisions in favor of the United States."

Not on board the departing sloop was the herd of ten merino sheep, two bucks and eight ewes "of the finest wool" that Forsyth had written to Roberts enthusiastically about several times during March, while *Peacock* was getting ready to deploy. "It is believed," he wrote on March 10 to push the bizarre project forward, "that the sheep which you have been instructed to purchase would be a particularly acceptable present to the Emperor of Japan, and it is therefore thought best to try the experiment of conveying them there."

Department folklore had it that the emperor once tried to obtain sheep from the Dutch, who'd demurred, reportedly explaining to him that "their sheep were hairy, and that the wool would not make cloth." An opportunity to slip past the Dutch into Japan in the company of these small, wooly beasts evidently excited Forsyth, who several weeks later raised the subject with Roberts again: "It is especially enjoined upon you to procure them of the best breed, to be very particular in their selection, and to have the greatest care taken of them when aboard the vessel."

John Forsyth was a lawyer and not a farmer, but he wasn't entirely ignorant of the trials *Peacock*'s amateur shepherds and any seagoing sheep would likely face during perhaps two years on salt water. "If it should be found to be impossible to carry them through the whole voyage," he granted, "they may serve as a part of the ship's stores." Considered in that light, there was no downside to the novel idea: either the emperor got the nucleus of a new Japanese fiber and fabric industry in exchange for American access to the home islands or *Peacock*'s people got mutton chops. Sadly, soon enough everything about the imaginative initiative was judged too hard, and the sloop of war left Brooklyn with only the usual menagerie on deck and without any gift sheep. Probably just as well. The aphorism "a sick sheep is a dead sheep" suggests the challenges that would have faced anyone trying to keep the delicate animals healthy during long months at sea.

Early Thursday morning, April 23, 1835, *Peacock*, now carrying rations for six months and almost 15,000 gallons of potable water (a ten-week supply in the unlikely event some didn't go badly foul before then), sailed from the New York Navy Yard, heading for the Narrows and open water beyond. Under way, *Peacock* drew fully fifteen feet nine inches forward and sixteen feet three inches aft. Good trim reflecting careful loading by the first lieutenant, if one neglected a several-inch list to starboard.

Rations, water, and all manner of spare parts for voyage repair or replacement of essential things were on board, but as Commodore Kennedy observed eighteen months later (after tens of thousands of miles sailing in the tropics), the flagship didn't have anything to advance "the unrestrained breathing of air" in the damp, confined spaces below decks. Neither the familiar wind sails nor the very new "Barron's Ventilating Bellows for Ships of All Descriptions," a mechanical device for pumping foul air from crew berthing spaces powered by miscreants from the crew.

Good experience in USS *Hornet* deployed to the West Indies had convinced Kennedy that Commo. James Barron's patented bellows could change the air in a ship's lower hold in fourteen minutes and in that time reduce the temperature below to that on deck.* Kennedy's November 14, 1836, letter to

* In 1835 James Barron (1768–1851) was second on the lineal list of U.S. Navy officers, junior only to Capt. John Rodgers, number one on the list and president of the Navy Board and twenty-three numbers senior to Kennedy. Barron was one of the century's most colorful American navy officers. In 1806 Commodore Barron surrendered USS *Chesapeake*, flagship of the Mediterranean squadron, to HMS *Leopard* after a fight so brief that a subsequent court-martial suspended him from active service for five years. Stranded as a merchant mariner in Denmark by neutrality regulations through the entire War of 1812, he returned to the United States after the war and in March 1820 fought a notorious duel with

the secretary of the navy written in Mazatlan, Mexico, well into the cruise but with much hot weather sailing still to come was an extended commercial for the device. *Peacock*, he concluded, "had she been equipped with such an apparatus" would have "escaped a great part of the diseases from which we have so severely suffered." But she was not.

A scant year after returning home *Peacock* was once again on her way to Rio de Janeiro, the first port call, chivvied out of home port on the twenty-third by the secretary of the navy, who on the eighteenth had pointedly written Kennedy, "I am not aware of any cause for your further detention" in New York. At 2:30 the next afternoon, the harbor pilot was put ashore, marking the true beginning of an impending around-the-world cruise. Ahead of her lay more than 54,200 miles to Hampton Roads, Virginia. She would arrive back on the U.S. East Coast on October 27, 1837, after two and a half years at sea as the flagship of the new U.S. East Indies Squadron, having in the meanwhile sailed the equivalent of twice around the globe and spent 424 days under way and almost as many days more, 414, in twenty-four ports on five continents.

Edmund Roberts was again on board, riding the by-now-familiar sloop of war to complete his next assignment, still commissioned as a "special agent" (he'd hoped to be named "envoy" or "minister"; but such more elevated status would have required consent of the Senate) but retroactive to January 1 paid better—five thousand dollars per year, negotiated up from the forty-four hundred dollars first offered—and no longer traveling under transparent cover as the captain's clerk. No longer on a secret mission, either, but one now publicized in *Niles' Weekly Register* and elsewhere in the American press.

Some of these accounts quoted from old news stories published in English-language newspapers in Asia that had warily tracked *Peacock*'s earlier movements, wondering what the troublesome Yankees were up to in such distant waters. First reported in the *Singapore Chronicle* while *Peacock* was in port there in June 1833 (a story based on an aggravating leak Roberts attributed to his interpreter, John Morrison), news of the American's covert embassy quickly reappeared in newspapers in Calcutta, Canton, and Batavia, and later in the United States.

---

the hero of Tripoli, Stephen Decatur, his successor in *Chesapeake* and a member of his court-martial. Their argument was over Barron's reinstatement on active duty. Decatur was killed in the duel and Barron wounded. His subsequent Navy career included command of two navy yards and of the Navy Asylum.

In uniform and out, Barron had moonlighted as an inventor; among his works were a rope spinning machine and his ventilating bellows for ships. His papers are held by the Earl Gregg Swem Library of the College of William and Mary in Williamsburg, Virginia.

Despite this, the new mission's sailing instructions emphasized the importance of avoiding publicity, "as indiscretions of this kind might endanger the success of [Roberts'] negotiations. I request therefore," the new secretary of the navy wrote, "that strict secrecy be observed on all Matters relating to the mission, and that it may be enjoined on the officers to abstain from all communications on the subject in writing of otherwise, that might find their way into the public newspapers."[1]

Virtually all the other chief players in this second adventure were new, as were men of the ship's crew. Roberts' patron and kinsman, Levi Woodbury, was now the secretary of the treasury. Nine months earlier President Jackson had replaced him at the head of the Navy Department with an afterthought, Mahlon Dickerson, of New Jersey. Dickerson (1770–1868), a former governor of and U.S. senator from that state, had been brought to Washington to become the U.S. minister in St. Petersburg at the Russian court, but a month later he declined the post. While *Peacock* was refitting in port Brooklyn and at sea on this cruise, two new secretaries of state, the second and third since Roberts' mission was first conceived several years earlier, passed through President Jackson's cabinet. The first was the short service Louis McLane, of Delaware, who clashed with the president over policy toward France and left office on June 30, 1834. The next (and much more durable secretary; he served both Jackson and Van Buren during seven years in office, 1834–41) was John Forsyth, an adopted Georgian. It was Forsyth who signed Roberts' several letters of instruction before *Peacock* sailed.

Master Cdt. David Geisinger had moved on too, certainly to Roberts' relief and satisfaction. He was home, collecting $150 per month salary while awaiting orders. In May 1848 Geisinger became the seventh commander of the Navy's East Indies Squadron, riding USS *Plymouth* as his flagship.

It's likely that reports of the antagonism between Geisinger and Roberts had made their way to Washington because Secretary Dickerson's long, April 2 letter of instruction to Commodore Kennedy, commander of the new squadron, included this guidance in its second paragraph:

> Your own views of propriety, and your desire to make those associated with you in the discharge of important trusts as comfortable as possible, will induce you to extend to Mr. Roberts all the accommodations in your power, compatible with the rights of yourself and your officers, as justly due his representative character. You will on all occasions regulate the movement of the ship as may according to Mr. Roberts' views be best suited to a correct performance of his duties.[2]

Somewhat redundant instructions came from the secretary five days later. "The great object of the cruise," Dickerson reemphasized on April 7, "is to enable Mr. Roberts to perform the duties entrusted to him. The other objects connected with the American commerce entrusted to your care, must therefore be considered as subordinate."

Yet another indication of Roberts' central role in the cruise to come came from the navy secretary a week after that. At first *Peacock* and *Enterprise* were to run up the west coast of Africa and visit the settlements of the American Colonization Society near Cape Palmas, Bassa Cove, and Monrovia once the two were back in the Atlantic and on the way home. But just days after these African port visits were laid on in the secretary of the navy's original deployment instructions to the commodore of the squadron, they were cancelled. "If, therefore," Dickerson wrote on April 15 (in a second amendment to his original orders), "Mr. Roberts shall not deem it absolutely necessary to return by the Cape of Good Hope, you will return from Japan by Cape Horn, agreeably in all respects to your first orders, except that you will not visit the coast of Africa, but reach the United States by the most direct course."

Francis Baylies and his entourage were, of course, no longer on board; the consul's status as senior ship rider was now filled by the first commodore of the new East Indies Squadron, Capt. Edmund Kennedy, USN. Kennedy was twenty-sixth in seniority among the Navy's thirty-nine captains. It was his blue, swallow-tailed pennant flying atop her mainmast, in place of the usual slender "coachwhip" commission pennant, that marked *Peacock* as the flagship of the U.S. Navy's fifth deployed squadron.*

After being denied command of the squadron in the West Indies the summer before, an offer months later to command the Navy's newest, albeit smallest, squadron must have come as welcome compensation. Kennedy, fifty-five when he came on board USS *Peacock*, had served at sea as a deckhand in merchant ships, an impressed seaman in HMS *Amphion*, and an enlisted man and officer in U.S. men-of-war, for the past forty-one years. His last assignment, before his death in 1844, was as the port captain in Norfolk, Virginia.

"It is contemplated soon to employ the U.S. Ship of War Peacock in cruise [*sic*] in the East Indies and along the coast of Asia," Dickerson wrote on January 26 to Kennedy at his home in Norfolk, Virginia, "and to associate with her on the cruise the Schr. Enterprise now on the coast of Brazil." The

* The other four were the prestigious Mediterranean Squadron (established in 1815), joined in 1821 by the West India and Pacific Squadrons and in 1826 by the Brazil Squadron. In 1843 the last squadron, the African, again put to sea to take on a unique mission—it had sailed for two years in the early 1820s before being disestablished. Like the other five, the African Squadron was at sea generally to protect American commerce and other interests and otherwise to show the flag, but unlike them it was also explicitly charged with the suppression of unlawful traffic in slaves across the Atlantic.

sweetener: "As this is to be a separate and distinct service from that of any of the Squadrons now employed, the Commander will be allowed to hoist his broad pennant and receive the allowances incident to command of a squadron." Not the better established and larger West Indies Squadron that he'd petitioned for, but a squadron nonetheless. Kennedy accepted four days later, asking to be allowed to nominate officers to sail with him, a usual courtesy extended to officers in command.

The new commodore's appointing letter came three weeks after that, with the secretary hinting inaccurately that perhaps the command would encompass more than two ships, and directing him to proceed to New York from Virginia, on arrival to prepare *Peacock* for sea with "all practicable dispatch."

To underscore his own elevated status—commanding the squadron, not merely its flagship—on his own authority Kennedy appointed Lt. Cornelius K. Stribling, USN, the senior lieutenant of five on board, to command *Peacock*. This would be Stribling's first command after his service as a midshipman in USS *Macedonian* and USS *Mohawk* during the War of 1812, later again in *Macedonian* and in USS *Constellation* with Commodore Decatur in the Mediterranean, and as a lieutenant deployed on antipiracy patrols in the West Indies in four different ships, among them the old *Peacock*.

Command at sea in the grade of lieutenant was an uncommon distinction. So for that matter, was service at sea. Nearly half of the Navy's lieutenants were usually on shore, either awaiting orders, on leave or furlough, or otherwise occupied. Commodore Kennedy's motives aside, the status of *Peacock*'s new commanding officer was at best irregular and unofficial. In late August 1835 (with *Peacock* months out of home port and then approaching Zanzibar), Dickerson wrote Kennedy a short note to acknowledge receipt of nine of the commodore's reports. He then added, without elaboration, "I regret however to differ with you in the necessity of appointing Lieut. G. K. Stribling Act'g Comdr. of the Peacock, which I cannot with propriety approve." The secretary's demurral seems to have changed nothing: out of the reach of Washington, Stribling, forty-sixth among 258 navy lieutenants on the 1835 lineal list, remained *Peacock*'s acting commanding officer during the cruise. (In Washington, however, the situation was visibly different: Stribling never appeared in the published annual register of officers and agents of the United States as in command of *Peacock*.) He later went on to eventual promotion to flag rank and to complete a distinguished half-century career in uniform.

The necessarily long voyage "through a variety of climates," with its uncertainties and dangers, prompted Secretary of State Forsyth to do some worst-case planning. "Captain Kennedy of the Peacock has been furnished with authority from the President to perform the service as your substitute in case of your death or physical inability," he wrote to Roberts five days before *Peacock* sailed. "It is hoped that the contingency may not occur which will call for the exercise of the powers thus conditionally conferred, but it has been thought proper to communicate to you the fact of its having been given, in order that you may impart to him such information and advice, if circumstances should in your opinion render it expedient, as would facilitate the discharge of the duty referred to should it improbably devolve upon him." If "hoped" and "improbably" were meant to reassure Roberts that official Washington judged that his death or disability during the next few years was unlikely, the words probably weren't enough.

A similar thought had occurred to Kennedy too, perhaps even before Forsyth had it. On April 20 he'd written the secretary of the navy to suggest that he be awarded authority to negotiate treaties "in the event of an accident to Roberts," but that power wasn't granted him. The "service" Forsyth had authorized Kennedy to perform was to accomplish the exchange of ratifications, nothing more.

Peacock's new ship's surgeon, William Ruschenberger, wrote a two-volume history about the cruise (*Narrative of a Voyage Around the World*), but because his was a more professional and less waspish account than was Surgeon's Ticknor's memoir, how Kennedy, Stribling, and Roberts shared *Peacock*'s very limited senior officers' accommodations and what was the state of wardroom morale isn't known.*

A letter from Roberts to Secretary Woodbury, written in Rio de Janeiro in early July after several months under way, confirmed that Roberts "was more pleasantly situated in this voyage than during the last one," and in mid-June 1836 Stribling gave room in his cabin to accommodate the fatally ill acting purser off *Enterprise*, J. (for John) Dickinson Mendenhall. Both are evidence

* At least the first chapters of Ruschenberger's book (original working title "A Trip to the East") were sent as letters to John J. Smith Jr., librarian for more than thirty years (1829–61) of the Library Company of Philadelphia.

Into the mid-1830s, Ruschenberger appeared to be happier at sea than was Ticknor, and that also accounts for the differences in the two surgeons' books about their cruise in *Peacock*. But ten years later, when Ruschenberger wrote *Hints on the Reorganization of the Navy, Including an Examination of the Claim of its Civil Officers to an Equality of Rights* (Wiley & Putnam, 1845), he sounded much less satisfied with his profession than he had a decade before. *Hints* argued that "civil officers" in the Navy (these men included surgeons, chaplains, pursers, and engineers) faced personal and professional prejudice from their counterparts in the line, officers eligible for command at sea, that could be corrected only by the former being assigned "equal footing," meaning assimilated rank, with the latter. The result of reform: higher status, better career prospects, and improved recruiting and retention of good performers in these professional specialties. Ruschenberger's pamphlet concluded with a farsighted twenty-one-point plan for the reorganization of the Navy. Some of the wise changes that he urged on the Navy's officer corps weren't implemented until the Spanish-American War.

of a kinder, gentler atmosphere in officers' country than had been the case under Geisinger's command.

William S. W. Ruschenberger, M.D. (1807–1895), the son of a merchant ship captain lost at sea months before his birth, spent forty-three years in the U.S. Navy. He joined as an eighteen-year-old surgeon's mate in 1826 and retired in 1869. During the years in between, Ruschenberger sailed in USS *Brandywine*, twice in USS *Peacock* (the first time in 1831–32), and in *Falmouth*, *Plymouth*, and *Independence*. He spent the Civil War as chief surgeon at the Boston Navy Yard.

Ruschenberger was the author of many books, among them memoirs of cruises in USS *Falmouth* and USS *Peacock*, and of articles on scientific subjects. In 1872 the British explorer Richard Burton, writing about Zanzibar and looking back three decades, dismissed Ruschenberger's *Voyage Round the World* for being "bitterly hostile to England," explained, he thought, by the fact that the surgeon was Dutch American. In fact, Ruschenberger's sharpest critique was directed at "the stubborn, blind, brutal tyranny of the Batavia Dutch," whom he described in connection with trade with Japan as "base panderers . . . ready to succumb to any terms for money."

A posthumous biographical sketch in the 1895 *Proceedings of the Academy of Natural Sciences of Philadelphia*, one of the half dozen learned societies to which he belonged, described Ruschenberger as a man of "striking individuality. . . . His prejudices were strong and his affections warm. He was a strict disciplinarian . . . frequently severe in his criticisms." Unsaid in the admiring sketch was the fact that the doctor was also an amateur phrenologist. He believed that the shape of a skull revealed personality traits of its owner. During the cruise Ruschenberger demonstrated his diagnostic skills in this popular pseudoscience to the credulous in Bangkok, Canton, and Honolulu.

He was also remarkably healthy in nasty places, and a hard worker. Ruschenberger usually held sick call twice a day, once in the morning and again in the evening, every day that *Peacock* was deployed and he was on board. On average, each member of *Peacock*'s crew consulted the ship's surgeon about four different health complaints during her thirty months deployed. The diagnosis and prescription for every patient Ruschenberger saw was entered in a daily journal, and at the end of the cruise, all these entries were carefully collated and transcribed by him into a volume of 853 individual case files—the medical history of the cruise. He also wrote a report at the end of 1836 that Commodore Kennedy described as "the best description that can be given of the different ports we have visited as far as relates to refreshing and refitting our Public Ships."

Personnel changes aside, *Peacock* herself was largely unchanged. During her first few days at sea, some seams in *Peacock*'s hull opened up, as they had several years ago, and these soon required extensive recaulking in Brazil. Once in Rio de Janeiro, *Peacock* was to be joined on deployment by the 10-gun schooner USS *Enterprise* and her crew of eighty officers and men, detached from duty with the squadron off the coast of Brazil for a cruise to the East Indies. This *Enterprise* was the fourth of that name in the U.S. Navy and the last not to have some form of steam propulsion. She'd sailed for Rio in July 1834 and arrived there in September to begin what was her second South Atlantic deployment since commissioning in mid-December 1831.*

Through that autumn and the winter of 1834–35, *Enterprise* tagged along behind the squadron flagship, USS *Natchez*, while the latter sailed between Rio and Buenos Ayres and touched at several of the station's ports: Santos and then St. Catharine's Harbor in Brazil, and later at Monte Video, Uruguay. To ensure that *Enterprise* would not be held on station as *Boxer* had been, orders to Commodore Renshaw from Secretary Dickerson dated February 24 directed Lieutenant Commanding Campbell to bring his schooner into Rio de Janeiro in early May "so that he may be completely equipped and in readiness to report to Comdre. E. P. Kennedy for a cruise with him in the East Indies." On April 27 *Enterprise* anchored in Rio to prepare for several years in the Indian and Pacific Oceans as ordered.

And so *Enterprise*, and not USS *Boxer*, was to escort the East Indies Squadron flagship's on this cruise, but three days out of Rio de Janeiro on July 12, the schooner being an "extremely dull" sailer said the commodore, the two parted company. On separation, *Enterprise*'s orders were to join *Peacock* in Zanzibar, and if not there, then in Bombay. That's where the two were finally reunited on October 22, when *Peacock* sailed into Bombay leaking seriously.

Despite the beginning of steam-powered industrialization and until the perfection of the electromechanical telegraph, the master clock of the early nineteenth century ran much slower than it does today.† People and small things moved on average no faster than a horse could canter. The best postal systems carried overland mail at an average just under ten miles an hour. Everything else moved more slowly still.

---

* *Enterprise*'s second cruise began July 17, 1834, and saw her in the Pacific through 1838, round Cape Horn in early 1839, and arrive in port Philadelphia for decommissioning that July after five years continuously deployed under four commanding officers. Built in New York in 1831 for $27,935, *Enterprise* sailed for the navy until 1845, when she was sold in Boston.

† An exception: once perfected during the Napoleonic Wars, British and French shutter and semaphore visual telegraph systems managed to exchange urgent, long-distance messages between the capital and the coast in minutes in good weather.

It could, and often did, take weeks to get anywhere, and months if the destination were distant. A year could pass between written question and answer if one came from North America and the other from Asia. All by itself, that slow pace was a disincentive to correspondence. After sixteen months at sea Commodore Kennedy had sent reports to the secretary only a dozen or so times, letters of a few pages each at the longest, and perhaps half were still on the way to Washington in August 1836. (Based on the holdings of "Captains' Letters" to the secretary in Record Group 45 of the National Archives today, it's likely that several of those few reports never were delivered.)

Not until railroads, steam packets, and the telegraph were put into service a little later in the century did that clock start to run appreciably faster and the pulse of life accelerate. Regular, biweekly steam packet service between England and islands in the Caribbean was introduced in the early 1840s. The same technology's effect on drawing together Europe and Asia was equally profound, even before the opening of the Suez Canal. By the mid-1850s (during the Indian rebellion and a generation after the pioneering *Hugh Lindsay*) England to Bombay via Alexandria, Egypt, and a five-day overland crossing of the desert to Suez was a thirty-six-day trip, of which the two overwater legs combined took one month.* Around the Cape of Good Hope by sail in the same decade took four months.

Enterprise was slower than *Peacock*—perhaps because the schooner was invariably trimmed aft when loaded, usually drawing a little over eight feet forward but fully twelve feet plus aft—but not by very much. *Peacock* herself lacked several knots from being considered "fast" by the standard of the day, which might have meant ten knots, a little over eleven miles per hour. The sleek tea clippers, at sea after midcentury, with their soaring masts supporting as many as thirty sails stacked in tiers five or six high, could make good fourteen knots or so in favorable winds. On their better days, clippers could cover four hundred miles—easily twice what could be optimistically expected from *Peacock*.

27

Roberts had spent most of the months between the time USS *Lexington* brought him to Boston in April 1834 and when USS *Peacock* put back to sea the following April, with him again on board, in Washington closing out his

* The East India Company's armed steamer *Hugh Lindsay*, Capt. John Wilson, appeared at Suez on April 22, 1830 after twenty-one days, six hours under way from Bombay, thirty-three days total, including stops at Aden, Mocha, and Jeddah. Her arrival concludes the first appearance of steam power in these waters. She sailed west across the Indian Ocean on this, her maiden voyage, dangerously overloaded and carrying only a single passenger. Thirty-five years later *Hugh Lindsay* broke apart on the rocks at Bassadore Harbor on the Persian Gulf coast.

first mission and maneuvering successfully—albeit much more slowly than he wished—for a second, more lucrative one. The interval was an anxious time for Roberts, in part because that spring official Washington was focused on two crises approaching their climax: Jackson's battle with the Bank of the United States and American relations with France, which country had just reneged on a three-year-old agreement to pay 25 million francs to indemnify American shippers for their losses during the Napoleonic Wars.* And in part because Roberts' interests—the treaties' ratification, compensation for expenses incurred, the possibility of further negotiations and his future status, and clearance to publish his journal—didn't rise near the top of anyone else's agenda until much later than he would have wished.

The Senate's resolutions of advice and consent for both his treaties didn't pass until the last day of June; the president didn't ratify them until the following January. Not until later that same winter, early 1835, were Jackson's and Forsyth's last reservations about a follow-on diplomatic mission finally put aside.

In the middle of March, Roberts learned from Secretary of State Forsyth that *Peacock* would be ready to take him on board in New York on the twenty-fifth and to sail soon thereafter for the Orient. A few days later, March 20, Forsyth sent Roberts the first of several letters of instruction, addressing the exchange of ratified treaties with Muscat and Siam and then the negotiation of such new "commercial arrangements with the other powers whose dominions border upon the Indian Ocean as may tend to the advancement or security of the commerce of the United States in that quarter."

"I now proceed to state to you more distinctly the objects of your mission," Forsyth continued, "and the means of effecting them which will be placed at your disposal, together with such instructions as are thought to be proper in respect to the mode of your proceeding":

> From Siam you will proceed to Cochin China, and use every endeavour, consistent with the dignity of this Government and with the means afforded you, to form a commercial treaty with that country. In the efforts which you are expected to make the accomplishment

* The United States pressed claims for shipping losses and violations of its neutral rights against France and against several of Napoleon's allies, Spain, Denmark, and the Kingdom of the Two Sicilies. In the Treaty of July 4, 1831, France had agreed to indemnify the United States for these losses. It fell to Forsyth in 1834 to press the French minister for satisfaction, and to restrain Jackson from taking rash action against the French as the president had threatened in his annual message to Congress.

Roberts had a personal interest in the resolution of the issue. In compensation for the loss of *Victory* in 1809, Roberts claimed that $7,310.50 was due him. Although the total amount was endorsed by the Treasury, his estate ultimately received a total of $5,562.87 for the claim after some $900.00 had been deducted from receipts to pay off a debt to a deceased shipmaster's widow.

of this object, much must necessarily be left to your own discretion. Everything has been done by this Government that suggests itself as likely to facilitate your negotiations with a people possessing habits and feelings peculiar to the East, and far different from our own. . . . You will of course accommodate yourself to the peculiar notions and customs of the country, however absurd they may be, whenever you can do so without such acknowledgment of inferiority as would be incompatible with the dignity of your Government, of which you will on all occasions assert the equality with the most powerful nations of the world.

You will studiously inculcate upon all those with whom you have intercourse the particular situation, character and views of this country: that it is an essential part of our policy to avoid political connexion with any other Government: that although we are a powerful nation, possessing great resources, an extensive trade, and a large fleet, all our past history shows that we are not ambitious of conquest: that we desire no colonial possessions: that we seek a free and friendly intercourse with all the World: and that our interests and inclinations alike lead us to depreciate a state of war with any nation, except in self defense, or in vindication of our violated rights or honor.

You will point out, where it may be necessary, the difference which exists between ourselves and other nations in these respects; and endeavour to remove the fears and prejudices which may have been generated by the encroachments or aggressions of European Powers.

Turning to Japan, Roberts' projected final assignment before returning home, Forsyth suggested that he plan to arrive not at Nagasaki (where the Dutch, who "might feel themselves interested in thwarting" his mission, maintained their factory) but instead, perhaps, at Owari, away from their surveillance and closer to the imperial capital, Edo.

28

Peacock made good an average of 115 nautical miles a day between New York and Rio de Janeiro, where she finally arrived at this crossroads of the South Atlantic in early morning June 11, after a slow and often rainy direct passage of just under 5,600 miles. Kennedy had asked for permission to stop at Hampton Roads on the way south, but his request had been denied.

Good days saw *Peacock* cover nearly two hundred miles in twenty-four hours, but light winds or poor weather occasionally reduced that to less than fifty, and once (on May 24, four days north of the equator) to as few as twenty-six. On her way south she hadn't come across *Palmyra*, a brig out of New York bound "ostensibly for Bahia" but suspected by the New York County district attorney "to be really intended as a slaver." He'd asked the Navy for help in locating her.

At Rio *Peacock* sailed into an anchorage already crowded with merchant vessels and the men-of-war of four navies, those of Brazil, France, Great Britain, and the United States. Among them was USS *Natchez*, the Brazil Squadron flagship, soon joined in port by USS *Erie* and USS *Enterprise. Natchez*'s presence with Commo. James Renshaw, USN, on board, prompted Kennedy to haul down his blue pennant on arrival and replace it with a red one, acknowledging Renshaw's senior status.

All these ships were attracted there not so much by the city itself (the center of trade in slaves, coffee, sugar, and hides), but because Rio was a convenient waypoint on sailing routes into the Pacific or Indian Oceans via Cape Horn or the Cape of Good Hope. Ruschenberger thought the port city was beautiful; he considered the population rather less attractive, which he attributed to an enervating atmosphere. "Everyone seems rather disposed to indulge the quiet animal enjoyments of eating, drinking, smoking, lounging, and sleeping," he observed, "leaving to slaves all kinds of manual labor hence the embonpoint [plumpness] amongst women and obesity amongst men of Creole and Portuguese residence." Slaves amounted to some 40 percent of the population of the city.

USS *Peacock* passed a full month in this land of lotus-eaters, between mid-June and mid-July 1835. Relatively few of the enlisted men on board had an opportunity to share in any animal enjoyments on offer, although a party of twenty-six was permitted liberty ashore one day. Until July 3 the crew's time was largely spent loading stores, refitting the rigging, and repainting their ship, while a team of twenty-one Brazilian caulkers swarmed over her hull stuffing parted seams. Seamen Jolly and Williams found the opportunity to desert; they were caught and flogged. A deserter from USS *Java*, one William Bond, surrendered on board.

"The boys on board the Peacock, at Rio de Janeiro, are amusing themselves by shooting one another," wrote *Niles' Weekly Register* archly on September 12 (p. 18). "Three duels have been fought between the midshipmen attached to her, by which one person was killed, and another had his leg fractured. So we learn from the Journal of Commerce." Two weeks later *Niles'* reported that the Navy Department had no confirmation from *Peacock*'s captain of any duel, but there had been one, involving Passed Midshipmen Leigh and Weems. Leigh was wounded, Weems unscathed. Such amusement wasn't unique to *Peacock* and Leigh got off lightly. Two midshipmen off USS *Natchez* had fought a duel that spring in Rio in which one, John Banister, had been killed.

On July 6 *Peacock* dressed ship, brought a band on board, and then hosted "the most brilliant affair that had taken place afloat in the harbor of Rio" for guests from ashore and other ships in port. The eating, drinking, and dancing went on until well into the next morning. Six days later, she sailed for Zanzibar.

Peacock's passage across the South Atlantic from Rio de Janeiro then around the Cape of Good Hope to Zanzibar took fifty-one days, as recorded in her deck log. Other than the loss of the lee quarter boat, torn from her davits by a rogue wave on August 5, so little happened on the way that not until the sloop was well inside of the Mozambique Channel, between Madagascar and the East African coast, did Ruschenberger have much to say about her passage from ocean to ocean. "One of those calm nights" in the channel "was exquisitely beautiful," he wrote then. "The sky was cloudless and so brilliantly starry, that its deep blue color was distinct. At the same time the surface of the ocean was tranquil, and like a polished steel mirror reflected the whole heavens and our ship, seemingly suspended between the two, floated among the stars."*

At sunset, September 3, *Peacock* anchored off Metony Palace, several miles north of Zanzibar's only town, guided there safely through one of the four passages into the harbor by an Arab pilot who wore only a waistband and a turban and carried his professional references in what had once been a box of Lucifer brand matchsticks.

Roberts had expected that the sultan was going to be at this island residence (Zanzibar would become his capital in 1840) and that the exchange of ratifications would happen here, but Sayyid Sa'id had to divide his attention between tranquil Zanzibar, Mombasa on the African mainland, where a rebellion against his rule had been percolating for years, and Muscat, with its complicated tribal politics and ambitious rivals. The sultan had left Zanzibar the previous April to quiet matters at home, where a cousin had been maneuvering to move up the political pecking order on the Arabian Peninsula.

Other complications distracted the sultan too. In late 1833, soon after Roberts had left Muscat with his draft treaty in hand, Sayyid Sa'id began to have problems managing his relationship with the British, who suspected that his new tie to the Americans might somehow threaten their own special status in Oman. That status dated back at least to January 1800—seven

* Ruschenberger's casual observations about the sea and its life gave an anonymous reviewer of his book in the winter 1838–39 edition of the *Edinburgh Journal* the opportunity to critique the surgeon's comprehension of natural science, sniffing at the same time that the U.S. Navy's four around-the-world cruises during the prior seven years "have added little to our knowledge of the earth" because of an absence of "vigilant and enlightened observers."

years before Sayyid Sa'id's rise to power—and the signature of an agreement between Oman and the East India Company that provided, almost poetically, for "an English gentleman of respectability" to live permanently in Muscat as a conduit for communications between the two "in order that . . . no opportunity may be offered to designing men, who are ever eager to promote dissensions, and that the friendship of the two States may remain unshook till the end of time and till the sun and moon have finished their revolving career."[3]

Was Roberts, the British must have wondered, one such "designing man," attempting to shake their relations with these Arabs? Reports of *Peacock*'s and *Boxer*'s 1833 port call in Muscat and the fact that a treaty had been negotiated with the Americans during the visit had reached Bombay almost immediately, where they prompted a quick legal review of the restrictions Oman had earlier accepted on its freedom to enter into foreign relations with third countries. These restrictions, it developed, addressed only France and Holland, Britain's historic competitors in the Indian Ocean, and said nothing about the United States. On the strength of that conclusion, and without knowledge of the text of Roberts' treaty, the governor general in Bombay was content to let the matter lie.

Not so Vice Admiral Sir John Gore, RN (1772–1836), commander in chief of the Royal Navy's new East Indies and China Station and then approaching the end of a fifty-five-year-long career, who assumed a proprietary interest in everything going on in the Indian Ocean. Without consulting with his political counterparts, in early January 1834 Gore dispatched Capt. Henry Hart, RN, commanding the 18-gun HMS *Imogene* (a nearly new sixth rate, very slightly larger than *Peacock*), to find out what mischief the Americans might have been up to in Oman.

Imogene sailed January 15 for Zanzibar, arriving immediately off the palace late on the thirtieth after an easy passage. She was back in Bombay on March 29, after less than a week in Zanzibar. As described in Hart's published report (*Extracts from Brief Notes of a Visit to Zanzibar . . . in H.M. Ship Imogene in the Month of January and February 1834*) the usual protocol visits between ship and shore were exchanged over several days and Hart met a few times with the imaum, always talking to his host through the same Bombay-educated interpreter, Captain Hassan bin Ibrahim of the Royal Omani Navy. No mention is made in Hart's "extracts" of any political talks, and the only subject of substance addressed was the imaum's desire to present his eight-year-old 74-gun flagship *Liverpool*, requiring a crew of five hundred, to the Royal Navy as a gift, she being too large for the Omanis to operate.*

* The gift was made in 1836 when *Liverpool* became HMS *Imaum*. All that remains of her is a handsomely painted wood figurehead, an Indian woman, now in the collection of the Nova Scotia Museum.

Quoting "a private letter," the end-of-year edition of *The Asiatic Journal and Monthly Register for British India, China and Australasia* reported somewhat more forthrightly, "*Imogene* has recently been sent to the Persian Gulf, on a mission to the Imaum of Muscat, relative to a treaty which his highness has recently concluded with the American government, by which they would be entitled to make a settlement at Zanzibar, or on any other part of his coast. The result of the mission has granted to England the same indulgence, should it become requisite. The Imaum testified his perfect satisfaction in the sought arrangement. He presented to Capt. Hart a Persian horse of pure breed."[4]

As explained by the late Hermann Eilts in 1990, the truth was, of course, more complicated.[5] Hart and the sultan discussed the treaty with the United States extensively over their several meetings in early February, during the second of which Sayyid Sa'id gave Hart the original document to read and keep, and indicated his instant readiness to abrogate or amend the treaty if it offended "his best friends," the British, or to sign one with them just like it. (The American treaty was later returned to Zanzibar by another Royal Navy ship on the East Indies Station, the 24-gun razee corvette HMS *Magicienne*.)* Abrogation raised the question of the American response, Sayyid Sa'id pointed out. If that were violent, would Great Britain support Oman with its Royal Navy? Captain Hart's reply was necessarily noncommittal.

Replying to Hart's insistence that the sultan should have obtained British permission before he signed anything with the Americans, or with any other foreign power, Sayyid Sa'id explained that prompt responses could not be had from Bombay on any subject, but that in the future he would ask. In all, the sultan was so accommodating to what he understood to be British concerns and wishes that Hart understandably judged his manner to be "remarkably pleasant and agreeable." That conclusion may have been reinforced by the sultan's obvious affection for Great Britain, and his assertions that the Americans "meant nothing" to him, and that Edmund Roberts was "an old, fat, blustering man."[6]

When the governor general in Bombay, and much later the India Board in London found out about the Royal Navy's freelancing in Zanzibar, both were horrified, not at what the sultan had agreed to with Roberts, but at Admiral

* "Razee" meaning a ship of the line reduced to a heavy frigate by removal of her upper deck. *Peacock* had run across *Magicienne* before, near midnight out of Krakatoa on the way to Angier in late November 1832: "On our passage across," Roberts wrote his children November 30, "about midnight saw a large ship bearing down on us, all hands were instantly piped to quarters—the Battle Lanterns were lighted, the guns loaded with rounds of grape shot, the Marines arranged on the quarter deck, the doctor and his mate in the cockpit with their instruments and bandages, ready for service. In five minutes we were prepared for a set-to—it proved to be his B.M. Frigate Magicienne from Batavia, so we parted as we met—friends."

Gore's and Captain Hart's rude intervention into what was strictly a civil, political matter under their cognizance. As quoted by Eilts, in August 1834 the Secret Committee of the India Board was unconcerned: "Americans are not the object of political jealousy to us in India, and the trifling trade which they may carry on in their small vessels with the territory of the Imaum of Muscat is not likely to interfere with our own." From high altitude above London, since the defeat of Napoleon the center of a self-confident, global empire and capital of the world, American traders in the Indian Ocean might well have appeared to be insignificant to the committee. By mid-1841, however, the merchants of Salem, Massachusetts, so dominated trade with the island that the new British consul, Capt. Atkins Hamerton of the Fifteenth Bombay Native Infantry, was chagrined to discover that the sultan's throne room in Metony Palace was decorated with paintings showing the defeat of Royal Navy ships by those of the U.S. Navy.[7] (As was, the visiting Americans would soon discover, the corresponding room in the royal palace in Oman.)

After four days in Zanzibar enjoying the gracious, open-handed hospitality of the same Captain Hassan who'd interpreted for Captain Hart the year before, USS *Peacock* put to sea for Muscat. On September 9 she crossed 5° south latitude and soon thereafter passed the clove plantations on the island of Pemba off to port, heading roughly northeast along the African coast, to deliver the ratified treaty to the sultan in Muscat, still some twenty-one hundred miles away.

One year later, on September 30, 1836, in a letter from Honolulu, Commodore Kennedy recalled USS *Peacock*'s call at Zanzibar and described the island to the secretary of the navy as the only safe place on the east coast of Africa to resupply:

> On the east coast of Africa, there is not a single port for obtaining water & provisioning, without risking the health of the officers & men. Zanzibar is a delightful spot, and fresh fruits, water, &c. can be obtained at moderate prices, but it can be visited safely only during the dry monsoon, and then no individual should be allowed on shore. From various authentic sources it appears, that in every instance where individuals, whether officers or men, have remained on shore during the night, they have been attacked with fever and several have thus lost their lives. With this precaution added to those usually recorded [resorted?] to the tropics, Zanzibar may be visited with comparative safety.

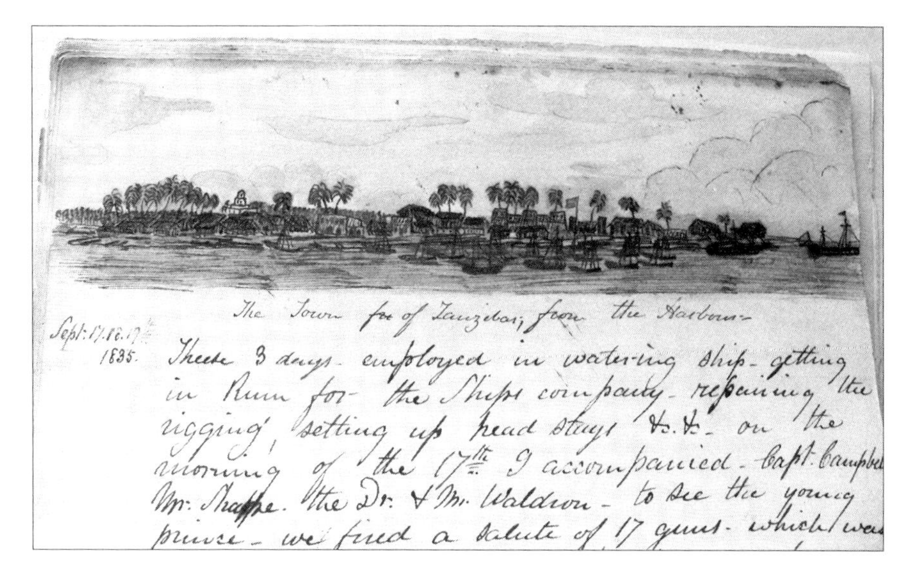

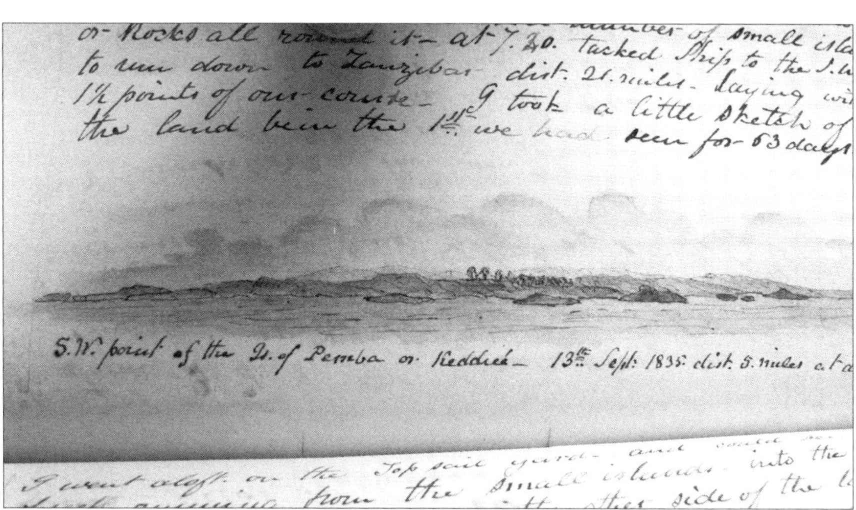

The Town of Zanzibar from the Harbor and *Pemba*. Pen and ink drawings by Midn. Henry Cadwalader, USN. Cadwalader (1817–1844) was one of four midshipmen on board the schooner USS *Enterprise* when she sailed as *Peacock*'s escort in 1835–37. His 32,000-word private journal of nine months on board, first in *Enterprise* and then in *Peacock*, reveals satisfaction with life at sea and a low opinion of *Enterprise*'s hard-drinking captain, Archibald Campbell.

Nearly two weeks behind *Peacock*, *Enterprise* spent September 14–20 in port Zanzibar, where she also enjoyed generous Arab hospitality before continuing past Pemba for Bombay, where in mid-October—now ten days ahead of *Peacock*—she became the first American man-of-war to visit that place. In Bombay Cadwalader happily transferred from the schooner to the larger sloop, thereby escaping Captain Campbell. Promoted to passed midshipman in July 1839 (the fifth of twenty-nine in that year's examination class), Cadwalader died in Philadelphia five years later of unknown causes, still on active duty.

Courtesy William Reese Company, New Haven, Connecticut

Once across the equator, for a while sailing over brilliant phosphorescent seas, Ruschenberger, looking aft, said the ship's wake resembled "a stream of fire" and explained the phenomenon as caused by "diminutive masses of animated matter, resembling jelly; as transparent as glass, and when troubled emit light like the firefly." With every sail set that would draw, among them studding sails rigged low and aloft to capture the least puff of wind, *Peacock* was making good seven or eight knots along her course for the Arabian coast.

8

Grounded!

On the voyage from Zanzibar to Muscat, the Peacock had the misfortune to strike upon a coral reef in the gulf of Mazeira, with the pleasant prospect of the ship and its gallant armament, together with the diplomatic representative of our country, becoming the prize of Bedouin Arabs. In this sad disaster, the second cutter was equipped with a crew of picked men, and dispatched to Muscat to obtain relief, Mr. Roberts volunteering to accompany this perilous boat expedition; which, after having encountered many of the dangers of Captain Bligh's famed adventure on a similar bottom, arrived in safety at its place of destination.

North American Review, October 1838

29

Just after 2:00 a.m. on Monday, September 21 (Roberts: while "we were reposing as we supposed in perfect security in our cots, in fine weather, every sail being set on the ship that would draw"), *Peacock* suddenly struck hard on a reef in the Masirah Channel. After scraping along for a short distance, she stopped, impaled and immobilized. It was the sloop's misfortune to have been sailing off the unfamiliar Arabian coast in near-complete darkness on the night before the new moon, almost exactly between the last full moon over these waters, on September 7, and the one that would become visible the evening of October 6.

Many weeks later, on November 10, Captain Stafford Haines, RN, commanding the East India Company's survey brig *Palinurus*, helpfully provided a written exculpatory statement about the grounding to *Peacock*'s sailing master, Passed Midn. John Weems, USN, when the two met in passing in Bombay:

> I conceive the United States ship of war *Peacock* run aground, as have many British ships in previous years, on and near the same spot; when at the changes of the monsoons, and sometimes at the full and change, you have such thick weather, as to prevent the necessary observations being taken with accuracy and the navigator standing on with confidence as to his position, and with no land in sight, finds

USS *Peacock*'s deck log entry, September 21: "At 2:40 ship struck on a reef put the helm up and took in all the starboard steering sails. At 2:50 ship grounded in 2 1/2 fathoms water coral bottom." Lt. William Green, who had the early morning watch, signed the entry that coolly described the grounding and the crew's first attempts to save their ship. Roberts thought that shifting her helm was intended to turn *Peacock* to the east, toward what was thought to be open water. "The ship rolled with an uncertain, wavering motion," Ruschenberger described in his *Narrative*, "grinding and tearing the coral as her sides alternately came against it. The uncertainty of our situation, threatened as we were with destruction, the crashing of coral, the darkness of the night, the wallop, wallop of the sails; the fast succeeding orders of the officer of the watch, and the piping of the boatswain and his mates, produced an impression not easily described nor forgotten" (p. 54).
NATIONAL ARCHIVES AND RECORDS ADMINISTRATION

himself to his sorrow, often wrong, owing to a deceitful and imperceptible current, which has set with rapidity upon it.

The cause of the grounding wasn't inept navigation; it was, Haines concluded, largely the fault of a "deceitful and imperceptible" current.

The 8-gun *Palinurus*, 190 tons, a Bombay Harbor pilot boat, had been pressed into survey duty when the company decided in the early 1830s to establish a coal depot somewhere on the thirty-one-hundred-mile passage between Bombay and Suez, evidence of the importance of steam propulsion on those waters decades before the construction of the canal. (The choice, between Jeddah and Mocha on the coast of the Red Sea and Aden on its eponymous gulf, was made in favor of Aden, partly on the basis of inspection visits by the company's first armed steamer, *Hugh Lindsay*.) Haines (1802–1860) was in command of *Palinurus*' survey, and the data he collected were incorporated into more accurate charts of Indian Ocean coastal waters, updating a survey of the Arabian coast then-lieutenant Haines and another Bombay Marine officer, George Brooks, had completed in 1825. In 1835 his expertise would have lent special strength to his attempt to exonerate Weems should there have been an investigation.

Captain Haines elaborated on why *Peacock* might have run aground early that September morning. "The position of Mazeira Island is laid down by Owen many miles too much to the westward," he asserted, referring to a chart based on surveys done in the early 1820s by HMS *Barracouta* and her tender, *Albatross*, under the overall command of Captain William Owen, RN. Until *Peacock*'s grounding, Passed Midshipman Weems had been using these ten-year-old Owen charts to navigate in the Indian Ocean without any serious problem, overlooking what a deck log entry earlier presented as two gentle groundings on uncharted coral reefs a mile off Zanzibar.*

Commodore Kennedy adopted Haines' theory about the causes of the near-disaster when he later explained the grounding to Secretary Dickerson. His flagship, he wrote to the secretary on the first of December, had been safely seventy-two miles east of Mazeira, well off "the desolate coast of Arabia," at noon the day before. Unknown and "violent and uncertain currents" and an error that placed the island "upwards of thirty miles too far to the westward" of its actual position were responsible for his embarrassment and the danger to his ship. Kennedy said nothing about the possibility that errors rating *Peacock*'s three chronometers—the source of Weems' longitude calculation—accurately could have been responsible for an erroneous noon fix half a day before impact.

When *Peacock* sailed from Brooklyn in April, more than a quarter of her crew was landsmen and boys who had never been to sea before. Standing port and starboard watches during the five months at sea since then had turned

* According to James Horsburgh's *India Directory*, in 1824 Owen described Mazeira, or "Massera," Island as twelve and a half or thirteen leagues long (thirty-seven to thirty-nine miles) and oriented north northeast-south southwest. From the sea its two hills joined by lowland appeared "rather low and rugged." Owen fixed the island's western (landward) side as lying between 20° 40 1/4' north 58° 54' east and 20° 7 1/2' north 58° 38' east.

Horsburgh (1762–1836) had suffered through a grounding also, one even more punishing than was *Peacock*'s. In May 1786, while first mate in *Atlas* sailing between Batavia and Ceylon, his ship ran aground on Diego Garcia in the Chagos Archipelago, misplotted in the charts of the day. The incident, which saw him stranded on a tiny island eight hundred miles off *Atlas*' intended course, inspired him to a career as a hydrographer. After many years at sea and in command, in 1809 Horsburgh published the first edition of *Directions for Sailing to and from the East-Indies*. In 1810 he became the East India Company's hydrographer, and he remained in that post until he died, publishing charts and sailing directions all the while.

these landlubbers into sailors, if not yet into able seamen. In this emergency evidently the crew's response was swift and capable. It had two objectives. The first was to save their ship by freeing her from the reef before she was holed and destroyed. The second was to save themselves, should *Peacock* have suffered damage beyond recovery, by improvising a raft from spare masts and spars loaded with barrels of food and other essentials, to which they could escape if their ship broke apart around them.

For the next two days her hull ground against the reef while the tide rose and fell beneath her and the Peacocks worked purposefully to free their ship from the grasp of the coral below. The first falling tide threatened to let the sloop keel over, a careening not entirely escaped by hastily propping her upright with a spare topmast poked into the reef and lashed at its upper end to a rail.

After pumping five thousand gallons of drinking water (two-thirds of all the water on board) and dropping two of her carronade guns, 401 rounds of 32-pound shot, and chains and cable over the side, and even after jettisoning all the molasses and vinegar and all but 250 precious gallons of whiskey, attempts to warp (drag) *Peacock* free with her kedge anchors were unsuccessful. Continuing the effort to reduce *Peacock*'s draft and ease her off the reef, the next day nine more guns, now most of her battery, were dropped overboard, buoyed to mark their positions for recovery.*

A navigation fix at noon on Tuesday—*Peacock* by then being worried by several small boats orbiting around her while their armed Arab crews eyed the stranded foreign vessel hungrily—put the sloop on a reef located at 20° 20' north, 58° 52' east, midway up and perhaps a mile and a half off Masirah Island's western side, in the channel between it and the Arabian mainland. At one point, as many as five such boats bobbed about *Peacock*, just out of range of musket fire, scavengers looking for an opportune moment to make away with something valuable.

Earlier that same morning, after more than a full day aground and uncertain about breaking loose, Commodore Kennedy had the ship's number two cutter launched for Muscat with Passed Midn. William Taylor, USN, in command of a crew of six. Roberts was the eighth man on board, carrying the

* This desperate weight reduction successfully reduced *Peacock*'s draft forward by more than two feet, as measured on September 30 after the crisis. Each of *Peacock*'s carronade gun barrels weighed about two thousand pounds. "Dropped overboard" makes this heavy lift sound deceptively easy. Three paragraphs of dense instruction ("Remove the pin and chock from the cascable, into the jaws of which place a selvage strap; hook the double block of the train tackle into the housing bolt over the port, and its single block over the selvage strap; remove the cap squares . . .") and a full-page illustration in Lt. Cdr. S. B. Luce's *Seamanship* (D. Van Nostrand, 1877) describe how this evolution, invariably under emergency conditions, should be done.

ratified treaty in hand hopefully toward shore. *Peacock*'s location meant her small cutter had ahead of her a four-day sail, the first miles through waters thick with aspiring pirates, before reaching sanctuary in Oman's tiny port and capital.

Weeks later Kennedy explained to the secretary of the navy his decision to send the eight off to distant Muscat:

> After several ineffectual attempts to heave the ship off into deeper water, (which failed, owing to the anchors breaking and coming home), we became fearful that we would be destroyed by the first gale, when no succor could be had short of Muscat, a distance of upwards of four hundred miles. The boats being incapable of saving one-third of the crew; were constantly beset, too, by numerous piratical vessels, who attempted, in a most audacious manner, to cut off the launch and cutter, when carrying out anchors—using, also every stratagem to plunder our raft of provisions, &c. And while their numbers was hourly augmented, they clearly manifested the purpose of destroying us and making prize of the ship, so soon as they were in sufficient force. Placed in the perilous situation, with very slight hopes of saving the ship; having on board only a small supply of water, in a climate where the sun burns with an intensity which can scarcely be surpassed; I could only look to Muscat for assistance. Being unable to spare either of the large boats, on which rested our only hope of saving the ship and crew . . . Mr. Roberts, our envoy to Asia, with a promptness and fearlessness which mark all his movements, most kindly volunteered his services, to proceed on this most dangerous expedition, in an open boat 20 feet in length, amidst numerous piratical craft, and on a boisterous sea, accompanied by Passed Midshipman Wm. R. Taylor and six men.[1]

If *Peacock*'s second cutter had followed the usual U.S. Navy rule, she would have been twenty-five-feet long, not Kennedy's twenty, either one still very near the length of the twenty-three-foot launch that carried Lieutenant William Bligh, RN, and his loyalists from HMS *Bounty* to landfall on East Timor nearly fifty years earlier. The length of their respective boats and the fact that Bligh in 1789 and Roberts in 1835 were both afloat on warm salt water, however, were the only similarities between the two passages, despite what this chapter epigraph's nameless author imagined. The eight in *Peacock*'s cutter cruised for four days in baronial comfort compared to the eighteen crammed into *Bounty*'s launch for forty-eight desperate days on starvation rations.

Peacock remained aground for another two days, leaking continuously—from soon after impact until safely in dry dock at Bombay, and despite hasty repairs to her hull attempted by pearl divers in Muscat, seawater continued to flow through leaks into the hold at the rate of about a foot an hour—while the crew continued to work to pump her down and break loose toward deep water. Finally, they succeeded. The evening of September 23, after fifty-six hours stranded atop the reef, *Peacock* managed to move under her topsails some ten to twelve miles away and anchored there overnight in six fathoms. At the last cast of her lead at sunset the next day, September 24, *Peacock* had thirty fathoms under the keel under way and open water before the bow while Masirah (Ruschenberger: "a pile of dark, arid rocks, rising perhaps five or six hundred feet above the level of the sea, without a single spot of verdure upon it") disappeared astern. The crew had saved their ship and themselves.

30

To his children, Roberts piously credited the cutter's safe arrival at Muscat to God: "He who protects the Wanderer to far distant lands against the perils of a tempestuous ocean, the bands of the sanguinary descendants of Ishmael & the Egyptian Hagar [the reference is to Genesis 16's story of the origin of the Arabs], not only conducted us in safety, but mercifully has preserved my health wholly unimpaired." He said nothing about God in his report of the near-catastrophe to the secretary of state a month later.

"We were chased by a pirate a distance of 25 miles, but darkness favored our escape, and on the same night the boat was nearly lost by a sea boarding us," Roberts wrote Secretary Forsyth from Bombay, describing his passage to Muscat and all that followed. The boat crew's reception at Muscat was extraordinarily generous, the secretary was told:

> Immediate information was given to the Sultan of the situation of the *Peacock*. As soon as the sad tale was related, His Highness ordered the *Sultana* Sloop of War to be equipped for sea. An order was also sent to the Governor of Zoar to proceed to the ship with four armed dhows and 300 men for the protection of crew and property. Two couriers were also sent across the country to the Governor of Mazeira and the principal Chiefs of the Bedouins along the coast, holding them responsible with their heads for the safety of every individual of the

> crew and the property of the ship. A troop of 350 Bedouins . . . were ordered to the coast to protect the crew if it became necessary to land.

Within hours, hundreds of "wild Bedouin" horsemen were on the way to the coast to protect any of the crew who might have made it ashore. The next day *Sultana* was at sea, being guided to *Peacock*'s reef by tireless Midshipman Taylor.

"Light breezes and pleasant weather," *Peacock*'s deck log records for Monday, September 28, a week exactly since she ran aground. The entry continues: "Beating up [tacking into the wind] for Muscat. At daylight discovered a sail coming out of the harbor of Muscat. At 7:15 the strange sail fired a gun, which was answered by us. Hoisted our colors. At 9 backed the main topsail. Mr. Taylor and the 2nd cutter crew came on board from the strange ship which proved to be the Sloop of War *Sultané* sent by the Sultan to our assistance. Received from her a present from the Sultan consisting of 3 cows, 6 sheep, 5 goats, fruit, &c."

31

Four days after *Peacock*'s cutter sailed into Muscat and the day after the cutter's parent sloop was shepherded in port by *Sultanah*, Roberts told the sultan he was ready to proceed with the exchange of treaty documents, the mission that had brought him to Arabia. Roberts must have assumed that what followed would be a brief formality, and that he'd soon be back at sea on the way to Siam to repeat the diplomatic ritual in Bangkok. In fact fully ten days passed before *Peacock*, this rite accomplished, headed back to deep water on the way for Bangkok via stops in Bombay, Colombo, and Batavia. She would not appear at the bar of the River Menam below the Siamese capital, her second destination, for another six months.

For the ceremony in Muscat he imagined was soon to come, Roberts had in hand the original treaty with the sultan, ratified a full year earlier, together with a certificate attesting to the formal exchange of the treaty copy held by the Americans for the one the sultan had presumably retained. He also had a generous assortment of gifts for his counterpart. These included a major general's dress uniform, chapeau, and sword, part of a wardrobe of elegant and ornamented costumes that included dresses, shoes, hats, and gloves (all unsuitable for hot weather wear); patent firearms; "a map of the U. States with richly gilt rollers and upper frames"; two "richly mounted cut glass lamps with new form shades"; and a complete display set of American coins struck at the Philadelphia mint.

It developed that Sayyid Sa'id had nothing: the Omani original of the treaty rested with Captain Hassan in Zanzibar, months away. It had been returned there by Captain James Plumridge, RN, of HMS *Magicienne* after—unknown to the Americans—Bombay had completed its ad hoc review.

Over the night of September 30, Roberts hastily wrote a duplicate by hand on blank parchment from the "scanty" nine page supply that the State Department had sent him off on his mission. Translation into Arabic took the next two days, but not until October 10 did the sultan and Roberts actually sign and seal the new original, when they agreed that September 30 of the year before would be the effective date of the new treaty and its lower customs duties.

At sunset on October 10, riding a breeze blowing offshore, *Peacock* set out for Bombay, twelve days away across a phosphorescent Arabian Sea. She sailed during the change of the monsoon winds, from summer's southwesterlies to winter's northeasterlies.

32

Following a slow passage from Muscat (averaging only sixty-four miles per day while manning her pumps around the clock), *Peacock* limped into Bombay the morning of October 23, once two weeks ahead of *Enterprise* into Zanzibar but now ten days behind her. The grounding and all that followed had cost the Peacocks three weeks. Remarkably, on board everyone's health had remained generally good through the trial and passage to and from Muscat. Everyone's but Midshipman Taylor's. His brief tour in command at sea had caused him, Ruschenberger later wrote without elaboration, to suffer "a slight indisposition of two or three days, of a nervous character."

That same day Roberts wrote Secretary Forsyth, reporting details of the near disaster and of subsequent events, a day after he'd sent his "Dear Children" much the same news.* "After two ineffectual attempts to heave the ship off into deep water," Roberts wrote them in Portsmouth, New Hampshire, and Delhi, New York,

> Expecting she would go to pieces the first gale on a coast where no succor could be had short of Muscat, a distance of 400 miles—being beset by a great number of Piratical Dows [dhows], who plundered

* Both of Roberts' letters, and other ship's mail too, left Bombay in the Glasgow-based merchant ship *Kirkman Finlay*, in from Liverpool on July 29 and finally returning there with a load of tea via St. Helena, the usual en route stop for East Indiamen. At St. Helena the U.S. commercial agent transferred the mail to the next ship bound for the United States.

> our raft made of the ship's spare spars, on which were placed barrels of provisions, naval stores, &c, &c, &c, they also made a very bold attempt to cut off the launch of the first cutter in which had they succeeded the ship would have been deprived of the means of carrying out anchors to heave off the ship, & they (the pirates) were accumulating a large force for the purpose of destroying us, of making a prize of the vessel, & the ship's boats being insufficient to save one-third of the crew & conduct them to either Bombay or Muscat—Matters being placed in this critical & painful situation, I volunteered my services to proceed to Muscat in a small open boat (being the 2d cutter of 20 feet in length) to procure aid & assistance from the Sultan.[2]

As he told the story, the cutter's first hours away from the mother ship were especially perilous. "We were chased upwards of five hours that day [September 22] by a piratical Dow to the distance of 25 miles," news that likely provoked equal measures of anxiety and admiration at home. Had the dhow caught up with them, the Americans' bold plan was to fire a "volley of musketry and board her with our cutlasses & pistols & make a prize of her if possible & I am satisfied that not a man in the boat would have submitted so long as he could have wielded an arm in his defense for death awaited us if taken, & it was much better to have died with the arms in our hands, fighting for self preservation, than basely to have submitted to an ignominious death." Saved such excitement by escaping in darkness, only later that evening to be "all but lost in a heavy sea," the cutter sailed on toward Muscat and help, her eight on board living only on "a small quantity of damaged bread, and some tepid water."

If artist José Gonsalves, working in Bombay in the 1820s and 1830s, had it right when he drew *View of Bombay, from Mazagon Hill*, *Enterprise* and days later *Peacock* sailed into a busy harbor densely packed with ships and boats of all sizes. Gonsalves' drawing, published locally in 1833 as the first of six hand-colored lithograph plates in a bound volume, is a perspective of the harbor from the heights to its north, showing masts standing thick as stubble in sheltered, placid waters below.*

* Not much is known of Gonsalves, other than he probably came to Bombay from Portuguese Goa. Two six-plate collections of his drawings of Bombay buildings and scenes were published by John Morris, one black and white in 1826 and the other hand-colored in 1833. Gonsalves' drawings, largely of public buildings but also including St. Thomas' Church and a formation of British Marines on the Esplanade, were clearly designed to appeal to British buyers.

Morris' General Lithographic Press opened for business in Bombay in 1826, very soon after the new, low-cost European illustration technology was first introduced to India, an introduction accelerated by the availability of suitable porous limestone printing stones domestically.

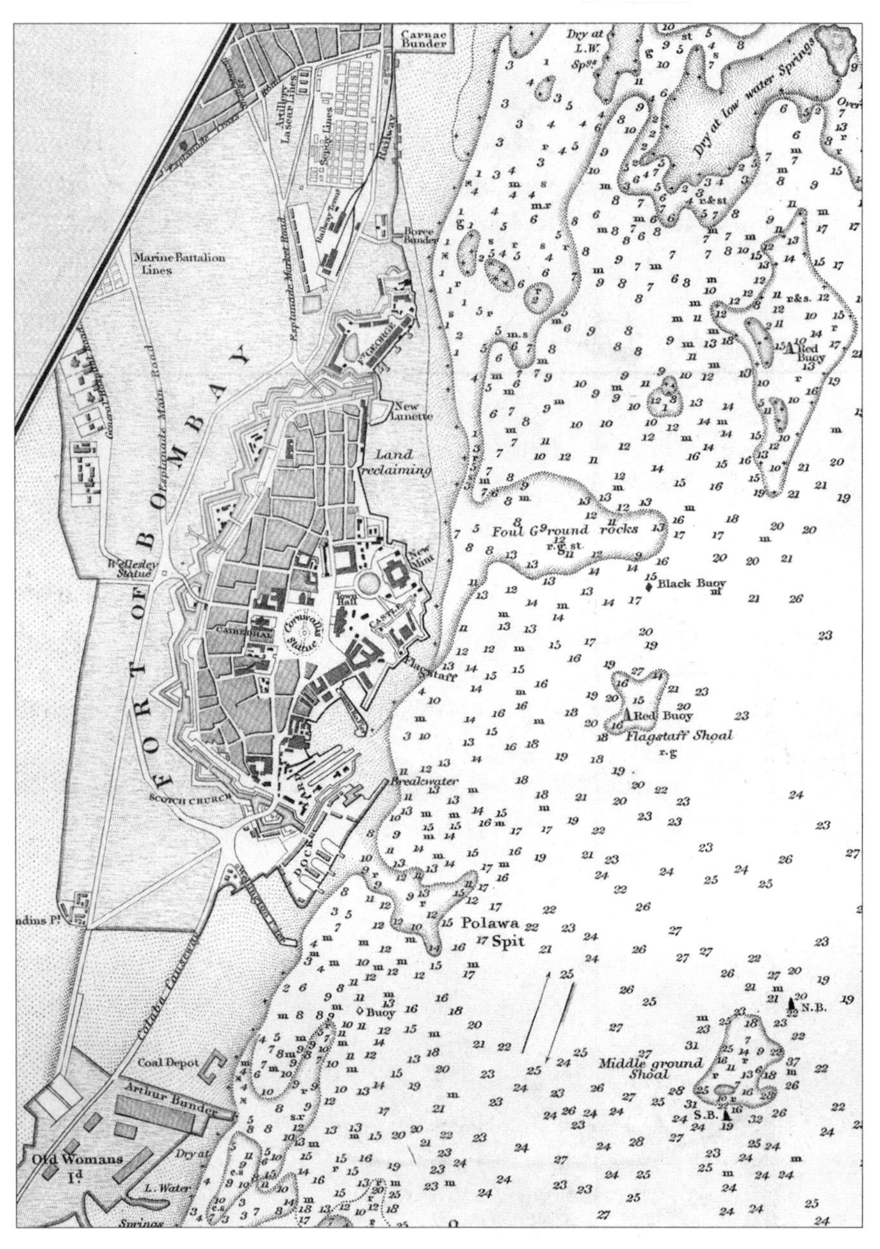

Chart 3. "The Fort of Bombay." Steamy, exotic Bombay, British since 1661 and once the East India Company's major port on the Indian Ocean, was in 1835 capital of the British Bombay Presidency and home to an estimated 230,000 souls. The port offered a harbor sheltered from the winter monsoon and was the place to do heavy marine repair work in waters east of Africa. Sited on the east side of one island among a cluster of seven that in time would be joined, Bombay's harbor had good access to stands of teak (more stable and resistant to marine parasites than even the American favorite, southern live oak) on the Malabar Coast. The harbor had, moreover, a fourteen- to eighteen-foot tide. This tide was the engine that made Bombay's dry docks work: a ship warped into the dock and onto keel

"Bombay has been unhealthy since time immemorial though very much improved in this respect since its occupation by the English," Commodore Kennedy reported to Dickerson months later in a long letter from Honolulu that amounted to an overview of the new squadron's operating area for the secretary. "The crews of vessels in the port, the troops in garrison, and the inhabitants generally are subject to miasmatic fevers and dysentery to a greater or less extent throughout the year, but more particularly after the breaking up of the wet monsoon. In other respects, no port offers greater facilities for refreshing & refitting than Bombay."[3]

After sending her black powder off for storage in Bombay Castle (opposite the dockyard, beyond the Customs House pier) transferring her enlisted crew, and her rigging, gun carriages, provisions, and what remained of her spirits, and ballast into HMS *Hastings*, *Peacock* went into dry dock the afternoon of Tuesday, October 27. The first task, to assess damage to the hull and define the scope of work required to make *Peacock* seaworthy once again, fell to a team that included the captain of the steamer *Hugh Wilson*, a second Briton, and the yard's chief builder, a Parsee Indian named Nowrogee Jamsetjee (1774–1860), one of the Wadia clan originally from Persia that virtually created shipbuilding in Bombay and then dominated it for that industry's first 150 years.

Ruschenberger wrote that Parsees were ranked, next to the English, as "the most intelligent race in India." During imperial times the favored native peoples of South Asia—Sikhs, Pashtuns, Punjabis, and Gurkhas—usually enjoyed that special status because of their perceived martial virtues and loyalty to the Raj. Not so the Parsees. They were flattered in the *North American Review* as "one of the finest races of men in the world, demigods and Apollos to the Mohommedan and Hindu casts around them," not warriors, but men who "constitute the only commercial class of the unmixed Orientals, who can pretend to even a distant rivalry of the Christian residents in intelligence, honor, or comprehensive views of commerce."

---

blocks with the high tide and rested there while the tide ran out. When the dock's gates closed at low water, the hull was left fully exposed through ensuing tidal cycles to the experienced carpenters, caulkers, and drillers who constituted the yard's skilled labor force. As many as sixty such craftsmen worked on *Peacock*'s hull at one time.

This chart of the Fort of Bombay, showing the dockyard and dry docks at its southern end, is an inset on the British Admiralty's chart no. 2621, "India West Coast Bombay Harbour," printed in September 1858 from information dated 1829–55. Bombay proper lay to the north of the fort. Credited to Lieutenant William Selby (d. 1876), an Indian Navy surveyor who earlier sailed in *Palinurus* under Haines' command, the chart was engraved by J. and C. Walker.
Courtesy Geography and Maps Division, Library of Congress

By the mid-1830s the Bombay shipyard had a century of construction experience dating back to a contract from the East India Company awarded in 1736 to Lovji Nusserwanjee, the first of the shipbuilding Wadias in Bombay, to build docks and ships. The port's first dry dock was built in 1750. It was doubled in 1762 and tripled in 1773, finally allowing Bombay to host a 74-gun ship. In 1806 Bombay built the fifth-rate 36-gun frigate HMS *Pitt* from the keel up; later renamed HMS *Salsette*, she was the first of more than thirty stout teak men-of-war for the Royal Navy to come from there before midcentury. One, the huge 84-gun HMS *Asia*, 2,289 tons and launched in January 1824, fought so well in October 1827 at the turkey shoot that was the Battle of Navarino, that Admiral Sir Pulteney Malcolm, RN, wrote the three Jamsetjees in Bombay to express his admiration of their work.[4]

The shipyard's building ways were also the source of Indiamen and country vessels built for local trade as well as combatant ships delivered to the Indian Marine, the Bombay Marine, and after mid-1830, the Indian Navy—all the same force under different names.

Predictably, the survey team's inspection report, delivered on October 31 to Commodore Kennedy by Capt. Sir Charles Malcolm, RN, then nearing the end of his ten years as superintendent of His Majesty's Indian Navy (and Admiral Malcolm's youngest brother), discovered significant damage to the sloop's hull. "We find," the survey officers had told Malcolm the day before, "the lower false keel entirely torn off, and the upper false keel so bruised and injured that forty feet will require to be shifted; the copper is torn off the larboard (port) bilge, and the bottom planking slightly rubbed in some places. There is a considerable leak along the garboard strake [the line of planks closest to the keel], and the caulking is slack, from straining when on shore. The copper nails in the starboard bilge appear started, and the copper looks rumpled."

"It appears quite evident," their report concluded, "that the ship has strained and the caulking is slack. We therefore recommend that the whole of the copper be taken off, the bottom well caulked and recoppered." A consolation, except where "rumpled," much of *Peacock*'s copper could be reused. Work began right away.

On Monday, October 26, Commodore Kennedy shifted his flag from *Peacock* to *Enterprise*, a formality given that neither ship was going back to sea until both sailed together five weeks later, after the yard finished voyage repairs to the sloop. Those weeks passed slowly. Ruschenberger began his chapter on "Sketches in Hindoostan, describing *Peacock* in Bombay," with a medical note:

> For a long time after [Bombay] was first visited by Europeans, it was regarded with horror; few persons had the courage to reside where the climate was so fatal, that it was a proverbial saying "the life of a man was equal to the duration of two monsoons." When first taken possession of, the fields were overgrown with bamboos and palms, and were manured by decaying fish; and marshes and pools infected the atmosphere with their exhalations. These destructive miasms would have driven the English away, had it not been that the island has the best harbor in all Hindoostan, the only one, except that of Goa, capable of admitting ships of the line.

Drained and dried out, and presumably minus its once infected atmosphere, Bombay was still unhealthy. Ruschenberger's daily medical journal shows that ten or fewer men went to sick call every day during the first week or so that *Peacock* was in Bombay. By the last week in port, however, Ruschenberger was seeing thirty to forty patients daily, and to accommodate demand sick call was being held every morning and twice in the afternoon.

When Midshipman Cadwalader stepped off *Enterprise* onto India, he was charmed by all that he saw. "I like the place very much indeed," he wrote. "The harbour is a fine one & a good deal of fun on shore, the people are very hospitable." A week later the fun on shore for tourists and natives alike was heightened by the celebration of Diwali, the annual festival of lights that signaled the start of the Hindu new year. *Peacock*'s other officers enjoyed Bombay too.

While their ship was in dry dock, *Peacock*'s officers lived handsomely in a rented house on Rampart Row, the road along the fort's interior wall that wags likened to Regency London's New Bond Street. The officers' establishment was sustained by a butler, a cook, and perhaps half a dozen other full-time servants, including a Parsee named Cowasjee who Ruschenberger soon described as his "right hand man." When off duty, the officers of the wardroom seem to have spent their time in Bombay and around the neighboring islands grandly touring. Breakfast was in the stone temple on Elephanta Island, catered by servants sent out the night before to prepare the repast. Dinner was on Salsette Island, following a morning visit to view its "celebrated" Buddhist caves of Kenery, when thirty servants waited on *Peacock*'s party of tourists, and the menu included wine chilled, improbably, by some of the first ice brought to India from the United States.

Thanks to the imagination and zeal of one Frederick Tudor, a Boston entrepreneur, in the early 1830s "frozen water" from Cambridge, Massachusetts' Fresh Pond became New England's most unusual export and India's most unusual import. During an era when really strange stuff (think bêche-de-mer, or sea cucumbers, "that disgusting-looking fish," Roberts said, "with a taste somewhere between the green fat of a turtle and the soft grizzle of beef when boiled") moved regularly through ocean commerce, common ice might yet have been the most exotic product in international trade. Deliveries had begun to the Caribbean early in the century. Drawing on that experience, by the early 1830s ice was being shipped to Bombay and Calcutta, sent around the world in specially insulated ships and stored there in heavily insulated houses. Ruschenberger said nothing about ice's supposed medicinal qualities, a specific for the fevers of this climate, but he clearly enjoyed the wine.

Not long after this excursion, *Peacock*'s officers rode cross-country to visit the caves of Jogheyseer, where again Ruschenberger marveled that the servants, "with their loads of furniture," had somehow again beat them to their destination and were busily preparing breakfast.

For two weeks, until Monday, November 9, *Peacock*'s "people," her enlisted crew, were crowded on board the port's guardship, the 74-gun HMS *Hastings*.* Not for them the cooks, servants, and bearers found to be essential for the comfortable accommodation of *Peacock*'s wardroom officers. One response was a spate of desertions; the first deserters were two Marines who ran off with their prisoner the day *Peacock* entered dry dock. Six more fled from HMS *Hastings* two days later, and others followed. *Enterprise*, part of the time at Bombay in dry dock for recoppering of her bow and the replacement of wormy stern timber, also experienced men vanishing ashore, if only temporarily. Both groups of absconders joined the 10 percent or so of navy ships' crews who typically deserted during deployment every year of the nineteenth century.

The reaction to this erosion of discipline came in the form of a six-officer, general court-martial presided over by *Enterprise*'s captain, Campbell. The court first met on his ship November 3. It then shifted to *Peacock* on November 9. The court sat, off and on, during the first half of the month and heard eighteen cases. Surgeon Ruschenberger acted as the court's judge advocate, the prosecutor, an appointment that suggests he was credited with some knowledge of Navy legal procedures. Punishment of the guilty, flogging—the practice wasn't outlawed until September 1850, thirty years after Congress first considered the reform and twenty after then-secretary Woodbury urged the use of fines, "badges of disgrace," and other "mild corrections" instead of

* *Hastings*, named after the then-serving governor general of India, was built in Calcutta in 1818 for the East India Company. She was sold the next year to the Royal Navy and not sold out of the navy until 1886, thirty years after she was converted to screw propulsion—her longevity evidence of the good work of the building yard. *Hastings* lives on only as a handsome model at the National Maritime Museum in Greenwich and as the figurehead of her namesake at the Merseyside Maritime Museum in Liverpool.

corporeal punishment—began on Friday, November 27, and continued on the following Monday and the Wednesday after that.

James Harvey got forty-two lashes with the cat-o'-nine-tails; eight others got thirty-seven, and nine others got fewer yet. The lightest punishment fell on Midn. John Chambers, USN, who was flogged at the grate nine times. Normally twelve lashes would have been the maximum, but deployed captains and commodores had the authority to impose harsher punishment, subject only to the secretary of the navy's review long after the fact.

Soon after daylight, Friday, December 4, after six weeks in port Bombay and now finally ready for sea, USS *Peacock* and USS *Enterprise* departed for Colombo, nearly nine hundred miles away. *Peacock* sailed with her full battery back on board, all her carronades fixed on their carriages behind closed gun ports. The eleven guns hauled over the side weeks ago, when the sloop was struggling to free herself from the reef, had appeared in Bombay at the end of November. They'd been recovered by the sultan's divers, received in Muscat on November 6, and delivered in Bombay at the end of the month on board the ship *Lord Castlereagh.** The guns' unexpected arrival—replacements had already been procured from the shipyard—prompted a fulsome letter from Kennedy to the sultan, extending "the homage, respect and gratitude which every officer and man, on board the Peacock, personally feels, for Your Highness' never ending exertions in rendering so many prompt and more than friendly acts for our benefit." Those acts had encompassed more than unusual generosity. Before *Peacock*'s fate on the reef was known in Muscat, Sayyid Sa'id had offered a ship from his navy to carry survivors home to the United States, and another to carry Roberts east on what remained of his mission.

For the next ten days or so, *Peacock*, averaging barely three knots with *Enterprise* easily trailing in her wake, navigated along the Indian coast largely by noting the passing off to larboard of historic places one after the other, ports—Goa, Calicut, Cochin—that had been the bases for Portuguese and later Dutch colonization of the subcontinent.

The 1836 edition of Horsburgh's *India Directory* described Colombo, the squadron's next destination, as "the seat of the British Government of Ceylon, and the principal emporium of the island," and "one of the most healthy places in India, abounding with good water and other refreshments." Not like Bombay, where drinking water drawn from large cisterns was known to carry a "singular disease."

---

* *Lord Castlereagh*, 800 tons, usually sailed in the country trade between Canton and Bombay via Singapore. She sank with great loss of life at Bombay in mid-1840. Commodore Kennedy said *Peacock*'s carronades were delivered by *Bagelah*, an otherwise unidentified ship. I cannot explain the discrepancy.

"An insect or worm is conveyed from [the water] into the system," Ruschenberger wrote, precisely describing guinea worm disease, "which after a time makes its appearance upon the surface of the body, in a vesicle, frequently as large as half a hen's egg. When this is opened, the extremity of a white, thread-like worm is perceived, surrounded by a gelatinous fluid. To remove the disease, the end of the animal is seized, and gradually wound on a dossil of cotton wool, a few turns being taken daily until the whole is extracted. . . . The animal occasionally attains several feet in length, and it causes severe pain to the patient."

The Tuesday before she sailed, *Peacock* took drinking water on board.

9

Colombo, Batavia, and Bangkok

> The adoption of Colombo, as the site for the Capital and the seat of Government, is altogether anomalous. The locality presents no single advantage to commend it. Compared with other parts of the island, the country surrounding it is unproductive, the coast is low and unsheltered, and the port is less a harbor than a roadstead. . . . Ships waiting for cargo are forced to anchor in the offing where disasters have frequently occurred during the violence of the monsoons.
>
> SIR JAMES EMERSON TENNENT, *CEYLON: AN ACCOUNT OF THE ISLAND*, 1860

33

At around ten o'clock Monday evening, December 14, a hand aloft at the fore topsail yard spotted the lighthouse at Colombo, Ceylon, through light rain. Before noon on Tuesday, both ships of the squadron were safely anchored a mile offshore the port, joining two British merchant ships in its small, open roads. Moments after *Peacock*'s anchor touched bottom at seven fathoms, she fired a twenty-one-gun salute—perhaps using the carronades recently returned by the sultan—which the fort answered gun for gun.

There would be more such salutes exchanged during this short visit: thirteen guns when Commodore Kennedy went ashore Wednesday on an official call and seventeen more when the governor and captain general of Ceylon, Sir Robert Wilmot-Horton, visited *Peacock* the following Tuesday to return the commodore's courtesy. Wilmot-Horton, having learned from Kennedy of Roberts' official status, graciously hosted him at Governor's House, his residence, for all ten days that the Americans were in port. (That building, since 1972 called President's House, stands today inside of the one-time high-security precinct of the modern capital's central Fort District. The fort's ramparts, built originally by the Dutch and described by Ruschenberger as a mile and a quarter around with six gates and seven bastions, and defended by three hundred guns, were taken down before the end of the century.)

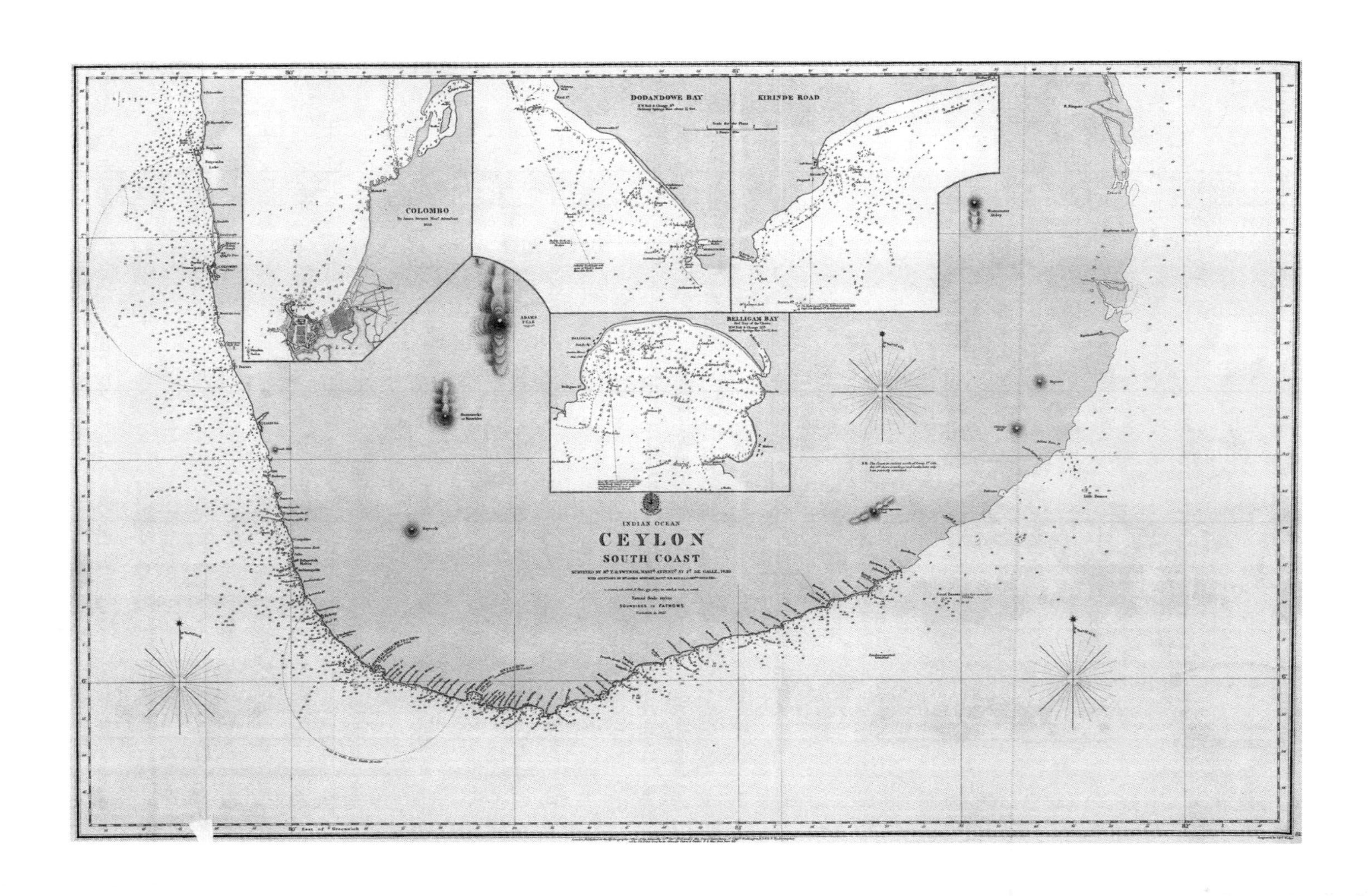
INDIAN OCEAN
CEYLON
SOUTH COAST
SOUNDINGS IN FATHOMS
COLOMBO
DODANDOWE BAY
KIRINDE ROAD
BELLIGAM BAY
ADAMS PEAK

A single, attention-getting carronade was fired just before Christmas Eve at 5:15 p.m. At the same time *Peacock* hoisted the cornet to the fore; that small, checkerboard flag signaled to *Enterprise* the flagship was preparing to get under way. An hour later both sailed in very light winds for the coast of Sumatra. "I have the honor to inform you . . . ," Commodore Kennedy wrote on the day of departure from Colombo to the secretary of the navy, "in consequence, as is believed, of the extremely bad water taken in [at Bombay] much sickness appeared on board, and seemed daily to increase, which induced me to touch at this place, for the purpose of obtaining a supply of good water. . . . Since our arrival here, I am happy to say, the health of the crew has somewhat improved."

Beyond taking on really potable water—remarkably no squadron sailor came down with guinea worm disease—not much other public business got done while the squadron tarried in Colombo, happily enjoying what the flagship's deck log recorded as "light airs and pleasant weather" of the early northeast monsoon season every day in port and what Roberts described in a Christmas Eve letter to his daughters as "feasts upon feasts, balls upon balls, tiffins upon tiffins, & rides without number."

Those two letters and *Peacock*'s other mail moved from Ceylon to the U.S. East Coast on board an aptly named bark, *Shepherdess*, Captain Kinsman, out of Salem for Sydney, Australia, hauling missionaries eastbound (four got off at Colombo to bring Christ to the "Tamuls") and Australian wool for the

Chart 4. "Colombo Roads." Colombo lay directly on the important nineteenth-century trade route connecting the Arabian Sea, Bombay, and Singapore to Canton, but its harbor suffered from all the disadvantages Tennent mentioned, and one he did not: a large shallows ("the Great Bank") that obstructed easy access to the shore. For those reasons Trincomalee, the best natural harbor on the Bay of Bengal and British after 1795, after 1810 grew to become the Royal Navy's principal base on the island during the long British colonial era.

This inset from the Admiralty Hydrographic Office's chart no. 813, "Indian Ocean, Ceylon South Coast," depicting Colombo Roads, is dated 1838. The parent chart, surveyed five years earlier by T. H. Twynam, master attendant at Point de Galle, Ceylon (the island's principal port then) and engraved by J. and C. Walker, was published in London in 1858. Soundings are in fathoms. The hook of land embracing the Roads on the west is Custom House Point. Governor's House is the quadrangle inside of the fort's northern wall. Colombo's ninety-seven-foot-high lighthouse is midway along the fort's western wall. An annotation on the master chart indicates the port's light was visible out to sixteen miles at sea.

The chart inset is credited to Captain James Steuart (1791–1870), a British merchant banker in Colombo beginning in 1818 but after 1825 in office for the next thirty years as master attendant of Colombo Roads (Twynam's counterpart seventy miles up the coast), with authority over the port and its customs collection. Steuart boarded *Peacock* on her arrival in the roads and escorted the squadron's officers to their courtesy call on the island's governor.

Geography and Map Division, Library of Congress

mills of New England on the return trip. She was the third American merchant vessel to sail this new route.

In addition to the squadron's mail, *Shepherdess* carried Roberts' presents to his children, including otherwise undescribed "curiosities," five sacks of Arabian dates, a keg of pickled mangoes from Bombay, and what he called two beautiful work boxes. She also provided transportation to the United States for Passed Midn. Hendrick Norvell, USN, returning home from USS *Enterprise* on a sick ticket. Young Norvell had transferred to *Enterprise*, his fourth ship during what was a short career at sea, from *Erie* in Rio de Janeiro.

"To afford him an opportunity to regain his health," the medical survey board chaired by Ruschenberger had concluded after examining Midshipman Norvell, "we think he should immediately be sent to the United States." Kennedy had agreed. That opportunity never existed: coughing up blood, exhausted and emaciated (in the advanced stage of consumption, although the board made no explicit diagnosis), and already terribly ill when he left *Enterprise*, Norvell, then twenty-nine, died of tuberculosis at home in Tennessee in mid-March 1837—nine months before his last ship arrived at her homeport. Ironically, the usual prescription for a diagnosis of consumption in the first half of the nineteenth century, America's chief fatal disease during those decades, was an ocean cruise. Pure, salubrious air at sea, the direct opposite of the poisonous miasmas thought to waft over wetlands, was believed to be both the prophylactic against and cure for consumption. (And for other conditions as well. Author Richard Henry Dana went to sea for several years seeking a cure afloat for "the weakness of my eyes.")

In Ruschenberger's memoir of the cruise, he would recall that sailing out of Bombay few in *Peacock* regretted departing the British capital of western India. "A large number of officers and men were suffering from fever," he remembered, "brought on by exposure during their night watches to the land winds, which came to us loaded with miasma exhaled from the marshy lands over which they blew. Scarcely an individual on board escaped attack, and for [the next] three months the sick list numbered nearly one-fourth of the crew." Elsewhere the surgeon described the process of infection more colorfully, as a consequence of "snuffing up the morbiferous effluvia from some neighboring marsh."

Colombo was much better. "Compared with continental India," Sir James Tennent wrote in 1859, "the securities of health in Ceylon are greatly in favor of the island":

> One of the most important inquiries is the probable effect on the health and constitution of a European produced by a prolonged exposure to an unvarying temperature upwards of 30 degrees higher than

> the average in Great Britain. *Mere heat, even to a degree beyond Ceylon, is not unhealthy in itself.* . . . In numerous cases heat may be the means of removing the immediate sources of disease. Its first perceptible effect is a slight increase of the normal bodily temperature beyond 98°. . . . To this everything contributes an exciting sympathy—the glad surprise of the natural scenery, the luxury of verdure, the tempting novelty of fruits, and all the unaccustomed attractions of a tropical home.

Tennent (1804–1869), a British politician and civil servant, enjoyed just such a tropical home, elegant Elie House, during the five years that he spent in civil service on Ceylon in the late 1840s.*

Three weeks after leaving Bombay, Roberts reported a slightly lower sick bay count to his children than Ruschenberger's tally. "Nearly every fourth man above 45 is now sick on board the P.," Roberts told them. Ages of the afflicted aside, the count was high enough that only a day out of Colombo, and then in open water and occasional wet weather, Kennedy considered the health of the crew and changed course, away from Acheen on northern Sumatra and directly for the Sunda Strait. Until then the plan had been to show the flag at three or four places on Sumatra (Roberts to his daughters: "*to show* our 22 teeth at them & 10 of the *Enterprise*'s—but hope we shall not be under the necessity of making *mince meat* of the savages") and only afterward to proceed to Batavia.

Enterprise fell behind repeatedly during the nineteen-day, nineteen-hundred-mile passage to Batavia, often forcing *Peacock* to heave to and let her escort catch up. On January 11, then past Krakatoa and in the Sunda Strait, Roberts reported 137 cases of fever on board to his children (he was "perfectly well" he wrote them, but not twenty others "in the whole ship have escaped") in a letter that went ashore at Angier on the mail boat, there to wait for a homeward bound ship.

* A handsome painting of Elie House by Andrew Nicholl, RHA, is among many done of sites on the island by the Irish artist while he was on Ceylon with Tennent, his patron. Sir James' observations are valuable, but his term as colonial secretary under Governor Wilmot-Horton was not a success, and his own hoped-for governorship didn't follow. In 1848 tax and other government initiatives the pair implemented produced a rebellion near Kandy, in the restive central highlands of Ceylon, that was harshly repressed. Tennent was subsequently recalled to London, and a parliamentary inquiry followed his return. He was the author of *Christianity in Ceylon* (John Murray, 1850) and ten years later of the magisterial *Ceylon: An Account of the Island* (Longman, Green, Longman and Roberts, 1860).

34

Commodore Kennedy's original sailing instructions from Secretary Dickerson had provided that after delivering the ratified treaty to the sultan of Oman, wherever he might be, the squadron was to proceed next to "the Island of Sumatra, visiting Acheen, Quallah Battoo, and such other places as the protection of our commerce may require making such a display of the force under your command as shall be best calculated to give confidence to our citizens engaged in the pursuit of their lawful trade."

February 16, just over a month after anchoring in Batavia Roads, Kennedy's next report to the secretary explained why this "display" off Sumatra's west coast hadn't happened and why the squadron had tarried so long at Java. "It was my intention to have proceeded to the pepper ports in Sumatra, in conformity to your instructions," he wrote, beginning a single, breathtaking sentence,

> but the winds proved very adverse in the Bay of Bengal, which pressed us to the Southward and Westward out of our course; and the rains, as we approached the Equator, were constantly increasing, and the fever on board, which was contracted in Bombay, by no means abating, it was strongly recommended by the Fleet Surgeon to proceed forthwith to this place, that we might curtail as much as possible, the time of our continuance southward of the Equator, where we could only expect at this season, a great deal of humidity, coupled with a hot, insalubrious climate.

The commodore consoled himself, and Secretary Dickerson, with the knowledge somehow gained that the sloop of war USS *Vincennes*, then at Lintin, would soon visit the coast of Sumatra to show the flag in his place.

Vincennes and *Peacock* might have overlapped off western Sumatra had Kennedy followed his orders precisely. *Vincennes*, then on her second around-the-world cruise, arrived at Lintin on January 2, 1836, from Peru, reprovisioned, and left China January 26, sailing for Sumatra via Singapore and the Malacca Strait. She left Kuala Batee unmolested on February 19 for the Cape of Good Hope on the way to Hampton Roads, Virginia, and the end of three years at sea. The first visit to Sumatra by the new East India Squadron, accordingly, didn't come until December 1838. That's when USS *Columbia* and USS *John Adams* arrived off Sumatra from Colombo and, in an echo of USS *Potomac*'s mission, bombarded Kuala Batee and Muckie in revenge for an attack on the American bark *Eclipse* and the murder of her captain the previous August.

Explanation offered, Kennedy's tone turned peckish as he described the frustrations of the squadron's past month in the notoriously unhealthy roadstead. On arrival he'd discovered that the provisioning ship carrying stores for *Peacock* and *Enterprise* had come and gone, sailing for Canton via Surabaya without landing anything at Batavia. This compelled Kennedy to direct the new American consul, Owen Roberts (Shillaber's successor), to purchase on the open market five months of supplies for both ships. Delivery of these stocks by small boat to *Peacock* and *Enterprise*, at anchor beyond the shallows and fully three miles off shore, Kennedy explained to Dickerson, was delayed day after day for "upwards of a fortnight, being interrupted by very tempestuous weather, accompanied by a dangerous surf on the bar." Just as well. On January 25 the ship *Gibraltar*, 152 days out of New York, unexpectedly arrived at Batavia with barrels of beef and pork, casks of bread, and other stuff from home for the squadron. These stocks were slowly loaded and the supplies just procured at Batavia were disposed of "at a trifling loss," Kennedy reported.

No less exasperating than the fumbling around with supplies *Peacock* and *Enterprise* needed to reach China was Kennedy's sense that his command was being neglected in Washington. He'd been a frequent correspondent, following Dickerson's instructions "to keep the Department regularly advised of all your operations, reporting as frequently as opportunities permit all your proceedings." But the flow of information had seemingly been largely one-way, prompting exasperation. "I regret to say again," Kennedy wrote, "that I have not received any communication from your Department, nor from the Navy Commissioners."

The itinerant reprovisioning ship at Batavia had carried no mail for the squadron, Kennedy discovered, nor had *Gibraltar*. Return communications from Washington came slowly, if at all. In August 1835 (when *Peacock* was already in the Indian Ocean) Dickerson mailed off to Kennedy acknowledgment of the commodore's letters to him of March through June, sent to Washington from New York and Rio de Janeiro. Kennedy's letter to Dickerson of mid-February 1836 from Batavia reporting on officer reassignments in the squadron forced by disease was received and answered by Acting Secretary of the Navy John Boyle early that August, by which time *Peacock* was in mid-Pacific heading for Oahu.* There's no evidence in archives that Boyle's reply caught up with the ship off the west coast of South America, or anywhere else.

* Like other acting appointments in the executive branch then, that of John Boyle, since June 1813 the chief clerk of the navy, to act for the absent secretary of the navy in August 1836 had to be approved by the president. In 1856, Boyle's son and executor sued in the Court of Claims for both the secretary's and chief clerk's salaries for the nearly fifteen months his father had been the acting secretary during nearly thirty years as chief clerk. He was awarded the difference: $4,976.

Managing the squadron's accounts in Batavia, even without the burden of buying and selling extra five-month ship sets of provisions, was complicated by the same problem—disabling disease—that in early summer would force the near-complete reassignment of officers to both ships' wardrooms. By February Charles Goldsborough, Commodore Kennedy's secretary since become *Peacock*'s replacement purser (the usual career path for these specialist officers), had been incapacitated for three months. Richard Waldron, off *Enterprise*, was transferred to the flagship in Goldsborough's place and Goldsborough was sent back to the United States on a sick ticket. "It may be the means of, at least partially, restoring his health. . . . I have my doubts of his ever reaching home," Kennedy explained.

Waldron's replacement on the schooner was *Peacock*'s former mathematics professor, J. Dickinson Mendenhall, who in midsummer would be buried at sea in the western Pacific, four days out of the Bonin Islands on the way to Oahu. Mendenhall had been ordered on board *Peacock* in New York to teach her midshipmen enough math during the coming cruise to be able to navigate the ship. He was to have shared the responsibility of training these junior officers with Rev. Addison Searle, a Navy Episcopal chaplain ordered to join *Peacock*'s commissioning crew on March 4 to provide for their and the men's moral instruction. "The joint labors of the Chaplain and Professor of Mathematics properly and unceasingly directed to the instruction of the young officers," the secretary's sailing instructions had intoned, "cannot fail to produce salutary effects in advancing their fitness and fitting them for distinguished usefulness in their profession." But Reverend Searle (who served in the navy for thirty years and died at sea in 1850) inexplicably never reported on board; he seemed to think that there was a charge against him, and so the squadron sailed without a chaplain. That had left it to the professor to inculcate morality by himself.

Also in Batavia, five sailors and two Marines sat before a medical survey board; all seven were "condemned as unfit for Service" and sent home on board the bark *Rosabella*, seven months out of Boston and heading back there from China.

35

On Wednesday, February 17, the squadron finally left Batavia for Bangkok, thirty-three hundred miles and five weeks away at the head of the Gulf of Siam. Roberts returned on board not long before departure. He'd again stayed in some comfort at Fancy Farm, Forrestice's country estate, a carriage ride away in Batavia's European suburbs. Nothing in Roberts' letters to his children—full of paternal advice about going out in Portsmouth's winter "thoroughly & warmly clad" wearing flannel hose and waterproof shoes, and family finances—says much about Java, only that storms and gales of wind continued to detain the squadron.

Ruschenberger, who might not have relocated to shore during this extended port call as Roberts had, was also affected by "the depressing effects of sultry weather and almost constant rain, coupled with the difficulty of getting to and from the ship." What could have been his sole extended excursion from *Peacock* took the surgeon thirty-five miles south of Batavia by fast carriage on the post road to Buitenzorg ("Carefree") in the hill country, the summer residence of the Dutch governor general and the site of a botanical garden famous even today. He traveled in the company of Consul Owen Roberts and with two unidentified others. The short trip prompted Ruschenberger to decry Dutch treatment of the natives, who'd built the excellent post road the party traveled on—stations for a change of horses every five miles—but were prohibited its use.

Consul Roberts and another American trader in Batavia, New Yorker Frederick Morris (who succeeded as consul there when Roberts died in 1848 only to die in the position himself two years later), were the sources for much of Ruschenberger's information about Dutch trade with Japan.

That trade—an exchange of sugar, tin, ivory, woolens, cottons, and earthenware from Batavia and other places for copper, camphor, lacquered ware, linens, "sakie," and soya from Japan—under highly restrictive Japanese rules moved in one or two vessels annually, leaving Batavia in July for Nagasaki and returning the following January. Had Edmund Roberts survived to undertake the last mission of his embassy, the opening of Japan to American trade, Ruschenberger's detailed data from Batavia customs house records on the goods moving between the ports, and the economics of that exchange would have been valuable commercial intelligence.

The terms of trade, Ruschenberger concluded, favored the Dutch by 300,000 florins per year annually between 1825 and 1833, for which benefit they accepted what he regarded as humiliating conditions. He believed that the exclusive arrangement, enjoyed by the Dutch and no one else, cost the Dutch their "independence and manly feeling":

> When we see a nation or a company of men consenting to be treated as menials, to hide their religious opinions, and subject themselves to the capricious and fantastical laws of a people they deem every way inferior to themselves, for the sake of gaining a hundred and thirty or forty thousand dollars a year, we must cease to regard them with the

> respect that is the right of every high-minded and honorable society. Whatever might be the advantages to the United States of commerce with Japan or any other nation, let us hope it will be established only on the basis of reciprocity.[1]

Ruschenberger's sermonizing was likely less useful than his data, but he echoed the same pridefulness that made all American contact with Asian courts such a complicated and often fruitless exercise.

Instead of sailing roughly north across the Java Sea, "unusually stormy and unpleasant" this season Kennedy explained to Dickerson, and passing Billiton Island to enter the South China Sea by either the Gaspar Strait or the Carimata Passage, the squadron's plan was to thread the hundred-mile-long Straits of Banca (between Banca Island and Sumatra) and come into the South China Sea from the west. A nice piece of navigation and ship handling, often into the wind. James Horsburgh took seventeen pages in the third (1827) edition of his *India Directory* to describe how this should be done, warning merchant ship masters of mud flats to the west and shoals to the east of the occasionally very narrow channel between islands, of "piratical proas" that threatened unwary passersby with boarding, and of past groundings in these same waters, mentioning by name twenty ships that had run aground over the years and describing their particular distress.

"I am happy to inform you," Kennedy had written Dickerson on February 16, hoping to sail the next day, "that our sick list is very considerably reduced since our arrival here." Not a week out of Batavia, a cook in the officers' wardroom, Seaman William Lewis, died and was buried at sea. His replacement, or perhaps a second cook in the wardroom mess, Charles Fisher, died ten days later in early March, just as *Peacock* finally reached the open sea and headed east toward Borneo Island before beating north up the Gulf of Siam toward the squadron's next destination. Ruschenberger thought the cause of the two deaths was dysentery ("that terrible scourge of armies and of ships") but said nothing about sanitary conditions in the galley that might have threatened the health of the entire crew.

36

On March 23 *Peacock* and *Enterprise* stood into Siam Roads, carefully feeling their way into the head of the Gulf of Siam behind the gig and third cutter, sent out ahead to sound the depth of water. Early the next morning the schooner was sent on to Paknam, the fortified royal government station on the lower river, carrying a letter from Roberts to "His Excellency the Chao P'haya

Klang, one of the first ministers of state to His Magnificent Majesty the King of Siam." The letter addressed three essential points. Roberts, "Special Envoy from the United States of America,"

- back with the treaty negotiated almost exactly three years earlier, and long since ratified, was now prepared to exchange his copy for the one held in Siam duly ratified "with the royal seal of the kingdom affixed";
- had with him gifts promised to the king, excepting the stone statues "which could not be obtained" (a "deficiency . . . repaired by purchasing an extra number of the most elegant and expensive lamps") and trees, plants, and seeds "destroyed on the passage" when *Peacock* went aground off the coast of Arabia; and
- now needed transportation upriver to Bangkok for the presents and his party of twenty-five "with as little delay as possible, as the Envoy has to visit many kingdoms, and has a great many thousands of miles of ocean to traverse; to accomplish which, will necessarily occupy at least twelve months."

Special Envoy Roberts' carefully phrased attempt at stage and schedule management failed almost completely. The Siamese had their own style and pace.

Not until April 5 did "the junk of ceremony," the delegation's transportation upriver to Bangkok, finally arrive, firing a thirteen-gun salute to honor the American envoy, at the anchorage where the squadron floated impatiently in the hot sun. During the frustrating delay, both American crews approached the edge of having to subsist entirely on salted meals washed down with rationed drinking water. A month later, with the condemnation of all the bread on board, found after inspection to be "decayed," the threatened short rations became a reality. The crews were then forced to subsist on hard salted meat and rice.

Ruschenberger admired the showy approach of "this piece of nautical architecture"—the junk's crew of thirty-two sailors handsomely outfitted in red, an equal number of soldiers in green, all sixty-four bare-legged and barefoot on deck beneath waving red banners. Among the crew stood its three officers, splendidly attired in costumes that the surgeon unkindly suggested must have come directly from the Bowery Theater following its final production of *The Last Days of Pompeii*. The large American delegation that boarded the junk in dress uniforms—twenty officers, several enlisted men, and *Peacock*'s nine-man band—boasted enough gold braid and gilt buttons to look suitably serious by Western standards, but it could not have matched its hosts for glitter. After spending the night at Paknam, the junk and its passengers started up the serpentine Menam River the next morning, towed toward the capital by three boats, each propelled by forty men at oars. The procession arrived in Bangkok late that night.

The following week passed largely in sightseeing and ceremony, punctuated on April 9 by the ceremonial delivery of the ratified American treaty to the Siamese and on April 11 by the advance gift of two splendid swords decorated with gilded elephants and eagles, heraldic symbols of the two countries. A day later Commodore Kennedy and Surgeon Ruschenberger departed Bangkok for *Peacock*, Kennedy ill since the day before (he'd slowly recover over the course of the next ten days, dosed with opium, Epsom salts, and calomel in the meanwhile) and Ruschenberger returning because of a report that Asiatic cholera had broken out on board the flagship with the deaths of a sailor, Daniel Thomas, and of a Marine, William Wagoner. Two more would die before all in the American shore party were back on board and *Peacock* was again under way.

Ruschenberger's time on shore had been long enough to persuade him to uncharitable views about the Siamese ("a race that has scarcely taken a step to emerge from ignorance and barbarism . . . disposed to indolence and animal propensities") but also to conclude grandly, on the basis of the little economic data shared by a resident British commission merchant, that "when the half-naked millions of Asia shall attain Christianity, and with it, all the new wants which the necessary change in their social condition will produce, the soil of our country, as rich and vast as it is, will be scarcely adequate to supply them. A new and extensive mart must be opened for our manufactures of all kinds, and even the literary will find an increased demand for their labors. Hundreds of ships will spread their sails to the westward of the cape of Good Hope, destined for the shores of Asia and the isles scattered in the southern ocean, and commerce will pour her wealth gathered in the old world, into the lap of the new." Pretty heady thinking in the face of the fact that in the past eight years only two American merchant vessels, the ship *Sachem* and the brig *Maria Theresa*, had called on Bangkok.*

On April 16 the rest of the Americans' gifts were presented to the king, and two days later in turn, the ratified Siamese copy of the treaty was delivered to the Americans, the centerpiece of a colorful procession afloat that included three flag-bedecked barges, each one manned by a hundred uniformed men pulling at oars toward Americans assembled in uniform on board the same barge of ceremony that had brought them to the capital two weeks earlier.

---

* *Sachem*, Captain Coffin, was the ship that in 1829 brought the soon-to-be famous Siamese twins, Eng and Chang, to Boston. *Maria Theresa* arrived in Siam soon after *Peacock* and *Enterprise* but was permitted upriver immediately, frustrating Roberts and company.

The lead royal barge carried the treaty like an offering, "in a box, covered with coarse yellow silk interwoven with gold. This was placed on a silver dish, which rested on a salver with a high foot of the same metal. Over it hung a scarlet canopy, itself shaded by a royal chat [a parasol with five canopies of diminishing size]. The scarlet uniforms of the men, and the measured stroke of their hundred oars; the flaunting banners, the music of their pipes and drums, and the glitter of gold and silver in the sun, formed a pretty pageant," wrote Ruschenberger somewhat more generously than usual about their hosts, "and indicated with what scrupulous ceremony everything is conducted at the Magnificent Court of Siam."

Roberts received the box from the second minister, raising it over his head portentously while the *Peacock*'s band played "Hail, Columbia," gestures that copied the American ceremony of treaty delivery one week earlier, but now were understood to be a salute to the absent king. This glitzy, theatrical moment when the ratified Siamese treaty was delivered to waiting Americans turned out to be the premature, last official act of Roberts' second embassy to the eastern courts.

Ceremony over and mission successfully concluded; ratified treaty bearing the personal seals of the emperor and each of his six principal officers now in hand; Roberts and his party rode a junk downriver on the ebb tide. Exhausted, ailing, and finally successful, the group reached Paknam at noon the next day, and boarded *Peacock* in the stream at midday on April 20.

Once again Ruschenberger celebrated the flagship's departure from port. Sounding much as he had sailing from Bombay and Batavia, he wrote,

> I believe no one in the squadron felt the least regret upon taking a final leave of Siam. In all probability not one of us will ever visit it again, and we hope it may be long ere any of our ships of war will be found in the waters of the gulf. The officers and crews now felt severely the effects of eastern tropical climates; all, with a few exceptions, had been seriously ill once, some of them twice; the past two months had been spent in contending against wind and currents; the ship was almost an hospital; four men had died since leaving Batavia.[2]

10

Cochin China and Macao

The climate of Indochina is very unhealthy for Europeans, who can never be acclimatized. . . . In no district can the European escape dysentery and anemia, but by avoiding heavy exercise and every excess, and by guarding against the extreme heat of day and dampness of the night, he can evade all the more serious attacks of the maladies. . . . Only the most careful avoidance of mid-day heat and all unusual exertion can safeguard the European. He must also take great care to guard against changes in temperature, for even the slightest variation at night often suffices to occasion attacks of dysentery almost impossible to cure.

The Catholic Encyclopedia, 1910

37

At sunset, April 20, 1836, *Peacock* and *Enterprise* left the mouth of the "most impure" Menam and sailed for Turon Bay in the second attempt in several years to open trade negotiations with the Cochin Chinese.

During his 1833 visit to the Siamese capital, Roberts had considered the uses of the Menam River, a combination highway, water source, and sewer. "The water used for domestic purposes is taken, with all its impurities, from the river," he (or someone) wrote in his still unpublished book, "in water tight buckets, neatly and strongly woven; it is put into unglazed jars of thirty or forty gallons, and is suffered to settle in the best way it can, without any foreign aid. The filth of half a million people, which is all emptied into the river, renders it most impure, and dead bodies are frequently thrown in to save the expense of burning."

On March 25 and 26, while still some twenty miles away from the mouth of the Menam, *Peacock* had put a party of officers ashore on Koh si Chang to search for a spring and water source. (An earlier search of the island for water, since forgotten, had also been unsuccessful when *Peacock* first visited it a few years earlier. The island's only source of fresh water even now is rain.) By then the sloop was down to less than 750 gallons, only a few days' supply to dry tank. Later, while waiting for Roberts to complete his mission, *Peacock* took water from the Menam often, once on April 5 and again on April 6, 8, 13, and 21. On May 4, off the tip of Cambodia and then approximately halfway to Turon Bay, she loaded one thousand gallons more from a stream on the north side of Pulo Oby Island, a good source described by Horsburgh as capable of flowing to fill one hundred casks ("butts") per day. This water, too, went into the same partly filled tank that held the ship's supply.

Most ships in that era had no means to treat river water other than by filtration through tubs of sand and dilution with vinegar. Neither process eliminated or killed pathogens, nor did simply waiting for contaminants to settle to the bottom of the cask. (Alembics, seaborne pot stills, could distill salt water into fresh, but the early-nineteenth-century version of this technology was impractical on the scale required for a combatant ship in the tropics and posed the danger of fire.) Another generation had to pass before physician John Snow's brilliant insight connecting Soho's Broad Street water pump to cholera in its London neighborhood first persuaded people that water carried disease. It was an additional twenty years or so before the durable idea that "miasma," the vapors of vegetable decomposition, was the source of disease began to lose sway for good.

By then, two weeks out of Bangkok, Edmund Roberts had already seen Ruschenberger at sick call ten times, the first time on April 22. The surgeon's case notes of a first consultation with his new patient describe a ten- to fifteen-day history of diarrhea, pain, disturbed sleep, and lost appetite, treated with what might have been a private stash of calomel, opiates, and ipecac. Roberts eventually became "Case No. 782" in Ruschenberger's medical journal, a case described in nine pages of handwritten entries that concluded with an autopsy report.

There wasn't much that surgeons on board ship (or ashore, for that matter) could do to improve the health of their patients in the early nineteenth century, little more than they'd done half a century earlier during the Revolutionary War era, when the distinguished Benjamin Rush—who believed there was only one disease—was bleeding his patients practically dry in an effort to restore their bodies to the imaginary equilibrium of humors that constituted good health. This despite a new American pharmacopœia in 1831 that contained fully 38 pages of "Materia Medica" (the raw materials of medicine, everything from *Acaciae Gummi* [gum Arabic], "chiefly used in solution in affections of the lungs, bladder, etc.," to *Zingiber* [ginger], "given as a stomachic, aromatic and stimulant for indigestion, typhus fever, etc.") and another 205 pages of prescription preparation instructions using these materials.

Medical science had advanced to the point that scurvy—as late as the mid-eighteenth century the scourge of cruises longer than several months—and dreadful smallpox could both be prevented, the first through diet, the second through vaccination with cow pox. Thanks to Peruvian bark ("cinchona" in that pharmacopoeia, available in yellow, pale, and red colors), malaria ("intermittent fever") could be prevented and cured, although other fevers that might be confused for malaria could not. If infection could be avoided, some injuries from accident and some wounds from combat could be treated more or less successfully, too; those to limbs often required horrifically painful amputation without anesthesia. A variety of techniques for resuscitating a drowned man existed—some, such as pumping smoke up his anus, were bizarre—but drowning, an occupational hazard for sailors, was almost inevitably irreversible.

But malaria aside, disease couldn't be cured. The pharmaceuticals that surgeons brought on board, opium aside—classed by their physiological effects as cathartics, narcotics, tonics, astringents, emetics, epispastics (blistering agents), refrigerants, diaphoretics, and escharotics—did much harm and little good. (Opium, however, actually worked. The narcotic was effective for controlling pain, inducing sleep, and treating diarrhea, and it was used casually for both medical and recreational purposes.) The usual practice of bleeding, sometimes in astonishing amounts, sometimes with the application of schools of leeches to strange places, did real harm and no good. So did the mercury salts, lead acetate, and sulfuric acid "elixir" packaged up as medicines. Sick sailors recovered, if they did, largely in defiance of their medical treatment, not because of it.

A further ten appearances at sick call with similar complaints and similar prescriptions passed by the time *Peacock* arrived at Turon Bay in mid-May after a voyage through pleasant weather marred only by the terrible health of the crew. The usual gun and small-arms drills, exercises for boarders and pikemen, target practice for the Marines, crew exercises at general quarters, all the evolutions that had enlivened boring ocean crossings in the past, were long forgotten. *Peacock*'s skeletonized port and starboard watches had all they could do to keep their ship under way on course and her hold dry.

"It would be difficult to present, to those who did not witness it, an adequate idea of the distressing state of things existing on board the ship," Ruschenberger recalled in his memoir, describing conditions on board *Peacock* after she left the Gulf of Siam ("Gulph of Siam" in her deck log) and sailed generally north-northeast between Pulo Condore Island and the Cambodian coast. "One fourth of the crew was confined, by sickness, to their hammocks, and those who were not under medical treatment, enfeebled by previous disease, were scarcely able to move about the decks; and, had we been so unfortunate as to encounter a gale, I doubt whether the physical force on board was sufficient to take care of the ship. It is the experience of contrasts like these which endears us to our home, and enhances its pleasures, showing the miserable chances which ever hang around a sailor's existence."[1]

Just before dark on May 13, after ten days sailing along the "beautiful and grand" Cochin Chinese coast off to leeward, Turon Point of Quang-Nam Province came into sight. The next day, Sunday, *Peacock* came around the point, anchored in the bay in five and a half fathoms, and lowered her boats. She was joined a week later by USS *Enterprise*. The schooner, twenty-eight on her sick list leaving Siam (a third of her crew) and sailing just ahead of the coming change in the monsoon, had been delayed by light winds and occasional calm air along the more seaward course her navigator had selected for the passage.

Once in this sheltered harbor close to the imperial capital the Americans, distracted by near universal poor health, briefly—almost halfheartedly compared to Roberts' first effort—tried again to open negotiations with the emperor of Cochin China. This attempt had two phases. The first, during which Roberts participated, was on board *Peacock*; the second was on shore, with Ruschenberger—curiously not Commodore Kennedy—representing the ailing special envoy attempting to sound out prospects for success. Both efforts were impeded by now-familiar cultural misunderstandings and by language.

No one traveling with Roberts spoke Chinese. In place of John Morrison, who'd interpreted for Roberts during the first embassy, was a Dutchman hired in Batavia named Jacobs, presumably at the forty dollars per month and two rations per day rate that had been approved by Secretary Dickenson for hired interpreters and harbor pilots the year before. Meneer Jacobs communicated with his American employers in French and with the Cochin Chinese interpreter in Malay, the only language the two parties found they shared. Even there, their dialects of Malay were different, guaranteeing frustration and confusion.

Nothing came of Roberts' brief meetings on board *Peacock* with provincial officials, although they did agree to transmit his letter reporting the Americans' arrival and purposes to the emperor. (It was later disclosed that no one in Hué could read Roberts' letter, written in English and French, or would confess to being able to read it.) On May 22, with no consequences of the earlier shipboard meetings visible in the interval, Ruschenberger, Midn. William Taylor (he of *Peacock*'s cutter once sent to Muscat for help), and the interpreter went on shore, where they met with two senior officials just arrived in palanquins from Hué, accompanied by a hundred-man, badly armed infantry escort. Ruschenberger's sole objective was to learn from them if a future third visit by a healthy Roberts with a capable interpreter could be productive. The conversation soon went beyond Ruschenberger's brief.

After the usual verbal maneuvering, complicated by filtering through four languages, just as he was getting ready to leave Ruschenberger was surprised by an abrupt offer from the senior mandarin, the "Laklak." "I repeated our regret that sickness on board of the vessels and want of interpreters required our departure," the doctor wrote, "and was about to take leave when the Laklak said, we might settle the matter at once":

> I told him this was out of the question, because the interpreters, who were our medium of communication, did not understand the language sufficiently well to treat on a subject of such moment. He nevertheless repeated we two might settle the matter now. . . .
>
> He again repeated we might settle it well enough, at least verbally. . . . He urged, that if Mr. Roberts would come on shore they might talk the matter over. I answered, that I would report what he had said, and requested to take leave; for I felt convinced, we were spending time to little purpose. . . .
>
> The Laklak asked whether I would not return again the next day to talk the matter over again; I replied, I would communicate what he said to Mr. Roberts, but thought it probable we should sail in the evening. . . .
>
> We shook hands, and I took leave impressed with the belief, that though a treaty might be effected, it would be at the expense of much time and patience, to overcome their vacillating and suspicious conduct. . . .
>
> We reached the ship near six o'clock, P.M., and preparations were made to get at once underway.

The squadron sailed later that night. On the evening of May 24, *Peacock* with *Enterprise* just astern, both heading for Macao at five knots, passed mountainous Hainan Island under a crown of thunderclouds. Four weeks after that Commodore Kennedy's next, his eleventh, report to the secretary of the navy, dated June 21, 1836, from Macao Roads, dismissed the squadron's port call at Turon Bay in a single sentence: "I have the honor to advise you of my arrival at this place on the 25 ulto. [last month], the Enterprise in company, having sailed from Siam on the 20th April and detained at Turon Bay, Cochin China eight days, from which place we sailed on the 22d ulto., owing however to the severe indisposition of our Envoy Mr. Roberts nothing was effected towards forming a treaty with the emperor of Cochin China."

To mark their centennial, in the mid-1930s the American vice consul in Saigon, W. Everett Scotten (1904–1958), there between postings at Juarez in Mexico and Palermo, Italy, managed with the help of the chief of the Surété to have the archives of the Cochin Chinese imperial court in Hué searched for records of the two Roberts embassies to the empire during the reign of Emperor Minh Mang. (Scotten's less sinister description of his helper, Léon Sogny, credited the French intelligence agent with being "a moving spirit in the local historical society, *Les Amis du Vieux Hué*.") Their search was successful.

What the pair found revealed that, unknown to the Americans, the first Roberts mission had prompted an undelivered imperial edict that posed no opposition to the opening of commercial relations at Tourane on the basis of rules already in effect, although it denied any right to build an establishment on land—a small, but perhaps sufficient first step toward Roberts' goal.

Roberts' second mission, in the seventeenth year of Emperor Minh Mang's rule, triggered a revealing discussion between the emperor and two senior mandarins when news of his arrival reached the court, a conversation recorded in the archive that suggested that a healthy Roberts might have managed to succeed had *Peacock* stayed in Turon Bay and he kept talking. Dao Tri Phu, a senior mandarin representing the treasury (and almost certainly Ruschenberger's "Laklak"), thought that talks in Hué with the foreigners might prove to be a good idea:

> The intentions and the words of these men seem to me to be filled with deference and courtesy. Would it not be fitting to acquiesce to their desire?
>
> Sire, these are foreigners, and we do not know whether the sentiments they have expressed are true or false. Your humble subject thinks that it would be well to authorize them to proceed to the capital and take up their residence in the [foreign trade ministry] and to order our mandarins to treat them well there and to seek out their real dispositions.[2]

The second, Huynh, a member of the household staff, thought not:

> Sire, their nation is very cunning, and it is advisable to break off relations with them. To tolerate them this time would be to make way for annoyances in the future. The men of olden times closed the frontiers of their country so as to shut out the nationals of Occidental

countries and so to defend themselves against the incursions of those barbarians. That is good politic. They have made a voyage of 40,000 leagues across the seas impelled by sentiments of admiration for the power and virtue of our government. If we resolutely break off all relations with them, we thus give them proof that good will is not to be found in our land.

Putting aside his usual xenophobia, the emperor determined to send Dao Tri Phu and one Le Ba Thu, representing the interior ministry, south to Turon Bay, this from the same archive, "to enter into friendly negotiations and examine the situation. Upon their arrival the commander of the vessel, giving out that he was ill, did not present himself in person to receive them. . . . The same day the vessel made sail surreptitiously."

"In haste they came," Dao's report to the emperor said, "in haste they departed, they have indeed shown themselves lacking in politeness." To which Minh Mang replied serenely, "Not to oppose their coming, not to pursue them upon departure, is for us to follow the rules of courtesy of a civilized nation. What brooks it to complain of barbarians from abroad?"

38

The squadron's short stop at Turon Bay explained, Commodore Kennedy turned in his report to the secretary to more current events, explaining, "Having sixty one persons on the sick report with dysentery & cholera it was deemed expedient on our arrival at Macao to procure a house on shore for a hospital under the direction of the Fleet Surgeon & his assistants, & on the 28th ulto. the sick from both vessels were removed to the hospital, since which there has been a gradual improvement in all, with the exception of a few."

During the last few days of May, when *Peacock* swung at anchor in Macao Roads before both ships sailed to the better protected anchorage a dozen miles away at Cumsingmoon Bay, and on the first of June, the flagship transferred a total of thirty-seven officers and men to a hospital quickly improvised in town. On June 1, Roberts moved ashore too, not to the hospital but to the home of William Wetmore, between 1833 and 1839 (when he moved to New York City) a wealthy American merchant whose company in Canton, Wetmore and Company, traded in tea, spices, silks, copper, coffee, and opium.

Lt. Archibald Campbell, *Enterprise*'s commanding officer, was one in the hastily assembled hospital who didn't exhibit the "gradual improvement" described by the commodore. He died there at 8:50 in the evening of June 3, exhibiting in his final days "fortitude becoming an officer," Ruschenberger said generously. None of the other sixteen men on *Enterprise*'s sick list when she entered Macao needed to be hospitalized ashore. Months later newspapers in the United States reported, perhaps correctly, that it was dysentery that had killed Campbell.

In a military ceremony presided over by the magnificently named colonial governor of Macao, Bernardo Joze de Souza Soares y Andrea, at the head of a battalion of Portuguese infantry, Campbell was buried the next day, very near to where Roberts would soon join him in death. Governor Soares y Andrea's proud show at Campbell's funeral was a vestige of his country's glory days in Macao. The crew of his ship, anchored in the roads, was represented at graveside only by Midn. Charles Richardson, USN, and the crew of the captain's gig.

Better known as a womanizer than as a divine, Rev. George Vachell conducted Campbell's internment service ("in a most impressive manner," judged the squadron's surgeon). It concluded with the traditional three volleys of musketry fired by the battalion. The monument over his grave, funded by an officers' subscription, suggests some held a better opinion of the man than did young Midn. Henry Cadwalader, who in his private memoir described his captain as "a most singular man. . . . He goes to bed at 8 at night and sleeps until 8 the next morning. Breakfast at 9, comes on deck and stays sitting on the taffrail until dinner time giving little orders about the crotch ropes, main sheet, and a little paint here and there. Perhaps he goes down and reads for an hour or so & takes something to drink & comes on deck again & plagues the officer of the deck."

When *Enterprise* sailed from Cumsingmoon on June 16, saluting the commodore with seventeen guns as she hauled away, a day ahead of *Peacock* on the short trip back to Macao before leaving China, Lieutenant Commanding Hollins, her new captain, stood on deck. He'd taken command ten days earlier, two days after his predecessor was buried.* The schooner's hastily reconstructed wardroom included four officers, among the total of nine, who held acting appointments. One, Acting Lt. John Weems, just off *Peacock*, had been the flagship's sailing master when she went aground, a near disaster the commodore obviously hadn't held against him.

During those late spring days, right around the time that Lieutenant Campbell failed and died, Roberts appears to have recovered his health. So he told his "Blessed Children" in a letter to Catharine, Sarah, Harriett, and Mary Ann written June 4, the day after he'd sent instructions to the American

* Hollins (1799–1878), of Baltimore, served in two navies. In command of the side-wheel frigate USS *Susquehanna*, in 1861 deployed to the Mediterranean Squadron, Captain Hollins returned home as ordered, resigned his U.S. Navy commission, escaped arrest, and boldly seized a commercial steamer on the Potomac with other plotters. He took a commission as a commander in the Confederate States Navy, in which he served at sea, on the Mississippi, and ashore with great verve and style.

Lt. Archibald Campbell's tomb reads, "Erected to the Memory of Lieutenant Commandant Archibald S Campbell by the Officers of the U. S. Ship Peacock and Schooner Enterprize 1836." Campbell's tomb stands next to that of Roberts. "To see an old, beloved Officer taken away by death from amidst his companions in arms, while in a useful and honorable career, far away from family and friends, draws strongly upon our sympathies, and is calculated to depress the spirits of those whom he has left, many of them afflicted by the very disease which has proved so fatal in this case." Squadron surgeon Ruschenberger's obituary of Campbell, of which this is a fragment, appeared originally in the *Canton Press* on June 10. It was quoted in full in the *Army and Navy Chronicle*, published in Washington, D.C., the following December 29.

Campbell's death June 3, 1836, created a career opportunity for ten-year Lt. George Hollins, USN, who in mid-March 1835 had volunteered to Secretary Dickerson to join the new squadron at the personal invitation of Commodore Kennedy—surely not with the intention of being one of four lieutenants in *Peacock* for all of the next three years.
PHOTOGRAPH BY SAMIYA ALLAN

commercial agents in Canton dealing with his personal account, other evidence of his improvement. "I have just recovered from a deathly sickness, diarrhea (chronic), which is incurable within the tropics," he told his daughters, two days before he collapsed:

> Our ship & schooner are very sickly, 80 in a state of starvation, having no bread nor a substitute for a fortnight. They are all in the hospital under the care of our fleet surgeon . . . , some recovering. Captain Campbell . . . dead and buried; Mr. Waldron [*Peacock*'s purser] better and gone to Canton.

> We shall sail in a fortnight for Japan, cannot return to Cochin China having no interpreters, and winds ahead, in four months we shall be in Valparaiso & in six at Rio.

And soon after that, presumably, at home.

Here Roberts turned his attention in the letter to other important matters, to his forthcoming book and to family finances. The continuing delay in getting his journal published made him fearful that someone else's description of the same cruise—Ticknor's perhaps, *Peacock*'s former surgeon had already written him about the idea—might beat him into print and so reduce his sales and its profitability. Next was the heady possibility that interest on the family account with Grinnell, Minturn and Company at home—he conjured up an eventual total of $22,000, including future deposits from the sale of pearls and cashmere, gifts from the sultan or bought recently on speculation—would be "more than enough to support us and save me from ever leaving home again."[3]

The next day, on June 5, soon after Campbell's death and while Roberts still seemed to be recovering his strength, Ruschenberger left for Canton, where he spent most of the next two weeks sightseeing, shopping, and collecting data on trade in opium and tea. Ruschenberger seems to have left care of the hospitalized Americans in the meanwhile to a British doctor in Macao, Thomas Colledge (medical missionary and surgeon to the British factory in Canton since 1826, famous for the charity eye hospital he ran in Macao and husband of Caroline Shillaber), and to *Enterprise*'s young assistant surgeon, William McClenahan.*

Roberts' brief recovery is difficult to explain. The arc of no disease that he might have been suffering from includes such a seeming complete but very short-term recovery. It was, in any case, illusory. An entry signed by Passed Midshipman Weems in *Peacock*'s deck log of Monday, June 13, reports that at 1:00 p.m. the ship "rec'd the news of the death of Mr. Edmund P. Roberts Diplomatic Agent of the United States. Half masted the colors. Baro. 29.85. Air 82°."

Five days later, June 18, and now back in Macao from Canton, Ruschenberger wrote former secretary of the navy Levi Woodbury a many-page letter about Edmund Roberts' health, or more accurately—since it reported Roberts' death—about his lack of it. His friend Roberts, Ruschenberger wrote to the new treasury secretary from halfway around the world, "had been more or less unwell during the whole cruise, and at Batavia he became much worse;

* Promoted to surgeon in 1841 McClenahan, a Virginian, was one of the fifteen (of sixty-nine) surgeons in the U.S. Navy who "went south," meaning they resigned or were dismissed in April 1861 to take commissions in the Confederate States Navy.

and at Siam he was severely attacked with the disease, which has been for years silently breaking down his once iron constitution":

> Several months previous to this time, I advised him to abandon his mission and return to the United States, and finding him to be more ambitious of performing his public duties than of preserving his health, I at last addressed him a letter on the subject! He was convinced of his perilous situation, and after leaving Cochin China, where nothing was effected, owing to Mr. Roberts' ill health and want of interpreters, he landed at this place and was entertained in the best possible manner, in the house of my friend, Wm. S. Wetmore, Esq. and I obtained the opinion of T. R. Colledge, Esq., a distinguished British surgeon of this place. We hoped, the change from the ship to the shore might have advantageous [*sic*] and appearances for the first few days justified this opinion.
>
> My public duties called me to Canton, and I left Mr. R on the 5th doing well, under the care of Dr. Colledge and Assistant Surgeon McClenahan. On the evening of the 6th his symptoms changed for the worse; delirium supervened; he gradually sank, and on the morning of the 12th tranquilly expired. . . .
>
> I have the consolation of knowing that every attention and care were given to our lamented friend and on reviewing the history of his case, my conscience charges me with no omission or misconceived opinion. . . .
>
> I herewith enclose a copy of the letter alluded to above, containing an outline of his case, together with a copy of the appearances presented after death, which justify the opinions I had long entertained and often expressed to him of the nature of his complaint. Had he followed my advice months ago and returned home, I think he might have been saved. But, true to his trust, he fell a sacrifice to his exertions for the public.[4]

The December after Roberts' interment at the Old Cemetery, news of what had happened was exchanged between two of Roberts' sons-in-law, Andrew Peabody and Amasa Parker. They must have found comfort in the belief that their father-in-law had died a "good death" according to the nineteenth-century model, reconciled to his end, at peace with God, and expiring among friends with dignity. December 19, 1836, Peabody wrote to Parker,

> Mr. Roberts contracted this disease at Siam, where it was especially epidemic, about the middle of May. He was left at Macao on account of his illness, and considered himself in a critical situation when he left the *Peacock*, as he remarked to a friend that he should arrange his papers and effects as if never to return to the vessel.
>
> We infer from his letter [of June 4, addressed to "My Blessed Children," in which he reported, "I have just recovered from a deathly sickness, diarrhea (chronic), which is incurable within the tropics"] that the disorder assumed a favorable aspect after his arrival at Macao, and that a relapse took place after the date of that letter. He was there at the house of Mr. [William S.] Wetmore, the most wealthy American resident in that port, and received every aid of friendship and of medical skill.[5]
>
> He was, we are informed, at the last, aware of his approaching dissolution, and entirely resigned and tranquil in the prospect of it.
>
> These accounts certainly give us much to be grateful for, in connection with so heavy an affliction: in the fact that he lacked not the comfort and sympathies of a home, though so far from his own home, and in the sustaining power of Christian faith, which, as we trust, gave him peace in death, and has made the loss of all others his gain.[6]

The flagship's departure a week earlier from Cumsingmoon had been marred by her grounding on a mud bank in fifteen feet of water a few hours after getting under way. It took eight hours of work by the ship's boats finally to kedge her free just before midnight that night, suffering only the loss of an anchor. The next morning, Saturday June 18, she arrived at Macao. On June 19, 21, and 22 men started dribbling back on board from the hospital.

As summarized by Ruschenberger on June 23, operating the hospital on shore from May 27 through June 22 had cost the United States $1,215.65, including $50.00 for rental of the house and $38.00 in undertaker's fees. At anchor *Peacock* continued to load foodstuffs from the stores ship—including 140 barrels of beef, pork, and flour—ship's stores, water, and galley stove firewood for the weeks to come at sea.

Roberts' death had ended it—not only his life but also USS *Peacock*'s second special mission. Three days after the surgeon's letter to Levi Woodbury was written, Commodore Kennedy ended his report to Woodbury's successor with the same news, reporting that Roberts had died either of dysentery or chronic cholera. "This disease has passed through the squadron & it is still among us, it is the third epidemic that we have had to encounter," he wrote, sounding at once weary and vindicated. "By the death of Mr. Roberts (as I am not authorized to act) the mission is necessarily at an end. I shall therefore proceed to put into execution, as governed by my original Instruction No. 1. I hope to sail tomorrow, all the sick having been brought on board today."*

On June 23 the squadron left Macao for the first leg of a Pacific Ocean crossing, happily this time without any visible ship-handling embarrassment on sailing away. Its next destination was three weeks off: Port St. William in the Bonin Islands. When the ships arrived at tiny Clarkston at the port on July 15, they found forty-two settlers (fourteen European and American men, the rest men and women from Hawaii) clinging like limpets on the north island's shore, catching sea turtles and living on the sale of food and firewood to visiting whalers.

Around sunup on Thursday morning, July 21, *Peacock* and *Enterprise*, after having taken on wood and water during their six-day port call, got under way for the Sandwich Islands, having paid Nathan Lavery twenty-five dollars for piloting *Peacock* into and out of Bonin Harbor. Later in the day the small squadron found itself sailing east into rain and thunderstorms under too much canvas. On board *Peacock* all hands were called away to reef the fore and main topsails and to furl the mizzen topsail.

Ruschenberger believed Dickenson Mendenhall, thirty-four, the schooner's acting purser, to be a practicing hypochondriac ("valetudinarian" was the word he used). Just before 4:00 a.m. the following Monday, July 25, Mendenhall proved the surgeon wrong: he died. "Departed this life," in the formulaic words of the entry in the flagship's log. One of the many on *Enterprise*'s sick list out of Siam, Mendenhall had appeared to be recovering when the squadron sailed from Macao. Near Formosa a relapse had prompted his transfer at sea to *Peacock*, where he'd been installed in the captain's cabin.

Before the age of refrigeration, great heroes who died at sea, Vice Admiral Horatio Nelson, RN, comes to mind, were occasionally shipped home for interment. Shot to death on board his flagship, HMS *Victory*, by a French marksman at the Battle of Trafalgar on October 21, 1815, Nelson was laid into a casket and submerged in brandy, soon topped up at Gibraltar with spirits of wine. His body arrived in England four and a half weeks later, more or less already embalmed for the autopsy and state funeral to come.

---

* Joseph Balestier, still consul in Singapore when Roberts died, belatedly saw the opportunity denied to Commodore Kennedy. In June 1838 (and again ten years later) he volunteered to complete Roberts' mission: "Not withstanding the personal inconvenience it may cause me, I shall be happy in being instrumental in enlarging our commercial intercourse with Cochin China, Siam, and the Malay States." In August 1849, Balestier got his wish: he was appointed a special agent "for the purpose of making treaties with the authorities [in Southeast Asia] and preparing for an extension of American commerce in that portion of the Eastern Hemisphere."

Not so the remains of lesser men, which were quickly slipped into the sea with sufficient ceremony to make the event look more like a rite than the sanitary disposal it also was. "A funeral at sea is always impressive," Ruschenberger assured his readers, describing the scene at 31° 50' north, 150° 28' east, where Mendenhall's body was committed to the deep at noon the day he died:

> The flags of both vessels were hoisted at half-mast high; the coffin, covered by a flag, was placed in the lee [downwind] gangway, the tolling of the ship's bell summoned the officers and crew on deck; a solemn silence everywhere prevailed, broken now and then by a slight swash of the sea against the vessel's side. While the service of the church was being read, the Enterprise, with tolling bell, passed under our stern, and came close under our lee. Her bell was then silenced; the officers and crew were gazing from the deck; one plunge—and the broad blue bosom of the Pacific Ocean closed over the mortal remains . . . leaving no trace to mark his grave.

Two days later, Mendenhall's personal effects were sold at auction on board *Enterprise*, the usual final act of a funeral at sea. (Reflecting Roberts' special status, his effects, packaged in a dozen or so crates, had been delivered in Macao to the store ship, *Lintin*, for shipment home.)

Late that autumn Roberts' obituary appeared in his hometown newspaper, just below a one-line item reporting Lt. Archibald Campbell's death and next to a story about a squirrel hunt the week before off to the west of Portsmouth, in Windsor. The winning party—its prize was an all-you-can-eat dinner—had shot 9,814 of the rodents, the losers only 7,543.

11

The Voyages Home

Died at Macao, in China, on the eleventh of June last, our valuable and extensively beloved fellow citizen, EDMUND ROBERTS, Esq. . . . At Siam the crew contracted a malignant disease, which proved extensively fatal. Among the persons attacked was Mr. Roberts. . . . He was immediately taken on shore to the house of the English counsel there, and, after a few days gave alarming proof of the power of his disorder. The best of medical ability and attention, and the utmost care and kindness were exerted to save his valuable life, but notwithstanding his strength of constitution, his abstemious habits and familiarity with hot climates, no human exertions could save him, and his spirit fled, as we trust, to a better world. . . .

Thus has fallen in a strange land, and thus has been by strangers mourned, one of the most noble, generous, honest, and benevolent of our citizens . . . a most able, judicious, and efficient public officer, who has long served his country most faithfully and successfully in advancing her commercial interests, and also has now yielded his life in her cause.

PORTSMOUTH, NEW HAMPSHIRE, *JOURNAL OF LITERATURE AND POLITICS*, NOVEMBER 19, 1836

39

Roberts' death in Macao on June 12, 1836, came four and a half years after he was first commissioned as President Andrew Jackson's special agent and went to sea as a joint venture of the State and Navy Departments. Back in China at his own instigation, Roberts died at age fifty-two, fourteen months—midway—into an extended second cruise in the sloop of war USS *Peacock* through the Indian Ocean, the South and East China Seas, and ultimately around the world.*

The second voyage, to finish the work of his first in Jackson's service, sadly for Roberts turned out to be one too many. His death abruptly terminated what

* Not the U.S. Navy's first circumnavigation of the globe, but nearly so. The first was by the sloop of war USS *Vincennes*, New York to New York between September 1826 and June 1830 westbound via Cape Horn and the Cape of Good Hope. After two years with the West Indies Squadron, *Vincennes* deployed again to the Pacific during her second around-the-world cruise in 1833–36.

had been until then a bold, complicated, but only partly successful mission that had begun some sixty-eight thousand sea miles ago, when in March 1832 he first left Boston in USS *Peacock* for Asia and promised not only to benefit New England's shipowners and sailors, and the young United States more generally, but also Roberts himself. Had it succeeded fully, Roberts might well have eventually been restored to the very substantial prosperity he'd gained through inheritance and beginning in 1806 watched diminish to near poverty through wartime losses, bad luck, bad investments, and poor business sense.

Success and prosperity would have also immeasurably eased the lives of Roberts' eight now-orphaned daughters—his wife of eighteen years, Catharine, had died six years before in early October 1830 "of pulmonic fever," likely tuberculosis—the eldest, Catharine, twenty-six, the youngest, Frances, eleven, living in New Hampshire and New York in almost perfect ignorance of what their father was doing during the long months while he was at sea.*

When news that he'd died finally reached Portsmouth, New Hampshire, it fell hardest on Catharine, since March 1834 the legal guardian of her five youngest sisters, the least not yet in her teens. Married that September to Andrew Peabody, pastor of Portsmouth's South Parish Unitarian Church, Catharine and the next senior daughter, Sarah, together with the Reverend Peabody were executors of their father's estate. The third daughter, Harriett, was living in Delhi, New York, with her husband of one year, Amasa Parker. The two had met in Delhi while her father was at sea.

Parker had charge of the rough journal manuscript left behind when Roberts sailed on his second embassy. He had not been enthusiastic about pressing ahead with the book in Roberts' absence, and in May 1836 Parker wrote to one of his sisters-in-law, likely Catharine or Sara, that he thought work on the manuscript should be delayed until her father returned and could superintend its publication himself. The response must have pushed him to go ahead, which he did reluctantly.

Parker then arranged to have the loose material edited by Jeremiah Reynolds for Harper and Brothers, which published it posthumously in 1837. In part Roberts' anodyne text is the result of censorship at the State Department to eliminate discussion of negotiation failures or to avoid tipping off the British about American objectives, and in part it's because Reynolds

* Tuberculosis is also commonly believed to have killed President Andrew Jackson in June 1845, then seventy-eight years old. Catharine's obituary, in the *Portsmouth Morning Chronicle*, October 9, 1830, described her death as following a long period of "severe suffering" and her in life as an "estimable and exemplary lady" whose "domestic virtues rendered her the ornament and delight of home, while her numerous and eminent Christian graces made her an invaluable blessing to the community." Three Roberts children, including their two sons, both named Edmund, died before the age of two, the first Edmund only two weeks after he was born.

pieced the book together from Roberts' personal shipboard journal and miscellaneous other, mostly uncredited sources. Publication, when it finally happened, contributed little to Roberts' estate. The book also added relatively little that was new to knowledge in the West about the exotic eastern courts Roberts described because, as discovered by the late Nan Powell Hodges in the course of her research in the 1980s, much of it was copied from already published sources.

The estate that was the Roberts daughters' entire patrimony turned out to be painfully scant after probate. In 1841 the eight daughters divided about $5,500 between them in equal shares. Each got $681. To give that number a scale, it amounted to some $20 less than a single year's salary for Nathan Eaton, the senior messenger in Secretary of the Navy Dickerson's office. Despite Roberts' efforts and sacrifices, the months spent at sea sailing to distant places and the risks to his health that he'd accepted, he'd failed.

Roberts managed to negotiate only two of the four treaties that had been his goal, and in the end those two contributed little obvious to the development of American trade in the Far East in the nineteenth century. Trade with Zanzibar was profitable regardless, but Oman's dates were an insufficient basis on which to base trade with Muscat, as the first American consul, Henry Marshall, quickly discovered. Siam's prohibition of the export of rice in its treaty with the United States turned out to mean that American ships had as little incentive to stop at Bangkok after the treaty as they'd had before.

It's tempting to speculate that if Roberts had survived disease and then gone to Japan as instructed on the final mission of his embassy, the state of "permanent friendship" between the young democracy and Tokugawa Japan established by the Treaty of Kanagawa might have begun earlier, nearly two decades before Commo. Matthew Perry steamed into Edo with USS *Susquehanna* and the rest of the U.S. East India Squadron, with unknown consequences for the future relationship.

If Roberts had survived and after leaving Macao had followed his instructions, riding an unarmed, chartered merchant vessel and (with sheep or without them) bringing with him only relatively modest gifts for the imperial court, he would have appeared before the Japanese in Owari without the cloak of power and authority that a generation later enveloped the commodore and permitted his success. Roberts' impression on the Japanese would have been much less imposing even than was Commodore Biddle's in 1846 and nothing remotely like Perry's two dramatic appearances, the first in July 1853 with four ships and the second the following February at the head of a squadron of ten that awed and intimidated his reluctant hosts.

The Roberts memorial window in St. John's Episcopal Church, Portsmouth, New Hampshire. Saint Edmund the Martyr faces Saint Catharine of Alexandria in this handsome stained-glass window presented to the church by their granddaughter, Anna Roberts Pruyn (Harriett's eldest daughter), in 1884. The saints' names and not the method of their martyrdom explain their selection for this memorial. The window is inscribed, "To the glory of God and in loving memory of Edmund Roberts and Catharine Whipple Langdon his wife married at Portsmouth Sept. 10. Both glorified God in their lives. One as a faithful wife and mother. The other died in the service of his country on his second embassy to Eastern Courts as Envoy Extraordinaire and Minister Plenipotentiary of the United States." In fact, although Roberts craved ministerial rank, he never held it.

In 1910 Pruyn's collection of more than one thousand of her grandfather's papers was presented to the Library of Congress.

Author's photograph

Commodore Perry's "black ships of evil appearance." Japanese art in midcentury (this detail from the wood block print *Black Ship and Crew Members*, 1854, is from the collection of the Ryosenji Treasure Museum in Shimoda, Japan) depicted Perry's ships belching smoke, bristling with guns, and churning the ocean into foam, conjuring up a visitation not from another country but from a fearsome underworld peopled by big, bearded men with large noses.

Perry's first port call at Edo had as one of its chief goals, according to Secretary of the Navy John Kennedy, writing in December 1852, to persuade this "populous and semi-barbarous empire . . . to abandon their unprofitable policy of seclusion, and gradually to take a place in that general association of commerce." Two years later the new navy secretary, James Dobbin, proudly reported that Perry had "by indomitable perseverance and remarkable management . . . succeeded finally in overcoming the obstinacy and prejudices of the Japanese government, and induced it to enter into a treaty of amity and peace, by which two of its ports, Hakodade and Simoda, were opened to vessels." And two years after that, in 1856, a six-hundred-plus-page *Narrative* of his expedition was published in Washington, D.C.

In retrospect, when events always appear clearer than they do in prospect, Roberts' instructions from the secretary of state concerning Japan were naïve. Absent a show of naval force in the 1830s like Perry's in the 1850s, diplomatic success was improbable. Instead, it's likely that at Owari, many miles from the Japanese capital, Roberts would have relived the frustrations of Cochin China before finally sailing for home.

In its edition of November 4, 1837, reporting the sloop of war's arrival at Norfolk a week earlier, *Niles' Weekly Register* reviewed *Peacock*'s two and a half years at sea, listed the countries visited and the ports touched, and mentioned that ten of her crew had died during the course of five different epidemics. The editor then concluded, "The visit of the Peacock to these different countries has no doubt been attended with considerable benefit to the interests of our commerce; and we trust that the attention of our government having been turned to this subject, the large amount of American property in the eastern seas will not again be left without the protection of our navy."

Niles' hope seems to have been realized. Roberts' two embassies to the eastern courts accelerated perhaps by two decades the deployment of a U.S. Navy squadron to this distant fifth station, and the more or less continuous presence of American men-of-war in Asian waters after 1835 further encouraged ship captains and supercargoes to venture there, granted without fundamentally changing the underlying economics of trade as Roberts had hoped his agreements would do.

40

Along the track that *Peacock* and *Enterprise* took in July and August 1836, nearly forty-eight hundred miles—and forty-nine days of "tedious and unpleasant" sailing in Ruschenberger's words—separated the Bonin Islands (the Ogasawara archipelago today) from Oahu in the Sandwich Islands (Hawaii today). On board the flagship nothing punctuated the routine of often-rainy days at sea: work aloft setting and trimming sails, crew drills on deck, divine services every week, and, several times, the flogging of a crewmember or two for drunkenness or insubordination.

Flagship and escort managed to remain in company only until late August 3, when they separated in a fog, not to be reunited until Wednesday, September 7, when *Peacock* discovered *Enterprise* south of Honolulu. The "dull sailer" had beat the flagship to Woahoo (Oahu) by a day. Thursday morning heading north under tow, both threaded the narrow channel leading from open water, past coral shoals off both sides, to the island capital's inner harbor.

The National Archives holds USS *Peacock*'s receipt for thirty-four dollars paid to the harbor master in Honolulu for pilot fees in and out.

To larboard in the anchorage, Ladd and Company's three-year-old general store marked the western limits of Honolulu, behind which lay fishponds and beachfront. (Soon the company's most important property would not be this store near Market Wharf but a new sugarcane plantation on Kaua'i, the first plantation anywhere in the islands.) To starboard, at Robinson Wharf, near the waterfront's eastern limits and not far from the small fort that had exchanged salutes with the newly arrived American men-of-war, was Robinson and Company's shipyard, the first on the island and then already ten years old. Between them, Ruschenberger noted in the beginning of his several chapters of "Sketches in the Sandwich Islands," "The belfry of the seamen's chapel stands conspicuous and imparts an air of civilization which one would scarcely expect to meet at a place so recently emerged from barbarism."

As further evidence of the advance of civilization, the surgeon noted wryly the availability on shore of "billiard tables, bowling-allies, grog-shops, livery stables, and *restaurans*," and with more enthusiasm, the appearance two months earlier of the four-page, weekly *Sandwich Island Gazette and Journal of Commerce* in English (printed on Saturdays, subscription six dollars per year).[1] A bold venture for Stephen Mackintosh, the paper's twenty-two-year-old publisher from Boston: in 1836 Honolulu probably had fewer than four hundred among its population of six thousand who could read English. Most who could were Americans, many of them traders supporting the whalers that passed through Honolulu and Lahaina, on Maui, each spring and fall while working the North Pacific grounds for several years at a time. The *Gazette*'s press run seems never to have exceeded one hundred copies for any issue during the few years that it survived.

Ruschenberger found Honolulu to be sun-baked, treeless, and cheerless, populated by "a mild race of people, tolerably docile, and capable of improvement" and governed by a "hereditary despotism"—currently by pudgy King Kauikeaouli, Kamehameha III, whom he judged after observation to be "genteelly dissipated but not vicious." Ruled by that same dynasty throughout, Hawaii was a kingdom from 1810 to 1893, during that period occasionally ogled by the ambitious officers of four navies, drawn there by the islands' strategic location, their charms, and the meager defenses of the capital on Oahu—a fort mounting 6-, 8-, and 12-pound guns on the waterfront at Queen and Fort Streets and eight 32-pounders standing on Punchbowl Hill. All in 1836 some twenty years old.

The surgeon's observations about the natives and their ruling family were kindly ones compared to the low opinion he had of the corps of Protestant missionaries (twenty-eight by his count, one for every thirty-nine hundred Hawaiians, and more coming) that manned Oahu's churches, ran its only schools, supervised public morality and a chaste dress code, and agitated to keep their Catholic counterparts off the islands. Ruschenberger judged the local clergy to be "inferior to all those whom it has been our fortune to meet at other stations during our cruise. Many of them are far behind the age in which they live, deficient in general knowledge, and . . . more of the lineaments of the Mucklewraths and Poundtexts of by-gone days than is desirable in divines of the nineteenth century."

During the weeks in port (*Enterprise* left for Mazatlan, Mexico, on Monday, September 26 in company with the American merchant vessels *Griffon* and *Raamauela*, arriving there on October 29; *Peacock* sailed for Monterey on Sunday, October 9) both ships' enlisted crews were allowed unusually generous liberty around the margins of the usual caulking and repainting, work on the rigging, loading stores, and taking on water. "Here the crew was allowed to go on shore for exercise, where they found abundant amusement," Kennedy's long September 30 report to the secretary said:

> This together with the fresh beef, vegetables and fruit served to them on board, has produced a remarkable change in the aspect of both officers & men for the better. Indeed never did men more require relaxation from the harassing toil of the past eight months, during which time they have been afflicted with severe disease, necessarily confined on board Ship, and passing through climates confessedly the most insalubrious on earth. They are much improved, and with one exception [Acting Purser Waldron], the officers and crews of the Peacock and Enterprise are all well.

Liberty on shore, however, didn't forestall several unsuccessful desertion attempts by men in search of even more abundant amusement. Seaman Van Dolsen tried to jump ship twice: first on September 11 from the crew of the gig and again on September 27, when he sportingly attempted to swim to shore from where *Peacock* was moored. Van Dolsen was flogged for his crimes, as were nine other men for their own offenses during the flagship's days at anchor. Seaman Robert Pravard, one of the black sailors on board *Enterprise*, paid a higher price for his offense: he drowned the night of September 20 while attempting to swim to land. Thomas Lowe, forty-three, a seaman in *Peacock*, "departed this life" on September 8 and was buried on shore. Three days later Bosun Philip Pachley from *Enterprise* also died. "Gastro-enteritis" was the diagnosis for both.

Taking advantage of the unexpected presence of U.S. Navy ships in port, on September 16 twenty-nine of the resident Americans delivered a letter to Commodore Kennedy appealing for help, telling him that "many serious outrages and unjust acts have been committed on by the government authorities" of California and Mexico "upon American vessels and seamen, and great losses and damages sustained in consequence" and detailing two specific "grievous embarrassments arbitrarily imposed on our commerce" by these same officials:

> We believe that no vessel of the United States government has, for many years, visited Upper California; and we have great confidence that, were a naval force to appear on that coast, and visit Lower California and Mexico, it would render valuable service to our citizens residing in those countries, and would afford needed succor and protection to American vessels, at present employed there, and be attended with results particularly advantageous to the general interests of our national commerce.
>
> With these sentiments and views, we have to express the hope that you may find it in your power to visit those coasts with the force under your command, before you shall leave the Pacific.

The twenty-nine did not include the colorful and combative first American agent for commerce and seamen in the islands, John Coffin Jones Jr. of Massachusetts, who, Ruschenberger reported, was "absent, engaged in his commercial affairs" while *Peacock* and *Enterprise* passed through the port.* Official position aside, Jones certainly would have been among the signers; one of his company's vessels was the second ship being held by Mexican authorities in Alta California.

Their letter offered Kennedy, finally, a chance to perform the U.S. Navy's principal mission, the protection of American commerce, to do something more than ferrying a civilian in failing health slowly around Asia. But first,

---

* Just eighteen months after disembarking on Oahu from the musically named brig *Tamahourelanne* out of Boston, young John Jones (1796–1861) was past ready to leave. "Woahoo," he wrote his employers, partners in the Boston trading house of Marshall and Wildes, in November 1822, "is becoming one of the vilest places on the globe, and if something is not done soon, murder and theft will be the order of the day, for my own part it will be the happiest day of my life, when I leave this miserable corner of the globe." Instead, he stayed and lived in Honolulu until 1844, representing the company, and until 1839 serving as the American consul, albeit without pay or that title.

Jones appears to have had three wives simultaneously, the second of which, Hannah Holmes, in 1838 sued him successfully for bigamy when the third appeared, a suit that prompted King Kauikeaouli in 1839 to withdraw his recognition of the agent's official status, thus ending his government career. Jones' casual approach to matrimony—he seems never to have actually experienced a marriage ceremony—was only one reason why Jones and the missionaries on the island were at odds.

while the squadron continued to prepare for sea, the commodore took on another task.

Kennedy spent part of three days in talks with the king, hoping to resolve trade, land ownership, and other disputes between the royal house and American expatriates. These issues had been thought resolved in December 1826 in a treaty signed by Kauikeaouli and Capt. Thomas ap Catesby Jones, USN, then riding USS *Peacock* as commander of the U.S. Pacific Squadron, but in fact were unsettled and continued to irritate relations.

Nantucket shipowners had complained to the president that mutineers and deserters were turning the Sandwich Islands into “a nest of pirates and murders.” Commodore Jones went to Oahu in part to deal with these bad actors and in part to press the royal family to honor its huge debts to American traders. His was the second U.S. Navy visit to Honolulu that year. The first had been by Lt. John “Mad Jack” Percival in the schooner USS *Dolphin*. Percival’s bullying of the Hawaiians foreshadowed his style of international relations twenty years later when in command of USS *Constitution* off Cochin China.

Days before sailing, Kennedy sent the king a letter describing his position on the disagreements. Kennedy wasn’t freelancing; a copy of this letter, “on subjects which appear to be of importance to the interests of our citizens,” went to Dickerson. Captain Stribling also left a letter behind. His was addressed to Kinau, high governor of Oahu, about the alarming decline in the population of the islands, its possible causes, and its recommended solutions.

Ruschenberger had been struck by the same phenomenon—the dwindling of the islands’ population since Cook’s arrival—since 1832 at a rate of 1.5 percent per year he calculated, this in a place with a healthy climate that had never experienced “a desolating epidemic.” “If no means be taken to arrest this alarming decrease,” the surgeon opined, “it is clear the Sandwich Islands, in the course of time, must be entirely depopulated.”* He attributed the decrease to “infanticide, intemperance, bad living, change in social habits, the state of political oppression, and . . . civilization . . . savage tribes fall before the march of improvement.”

Ship resupplied, crew’s health restored, and her dead buried, *Peacock* sailed for Monterey, capital of Alta California, planning later to join *Enterprise* on the Mexican coast in Mazatlan. The flagship arrived in Monterey on November 23, after a swift, twelve-day passage, appearing near the end of a crisis year in local politics that had seen three Mexican governors in and out of office (one, the incumbent Lieutenant Colonel Nicolas Gutierrez, twice, and now facing the other two in rebellion) against a backdrop of agitation for

* In 1836, 129,614 were thought to live on the seven populated Sandwich Islands. The 2013 population of Hawaii is estimated to have been 1.4 million.

California's independence similar to that which had finally torn Texas away from Mexico early that March.[2]

Americans would know much more about Monterey, the several ports of the Alta California coast, and the local hide and tallow trade after the publication in 1840 of Richard Henry Dana's *Two Years Before the Mast*, a memoir of his time mid-decade as a deckhand in the Boston brig *Pilgrim* and later in the Indiaman *Alert*. The first edition, published as No. 106 in Harpers Family Library, quickly sold thousands of copies, sadly netting Dana nothing in royalties.

"Monterey . . . is decidedly the pleasantest and most civilized-looking place in California," he wrote. "In the center of it is an open square, surrounded by four lines of one-storied plastered buildings, with half a dozen cannon in the centre, some mounted and others not. This is the 'Presidio,' or fort." And later in the text, "Nothing but the character of the people prevents Monterey from becoming a great town. The soil is as rich as man could wish; climate as good as any in the world; water abundant, and situation extremely beautiful." Then, sounding like the old salt that Harvard collegian Dana was slowly becoming, "The harbor, too is a good one, being subject only to one bad wind, the north; and though the holding ground is not the best, yet I heard of only one vessel's being driven ashore here."

Kennedy, on his just-adopted mission to protect and advance American commerce at Monterey, knew nothing of the political ferment boiling around the place, known east of the Mississippi chiefly as the distant hub of New England's trade in cow hides with Alta California. For his part, Colonel Gutierrez, back in office since midsummer, suspected the worst when a sloop of war anchored unexpectedly in front of the small town, joining six other American vessels there, four merchant ships, and two whalers. Notwithstanding his position as governor, Gutierrez's local command encompassed only three other officers, sixteen troops, and, according to Ruschenberger's count, not half a dozen field guns but only two—not enough to face *Peacock*'s broadside.

It never came to that. Instead, on October 27, 28, and 29, Kennedy fired off a letter each day to "His Excellency, Don Nicholas Gutierrez, Commanding General and Political Governor of Alta California," all on the hand-scribed letterhead of the "United States Frigate of War Peacock." In the first Kennedy described himself as a representative of his government, in Monterey to seek explanations and satisfaction for the seizure of the American schooner (actually a brig) *Loriot* in San Francisco from Honolulu, the mistreatment of her supercargo and another citizen, and an end to the practice of forcing Americans to serve unpaid garrison guard duty.* Kennedy's next letter raised a

* The brig *Loriot*, Captain Nye, allegedly seized in San Francisco in mid-1833 by Mexican authorities appears again as Richard Henry Dana's little *Loriotte*, "a lump of a thing, what the sailors call a

new case, that of the American "frigate" *Rasselas* being chased out of port after paying anchorage charges. His third repeated briefly the first two.

In his initial response, Gutierrez replied patiently, in beautiful calligraphy and at great length, that what had happened in these cases was not as described and was legal according to Mexican law. His next two letters were additional but shorter polite denials of everything charged. With those received on board, the intervention ended.

Kennedy's work done and nothing really accomplished other than an endorsement of Bostonian Nathan Spear's application to become consul in Monterey, *Peacock* sailed for Santa Barbara late in the afternoon of October 30. She left after the morning fog had cleared, replenished with a supply of bread, flour, and cheese. In the commodore's hand was a letter from the "American Residents, Masters and Supercargoes of American vessels in Monte-rey" expressing the humble thanks of these thirteen "for the lively interest you have been pleased to manifest for our commerce on this coast. . . . The appearance of a U.S. ship of war on this coast, after so long an intercourse between our vessels and this territory, has been highly salutary."

Four days later, two of Gutierrez's rivals, José Castro and Juan Alvarado, led a successful attack against him in the presidio of Montrrey—if Hubert Bancroft's *History of California* (History Company, 1886) is correct, the assault included not much more than parading about and a single cannon shot, and that barely managed with salvaged black powder. Soon afterward the birth of the Free and Sovereign State of Alta California was declared, a step, as it later turned out, on the way to American statehood.

41

Bad weather prevented *Peacock*'s planned port call at Santa Barbara, and so the sloop continued south to "miserable" (Ruschenberger's word) Mazatlan, Mexico. When she arrived there November 12 after a dozen days at sea, moved along for those nearly fifteen hundred miles by moderate breezes in pleasant weather, *Enterprise* wasn't anchored in the roads as expected. At the suggestion of the American consul, Samuel Talbot, Captain Hollins had sailed his schooner north five days earlier to call at Guaymas, 425 miles up the Gulf of California, where opportunities for American business were said to be opening. Hollins had not yet returned.

The planned rendezvous aborted, the flagship continued south three days later for San Blas. She did not join up with *Enterprise* until early in March

butter-box," manned with English-speaking officers and mates and crewed by Hawaiians, whom he admired. She was out of Oahu, and sailed in the hide and tallow trade, as did *Pilgrim*.

1837 at Callao, the port of Lima, the capital of Peru. In the interval *Enterprise* had been in Acapulco and Valparaiso, Chile, but never in Guaymas. The headwinds in the Gulf of California in November had been very strong, so she'd turned about, rightly fearing missing *Peacock* in Mazatlan.

On November 20, while *Peacock* was in San Blas, Mexico, long-suffering Acting Purser Waldron was sent home. The port call was for his medical evacuation. "It is absolutely necessary for the preservation of his life that he should leave us at this Port," Kennedy wrote the secretary, "for the purposes of returning to the U. States, as soon as his health shall be sufficiently improved." Too sick to ride astride, Waldron was loaded on board a litter and carried by shifts of hired bearers over the course of the next two days some seventy miles eastward to the town of Tepic, where he seems to have been turned over to either an expatriate American or the British consul. Presumably, this stop was the first stage of a five-hundred-plus-mile overland crossing of Mexico to the port of Tamaulipas (now Tampico) on the Gulf. There, if improbably he'd survived getting hauled recumbent over the corrugated tops of the Sierra Madre Mountains, the desperately ill American could have been put on board a ship for the "U. States," if one happened to be there.

At Tepic Richard Waldron was lost to history. *Peacock* sailed on from San Blas for Acapulco without him. The macabre game of musical chairs continued, however, with Edward Whelen now appointed as acting purser. He, remarkably, managed to survive the cruise.

Peacock arrived at Acapulco just before noon on December 3. Kennedy described the place to the secretary of the navy as perhaps one of the finest harbors in the world, but the once-celebrated eastern terminal of the Manila galleons—the last had sailed for the Philippines nearly twenty years earlier—was now exhausted and dilapidated. Acapulco's protecting fort was in such a state of neglect that it was capable of firing only a seven-gun salute to mark the Americans' arrival. The remaining fourteen guns were fired after an embarrassing delay of two days. Two explanations were offered for the pause: the fort had run out of powder or, alternatively, the guns had toppled from their mounts when they were fired. Eight days later *Peacock* sailed for Valparaiso, Chile, having taken on water, the only reason for her last stop in Mexico.

On December 5, early during *Peacock*'s port call at Acapulco, in distant Washington City, President Andrew Jackson delivered his eighth, and last, annual message to the Congress. Jackson, nearing seventy, was anticipating a quiet retirement in the Hermitage, his estate near Nashville, Tennessee, while at the capital his handpicked successor, Martin Van Buren, continued to move purposefully down the course "Old Hickory" had charted and followed during his eight years in the White House. Instead, Van Buren's presidency ran hard aground on the Panic of 1837, a five-year depression. Consequently, "the Little Magician"—Van Buren was five feet six inches tall—held office for a single term only, replaced briefly by the ninth president, William Henry Harrison.

News of Edmund Roberts' death in Macao had reached the United States the month before, but the two ratified treaties had not. The documents would not leave Callao, Peru, where *Peacock* spent several months off and on in port during the first half of 1837, for Washington until March 7. The ratified treaties finally arrived in the capital, delivered by Lt. William Green, USN, *Peacock*'s former first lieutenant, months after President Van Buren's inauguration.

Ignorant of the state of play, Jackson could say no more in his last message than "commercial treaties promising great advantages to our enterprising merchants and navigators have been formed with the distant Governments of Muscat and Siam. The ratifications have been exchanged, but have not yet reached the Department of State. Copies of the treaties will be transmitted to you [meaning the members] if received before, or published if arriving after, the close of the present session of Congress."

Later in his text Jackson gave the Navy, and the U.S. Exploring Expedition, not to deploy until 1838, a generous boost:

> In the construction of vessels at the different navy yards and in the employment of our ships and squadrons at sea that branch of the service has been actively and usefully employed. While the situation of our commercial interests in the West Indies required a greater number than usual of armed vessels to be kept on that station, it is gratifying to perceive that the protection of our commerce in other waters of the world has not proved insufficient. Every effort has been made to facilitate the equipment of the Exploring expedition authorized by the act of the last session, but all the preparation necessary to enable it to sail has not yet been completed. No means will be spared by the Government to fit out the expedition on a scale corresponding with the liberal appropriations for this purpose and of the elevated character of the objects which are to be effected by it.
>
> I beg leave to . . . urge upon your attention the necessity of further appropriations to increase the number of ships afloat and to enlarge generally the capacity and force of the Navy. The increase of our commerce in regard to the other powers of the world will always make it our policy and interest to cherish the great naval resources of our country.

"Always . . . our interest to cherish the great naval resources of our country"—Jackson had come a long way in his strategic thinking.

On June 24, 1837, Roberts' treaties were proclaimed by President Van Buren. The two were now a part of the law of the land.

42

Peacock's two-day stop at Payta (Paita) on the north coast of Peru just after the start of the New Year was unplanned, explained on March 4 to the secretary of the navy as required not by another health emergency on board but by a "deficiency in the Provisions for the use of the crew." It was at Payta that Commodore Kennedy learned that Peru and Chile were at war ("the War of the Confederation") and that the 44-gun USS *Brandywine*, flagship of the Pacific Squadron at Callao, would likely be returning soon to the United States without relief on station. *Brandywine* had deployed in June 1834, more than a year before *Peacock* sailed from New York, and the three-year term of enlistment of her crew was soon to expire. "Under the circumstances," Kennedy told the secretary, "it appeared to me for the interests of the Government that the *Peacock* should touch at Callao for the purpose of affording all necessary assistance."

Arriving in Callao on January 25, 1837, Kennedy discovered that "touching" wouldn't be nearly enough. *Brandywine* had indeed sailed for Norfolk earlier in the month. In the absence of the Pacific Squadron's departed commander, Commodore Alexander Wadsworth, USN, he was the senior officer on station until the eventual arrival of Wadsworth's replacement, Commo. Henry Ballard, USN, riding the 74-gun ship of the line USS *North Carolina*. Out of Hampton Roads on January 12, 1837, Ballard's flagship would not appear at Callao until May 26—precisely five months after *Peacock* first got there—after rounding Cape Horn in late autumn through tempestuous weather.

Three days after entering port, Kennedy received a letter from the American chargé in Lima, Samuel Larned, asking him to stay until "the present difficulties between Peru and Chile are adjusted" or until *Brandywine*'s relief appeared.* "Difficulties" was cool understatement. In mid-November 1835, Larned had described the same political situation much more colorfully to Secretary of State Forsyth: "We are still almost in a state of siege from the operations of the armed bands who rob and plunder almost daily," he wrote, "on the great thoroughfare between [Lima] and its port town, Callao, and,

* Larned (1788–1846), from Providence, Rhode Island, was by the 1830s an accomplished diplomat. He'd served as U.S. consul in Cadiz, as secretary to the American legation in Chile, and as chargé in Peru and Bolivia. In 1836 he was overdue for leave at home and soon rode USS *Boxer* to Panama as the first leg of that journey back to Rhode Island.

amongst others, some of our countrymen have been attacked and wounded."[3] The situation was exciting enough that *Brandywine* had put a few of her Marines ashore at Callao that December, and did so again once or twice in early 1836 before sailing home.

Larned's appeal to Kennedy was against the backdrop of open warfare between the two former Spanish colonies, the immediate trigger for which had been a coup attempt against Chile launched from Peru in July 1836 (while the East India squadron was in the Bonin Islands). Chile's response to that and to follow-on offenses was to send two men-of-war, *Aquiles* and *Colo-Colo* to Callao, where in August they seized three Peruvian ships, *Arequipeño*, *Peruviano*, and *Santa Cruz*, and to blockade Guyaquil.

Kennedy unwittingly sailed into this boiling cauldron—joining the French frigate *Flore* and HMS *Talbot* there, attracted to the unrest like flies to carrion—abandoned by *Brandywine* just in time to comfort Chargé Larned and the nervous agents of two American firms in the port, Alsop and Company and Edward M'Call and Company.

"I have consented to remain," Kennedy told the secretary, "until the settlement of these difficulties or the arrival of Com. Ballard may permit me to fulfill my remaining instructions." In the meanwhile, he ordered USS *Boxer*, part of the Pacific Squadron, to Panama to ease the anxieties of the American consul there; *Enterprise* to Callao from Valparaiso, a month-long passage; and once *Enterprise* was in Callao, *Peacock* to Valparaiso, Chile, and back via Pisco, Peru. The two schooners and the sloop of war sailed conspicuously up and down the west coast of South America showing the flag through most of the first half of 1837 until USS *North Carolina* arrived.

North Carolina, nominally seventy-four guns but likely carrying more, was enormous, a live oak forest afloat: nearly 200 feet long and more than 50 across her beam, she drew twenty-one feet. Her complement of 820 officers and men was three times as large as *Peacock*'s and *Enterprise*'s together. *North Carolina* was not, however, on arrival in Peru ready for sea. Her rudder had been damaged in the passage around the Horn, so much that either timber for repairs had to come from Talcahuano, midway down the Chilean coast and the source of a famous ironwood, Commodore Ballard explained to Kennedy, or a new rudder had to come from the United States.*

* Talcahuano's durable luma wood was one reason mariners worldwide knew of the place. (In 1827, for example, France ordered some from Chile for the reconstruction of its navy.) Another reason was the earthquake and tsunami that devastated the small port and its environs on February 20, 1835. Charles Darwin and HMS *Beagle*'s captain, Fitzroy, were there, Darwin on the ground and Fitzroy in his ship offshore. Darwin's eyewitness account of the temblors and the twenty-three-foot wave they produced could have been a script for Talcahuano's next quake, on February 27, 2010.

In the same letter to Kennedy, datelined "Harbour of Callao, June 1st, 1837," that delivered the bad news about his flagship, Ballard (seven numbers senior to Kennedy) also appealed to his junior for favors, but first, a grace note: "I cannot deny myself the pleasure afforded by this opportunity of tendering to you my thanks, for the very important service you have rendered our country, in consenting, at the request of our countrymen resident in Lima and at Valparaiso, to assume the command of the naval station, at a moment so important to our commerce in this sea."

His chief request was to keep *Enterprise* on the Pacific Station, "which is rendered, it seems to me, to be absolutely necessary by the belligerent attitude assumed by the governments of Peru and Chile, towards each other—by the prospect of a blockade of the ports of Peru by the Chilean squadron," but most of all by the fact that *North Carolina* couldn't put to sea, which until she could, reduced the squadron in the Pacific to a single schooner, little *Boxer*, the veteran of *Peacock*'s first Pacific cruise. "Under these circumstances," Bollard continued, "I beg leave to ask in all frankness, whether you have any thing of importance yet to accomplish, on your way homeward, that will be likely to suffer from my detaining the Enterprise in this sea."

Kennedy had not. Leaving *Enterprise* behind when *Peacock* sailed was agreed, but the logistic changes to implement the decision were not easy. The planned departure of one and not both East India ships resulted in a scramble of cross-decking, as sailors leaving, staying, or volunteering to stay were moved between ships, a reshuffling complicated by the arrival of those who weren't crew members hitchhiking home in *Peacock* on other authority. Their enlistments expired, most of *Enterprise*'s crew had been discharged at Callao in May, and replacements for them now had to be recruited from among the pool of available sailors. When *Enterprise* sailed for Valparaiso July 12, she did so with a crew drawn largely from the new, and for the time being immobile, squadron flagship.

Lt. George Hollins had been relieved of her command, replaced by Lt. William Glendy, USN, off *North Carolina*. (Hollins, together with Lieutenant Paige of USS *Boxer* and other officers, returned to the United States via Panama and Jamaica rather than around the Horn. They arrived in Baltimore just forty-seven days out of Callao, having ridden *Orbit* to New Jersey from Jamaica.)

Peacock's departure from Peru for home was further delayed by a court-martial that convened on Tuesday, June 20, and sat morning and afternoon, Saturday and Sunday included, through the first of July. Charles Field, a seaman on USS *Boxer*, was accused of the grisly murder on February 28 of a shipmate, Bligh Gryle, by cutting his throat and had been held in irons since then on board *Peacock*.

"A court competent to try a case of such importance," Ballard wrote Kennedy weeks earlier when he first learned of the murder, "should be composed of officers of more rank than those I could control, were you to sail." When the court-martial finally convened that Tuesday morning—the trial had to be delayed until *Boxer*, carrying witnesses to the crime, returned to port on June 18—Commodore Kennedy was its chairman. Its members included Captain Stribling and Captain Hollins and eight other officers from the ships in port, including at least one (Lt. Hubbard Hobbs, USN, acting as judge advocate) left over from the frigate *Brandywine*. Ruschenberger was counsel for the accused, who, no reflection on Ruschenberger, was condemned and hanged soon after the court-martial ended.

That last bit of official business done, water, stores, and firewood loaded on board, *Peacock* saluted Commodore Ballard with the usual thirteen guns and, cheered in passing by the crews of *North Carolina*, *Enterprise*, and *Boxer*, at 6:15 on July 5, 1837, stood out for sea. Her route home took her a day up the Peruvian coast to Huacho Roads (to take on four bullocks for meat and fresh vegetables); around Cape Horn in early August through rain, hail, and snow, at one point under only a single-reefed topsail; through Rio de Janeiro the last week of August; and, by Bahia in the middle of September, finally to Hampton Roads. There, just before noon on October 27, *Peacock* came to in five fathoms of water between Forts Norfolk and Nelson.

43

On October 27, 1837, Commodore Kennedy reported USS *Peacock*'s arrival at Hampton Roads to Secretary Dickerson, who by return mail congratulated him upon his "safe arrival to your country and friends."

At about the same time, Kennedy picked a silly fight with the commandant of the Norfolk Navy Yard, Capt. Lewis Warrington, USN, over status. Sailing into the roads, Kennedy refused to lower his commodore's broad pennant in deference to Warrington, seventeen numbers on the register his senior and then midway through a decade in command of the yard and station. He'd shown no similar reluctance five months before when Ballard had arrived in Callao, hauling down his blue pennant and replacing it with a red one minutes after *North Carolina* came into the harbor.

Former brilliantly successful commanding officer of the first USS *Peacock* during the War of 1812, Warrington was himself and with some reason a proud man (until taking command in Norfolk five years earlier he'd been one of the three Navy commissioners, senior captains holding offices created in 1815 by act of Congress) and unlikely to stand down in the face of a prickly junior just in from a cruise on a sloop of war.* Both captains referred the squabble to Secretary Dickerson, who rightly sided with Warrington, writing to Kennedy on November 8, "it appears that you did not change your pennant on arrival at Norfolk, nor report your arrival nor hand over your official communications to Comdt Warrington because you did not think that officer entitled or authorized to wear a Broad pennant or to take you under his command":

> It is the opinion of the Department that you could not rightfully assume that a senior officer in actual command displayed any pennant which he was not authorized to wear, but that you were bound to suppose it authorized and immediately change your pennant as required by the regulations until you could refer to the Department for information.
>
> By whom and under what circumstances a Broad pennant may be worn is a matter of executive regulation and liable to alteration or modification as the President may deem proper.
>
> Comdt Warrington was not only in command of the Navy Yard, but of the station also, but were he commander of the yard only it would have been your duty to wait upon him and to report yourself under the 5th article of the Chapter of Regulations entitled Rank and Command. . . . The Department is of the opinion that the order of Comdt Warrington was correct and proper.

On November 8 Midn. Louis McLane, USN, wrote and signed the last entry in *Peacock*'s deck log: "Sailed up to the Navy Yard, hauled into dry dock, stripped and received our leaves." So ended USS *Peacock*'s around-the-world cruise, tied up at Hampton Roads awaiting recommissioning while her former commodore maneuvered for position.

---

* Described in his *New York Times* obituary as "a hero of that war which satisfied Great Britain that she did not hold the supremacy of the seas," Commodore Warrington died in Washington, D.C., in October 1851, third on the Navy lineal list and holding office as the chief of the Bureau of Ordinance and Hydrography. He'd served for fifty-two years, the last thirty ashore.

Epilogue

Sultana in New York City and USS *Peacock* on the Columbia River Bar

A shock! A shout! their dream is o'er—
Sudden as bursts the thunder peal,
When the blue lightning gleams like steel;
Fearful, as when from mountain hoar,
Where the eternal snows are press'd
The loosen'ed glaciers, rushing, pour
Their storm on the green valley's breast—
So sudden, fearful, shock and sound
Hath told—the vessel strikes the ground!
Like hungry wolves that howl in wrath
On the benighted traveller's path,
The breakers foam on either hand;
With the fell boa's writhing bound,
The hissing waters close around,
And press the strong ship on the sand!
Like giant chain'd, she meets the strife
And struggling groans like thing of life!
What strength, what power her fate can stay,
When the roused ocean claims its prey?
And have those wanderers scathless come,
From polar storms and rock-sown seas,
To perish, where the warm land breeze
Seems laden with the prayers of home?

—Sarah Josepha Hale, "The Wreck of the Peacock," 1842

45

Near the end of April 1840, the 14-gun, 300-ton Omani bark *Al Sultana*, eighty-seven days out of Zanzibar via a stop at St. Helena six weeks earlier, wearily tied up at the Rector Street pier in the Hudson River, two long blocks north of the Battery at New York City. *Sultanee*'s arrival (that's what contemporary American newspapers called the vessel) with a cargo of coffee, dates, hides, ivory, and drugs for sale was unexpected, but she wasn't entirely unknown to Americans.

Despite being encamped on the southern margins of the great Arabian Desert, nineteenth-century Omanis were superb blue-water sailors. They'd long before cracked the secret to sailing the Indian Ocean, the fact that the reversal of the monsoon winds twice a year made possible round trips between the ports and markets that lined East Africa, the Arabian Peninsula, and South Asia. Their expertise accounted for the fact that beginning early in the eighteenth century, Oman's sultan boasted a distant property, the island of Zanzibar, gateway to rich trade with Africa, twenty to thirty miles away across the intervening channel. In 1840, reflecting the importance of this trade and the sere conditions at home, the sultan moved his capital from Muscat to Stone City, Zanzibar's largest settlement.

Al Sultanah's visit to New York, the first by any ship flying the red flag of the "Imaum of Muscat," came a full half-century after the *Boston Rambler* had brought the first American traders to his country but only five years after the United States and Oman had exchanged ratified copies of Roberts' Treaty of Amity and Commerce, which bound both parties to perpetual peace and free trade.[1] That treaty was effective until replaced in 1958, early in President Eisenhower's second term—124 years, not a record for treaty longevity, but close to one.

The idea of a ship visit to New York had been brewing for years, since before *Mary Ann* had brought Roberts to Zanzibar in 1827, according to the brig's captain William Stevens. The next year in May, Captain Stevens was quoted in the biweekly *New York Spectator*, saying that "it was the intention and desire of the Sultan of Muscat . . . to send a frigate to the United States for the purpose of forming a commercial treaty and placing us on the same footing with England. . . . The Sultan expressed much surprise that the government of the United States had not made the attempt to enter into a commercial treaty with him, the advantages arising from it would be wholly in favor of American trade."

Still, during that distant spring even New York's sophisticates were surprised to find their city hosting an "Asiatic ship of war" (the phrase comes

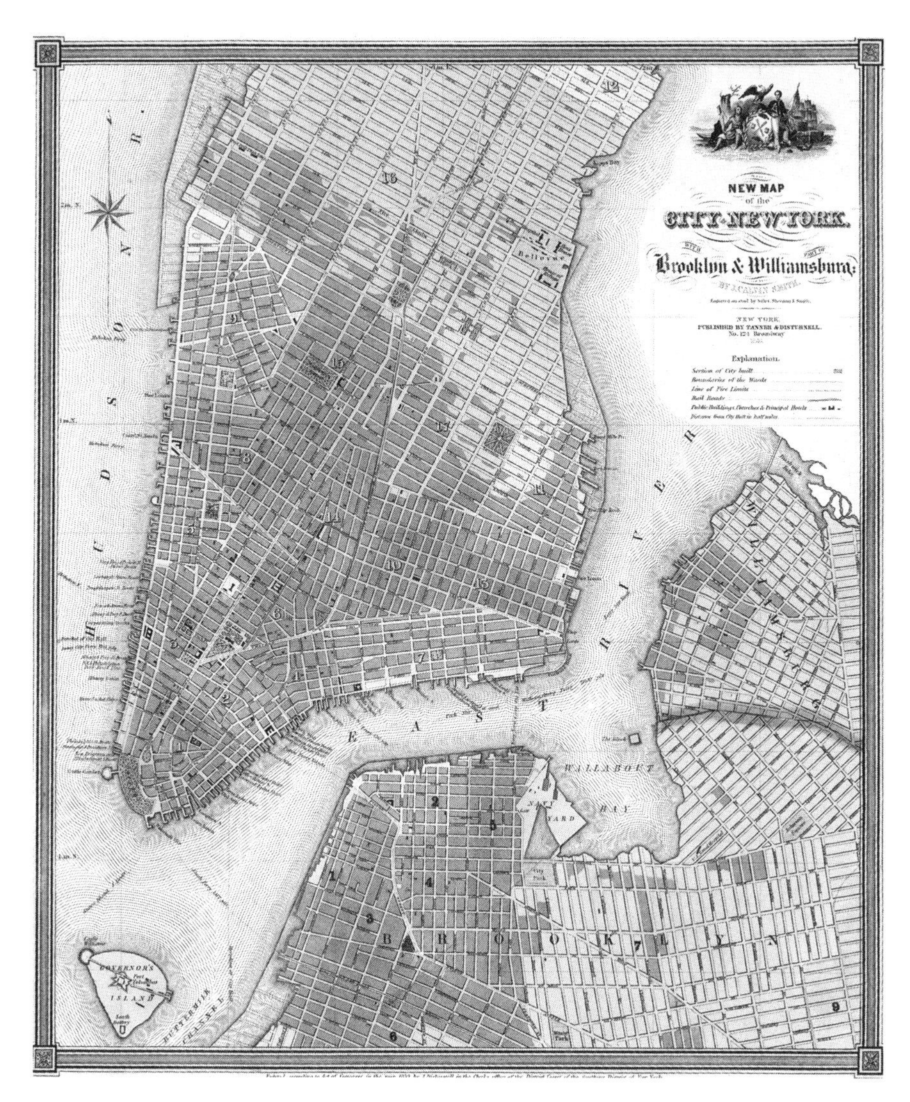

Map 2. "New Map of the City of New York, with Brooklyn & Parts of Williamsburgh." J. Calvin Smith, engraved by Stiles, Sherman and Smith. This 1840, 1:8,420-scale map shows Rector Street running roughly east-west between Broadway and the Hudson River riverfront. (The New York Navy Yard lines the west side of Brooklyn's Wallabout Bay.)

When *Al Sultanah* called, New York already enjoyed pride of place as the largest American city and principal port: its piers, lining both sides of Manhattan Island from its southern tip practically as far north as Fourteenth Street, handled nearly half of the country's international trade. Thanks to the fifteen-year-old Erie Canal, the total moved included much of the products and produce flowing between the outside world and the North American continent's interior beyond the Alleghenies. New Orleans on the Mississippi, with only a third of New York's population (102,000 versus 313,000) and focused on trade with South America, was a distant rival. No other Atlantic or Gulf Coast port even came close to experiencing the flood of people and cargo that passed through New York. Roberts' home town, Portsmouth, New Hampshire, population 7,900, fell at number fifty in the 1840 census of America's hundred largest urban places.

FROM *GUIDE TO THE CITY OF NEW YORK* (NEW YORK: TANNER & DISTURNELL, 1840).

"Zanzibar Town from the Sea." (1857?) Chromoxylograph. This view of Stone City, looking west from the anchorage and showing the town as it looked some two decades after *Peacock* called there, is the frontispiece of the first volume of Richard Burton's account of his exploration of Central Africa searching for the source of the Nile River in 1856–59. It turned out not to be Lake Tanganyika, as Burton thought, but rather Lake Victoria, as his colleague, William Speke, had surmised. Burton, geographer, explorer, linguist, pilgrim, and consul, was the author and is the subject of many books describing events in an extraordinary life spent in the exotic places of the world.

Chromoxylography, a late-nineteenth-century color printing process that used multiple engraved wood blocks, was capable of reproducing complex images at low cost.
FROM *THE LAKE REGIONS OF CENTRAL AFRICA* (LONDON: LONGMAN, GREEN, LONGMAN, AND ROBERTS, 1860).

from a contemporary issue of the *Floridian*), apparently commanded by an elegant, berobed Arab captain at the head of a crew of nearly sixty.[2] In fact, Ahmad ibn Na'amon, fifty-six, the Omani sultan's personal secretary, was not the ship's captain but rather his chief's ambassador to the United States, and while in port the ship served as Oman's temporary embassy afloat. *Sultana*'s master and navigator, Captain William Sleeman, formerly of the Royal Navy and one of the few known European faces on board, likely kept a low profile. He's gone down in the historic record as "intemperate," a hard drinker and poor performer responsible for *Sultanee*'s lubberly condition when she arrived after nearly three months at sea.

"Since last Thursday a perfect wonder to us Americans, in the shape of an Arabian ship, has arrived," gushed the *New York Morning Herald* on May 5, 1840. "She lays at the foot of Rector street on the North River, and has been thronged and the pier crowded with people anxious and pushing to get a peep." Built in Bombay's Mazagon Dockyard of native teak to a British design, the six-year-old, three-masted bark would likely have attracted no special attention under any other flag.

Her owner, "His Majesty Seyed Syeed bin Sultan of Muscat and his Dependencies," had good press in the United States, thanks in large part to Edmund Roberts, who'd reported to Washington that "the Sultan is a powerful prince, possessing a more powerful naval force than all the native princes combined, from the Cape of Good Hope to Japan." Not only powerful but also gracious: "He is of a mild and personable demeanor," the *Missionary Herald* told its readers in April (quoting the same Roberts report) while sizing up prospects for the work of saving souls, "and of unquestionable bravery—a lover of justice, humane, and greatly beloved by his subjects."

During the next three months *Sultanee*'s pioneering port call unfolded into a diplomatic and commercial triumph that began (as reported by Philadelphia's *North American and Daily Advertiser*) in the spring with a rush by members of New York's boards of common council "to extend the right hand of fellowship" to the captain, representing his ruler, and to tender to him "the civilities and accustomed hospitalities of the city," and ended in midsummer with cordial farewells.

Early in August, after more than three months in port, *Sultanee* cleared New York for the long trip home, carrying a cargo itemized in the *New York Spectator* as including among its boxes of muskets, kegs of gunpowder, and cases of glassware, crockery, soap, and sperm oil candles, a "splendid pleasure barge," the gift of the U.S. government to the imaum. But even including her voyage repairs at the navy yard in Brooklyn and the installation of a new main battery featuring heavier guns than those exchanged, she gave at least as good as she got. The imaum's presents for his faraway friend, President Martin Van Buren, had included two handsome stallions, bags of pearls, and other valuable gifts. Their magnificence raised an awkward question: what could self-consciously democratic republicans do with such royal presents that wouldn't offend the honor of the donor or the scruples of the recipients?

The diplomatic gift exchange could have been even more awkward, smirked the *Morning Herald*: "His Mightiness of Muscat keeps a splendid harem of forty beautiful women, Circassians, Greeks and Arabians, and he intended to select two choice ones and send them to Sultan Van Buren, instead of the horses; but when being told that there were no seraglios in this country he changed his mind.* We are sorry that the Circassian slaves have not been

* Earlier, in autumn 1834, the sultan had proposed to send two Arabian stallions and two mares home with Roberts as gifts for President Jackson but was dissuaded by Roberts, who explained that acceptance of such gifts would violate the Constitution of the United States.

sent. Although the constitution of the United States would not permit the President to receive them, his own constitution perhaps would."

Sultanee's warm welcome and the attendant exchange of flattering correspondence between Van Buren and the sultan reflected the good relations between the American Republic and the distant Arab sultanate, relations based almost entirely on trade between New England and Zanzibar, the gateway to the markets of Arabia, and—especially—the ivory, dyestuffs, and other exotic products of East Africa. New England's business interests lay behind the opening of the American consulate in Zanzibar in March 1837, not long after ratification of the Treaty of Amity and Commerce (but before it was officially proclaimed), and fully four years before the British established their own consulate.

For years Salem's traders, whose motives were believed by Omanis to be purer than those of the British, enjoyed a near-monopoly on trade with Zanzibar, exchanging New England's finished cotton for African exports while witnessing the island's booming trade in slaves. The first American consul in Stone City, Salem's Richard Waters, was employed by Bertram and Sheppard, which company vied with other Salem-based traders to dominate American trade with Zanzibar. Following the familiar nineteenth-century pattern of consular representation mixing near-seamlessly with private interest, his British counterpart, Captain Atkins Hamerton (1804–1857) of the Fifteenth Bombay Native Infantry, also wore a second hat. He was the local agent of the British East India Company.

There were, however, occasional rough moments in U.S.-Omani relations. In December 1851, with America's second resident consul, Charles Ward, back home in Salem in a snit over an insult to the American flag, the year-old side-wheel steamer USS *Susquehanna*, flagship of the East Indies Squadron, threatened to shell Stone Town with her big Dahlgren guns in reprisal for the slight. Tempers cooled; the flag eventually was suitably honored, and *Susquehanna* sailed on, soon to carry Commo. Matthew Perry on his first mission to open Japan.

America's, read "Salem's," commanding position astride Zanzibar's trade with the Atlantic world flourished until the Civil War. During the war years, maintaining its blockade of the Confederacy and chasing commerce raiders (largely unsuccessfully) took the Union navy's entire attention. At the same time, soaring marine insurance rates and the threat posed by predatory raiders caused the U.S. merchant fleet effectively to evaporate. Seven hundred American flag vessels switched to foreign (usually British) registry.

After the Civil War, the U.S. Navy's small South Atlantic Squadron, its responsibility to show the flag stretched into the Indian Ocean north to the equator, resumed port visits to Zanzibar. Even so, the sharply lowered level of visibility during the 1860s dramatically reduced American influence in the region going forward, allowing Great Britain's to grow unfettered. Moreover, next to the security of the home islands, never challenged during the century after Waterloo, Great Britain's chief focus was on its principal colony, India, the jewel in Queen Victoria's crown. That attention made the sea lane through the Mediterranean and the waters east of Suez second in importance only to the Channel. In contrast, America's interest in the Indian Ocean was regional, not national. Given the small, postwar U.S. fleet, anything east of Suez was necessarily a sideshow in American eyes. Approaching the end of the century, with the United States focusing its attention on close-in, restive Cuba, British influence over Zanzibar grew into a sole proprietorship.

Although USS *Susquehanna*'s threat in 1851 to bombard Stone Town never came to anything another such threat, this one by the Royal Navy decades later did. "Zanzibar did look very beautiful that night," Rear Admiral Harry Rawson, RN, wrote poetically about Stone Town as he saw it from the water the evening of Wednesday, August 26, 1897, "with the undimmed, clear moonshine, the white roofs whiter than by day, the harbor placid, the white ships resting on the blue water, the palace a blaze of light, and the garden of date-trees, with their still foliage." The old port city he was admiring as the sun went down behind it was only several generations removed from the small fishing village it once had been.

Admiral Rawson's observation was an obituary of sorts. Precisely at nine the next morning, his flagship, the British *Edgar*-class cruiser HMS *St. George*, and her consorts, HMS *Philomel*, HMS *Raccoon*, and the gunboats HMS *Thrush* and HMS *Sparrow*, opened fire on the government buildings, houses, and shops of Stone Town. Rawson (1843–1910) was then commander in chief of the Royal Navy's Cape of Good Hope and West Coast of Africa Station, and the ships shelling Zanzibar constituted about a third of the force under his command.

The short, shattering high explosives bombardment by 9-, 6-, and 4-inch naval guns tore the sleepy place from its historic roots as the African seat of Omani royalty and thrust it practically into the new century. What must have appeared as Armageddon to the fishermen and traders of Zanzibar—return fire from shore to ship was completely ineffective—was likened by Rawson's biographer, Geoffrey Rawson, a relative, as "more like a scene out of one of Gilbert and Sullivan's operas than an episode in real life."[3]

The goal of the bombardment was the quick suppression of a palace coup that challenged Great Britain's seven-year-old protectorate over the island. Britain's hand-selected sultan at Stone Town had suddenly died just days before—most suspected poison—and a cousin, Sayyid Khalid, had succeeded him, on his way into the royal palace brushing aside a relative and Britain's preferred successor, Sayyid Hamoud. Britain claimed a right to approve who sat on the throne, and when Khalid assembled several thousand badly armed supporters to keep him in office and ignored British consul Basil Cave's ultimatum, the shooting started. Almost all of it from ship to shore.

Zanzibar's navy boasted only a single vessel, the British-built royal yacht HHS *Glasgow*, and she was sunk minutes into the excitement with the loss of nine lives. Loyally but foolishly, *Glasgow* had fired on the British flagship, which answered with several fatal shells. The tips of *Glasgow*'s three masts and the top of her funnel were visible standing above water for many years thereafter. By Geoffrey Rawson's count, 500 Zanzibaris were killed or wounded in less than an hour on August 27, and another 250 were captured. One British sailor was seriously wounded in exchange.

Considering with satisfaction what his kinsman, the admiral, had done at Zanzibar, young Rawson concluded proudly,

> Action no doubt was singularly prompt, but it was suited to the swiftness of the emergency. Zanzibar was ours to do what we liked with, and it was only a question whether we should continue to maintain a nominal Sultan, whose rule was the centre of constant disturbing and distracting intrigues, or whether we should take the administration directly into our own hands. The bombardment was not a great feat of arms, nor a great feat of any kind, but it demonstrated the watchfulness of the Navy, the celerity with which its aid may be invoked in any corner of the world in which it may be wanted, and the self-reliance and presence of mind with which the naval might of England may be employed wherever necessary.[4]

During the years between Hamerton's appointment as Her Britannic Majesty's first consul in Zanzibar to *St. George*'s shelling of Stone Town, British influence over local government steadily eased the Americans aside, and moved deliberately from genteel recommendation to explicit direction. In 1890 Zanzibar was declared a British protectorate, not yet the end state of a process that—after Rawson's sharp correction—would eventually see local currency replaced by the British Indian rupee, Zanzibar's defense entrusted not to its army but to two companies of the King's Own African Rifles, and British jurisdiction imposed in place of traditional consular courts. In 1913 the Colonial Office assumed control of Zanzibar from the Foreign Office.

Fifty years later, in 1963, Zanzibar became independent. The following year it joined with Tanganyika to become Tanzania.

The Royal Navy's shelling of Stone Town, the nineteenth century's equivalent of a drive-by shooting, lasted just under forty minutes. When it ended, around a quarter until ten o'clock Thursday morning, August 27, what has been since judged to be history's shortest war was over. Arguably, Rawson's brief, midmorning bombardment tightened the British grip on Zanzibar just at a moment when local leadership might have led the country astray, and so strengthened the empire's hold on the nations and wealth of the Indian Ocean for decades to come. Seen from this perspective, it was a near no-cost, enormously successful exercise of gunboat diplomacy. That diplomatic style had another few decades to run, after which the price of inflicting shock and awe would grow dramatically more expensive.

46

On October 30, 1837, Secretary Dickerson sent a short letter to Commodore Warrington about USS *Peacock*, in at Warrington's yard several days earlier after two and a half years at sea. *Peacock*'s enlisted crew was to be paid off and discharged, the secretary instructed the commodore, the usual practice at the end of a cruise, and officers were to be granted leaves of absence as soon as they could be spared from the ship.

As for *Peacock* herself, Dickerson wrote, "Captain Kennedy having given it as his opinion that the Peacock could be made ready for any cruise in one month, it is the desire of the Department that she be not dismantled." She was not. Instead, after what soon proved to be insufficient attention in the shipyard (corrected near the end of the year by voyage repairs in Rio de Janeiro), *Peacock* left Norfolk on August 18, 1838, heading for Cape Horn and the Pacific Ocean, ten years after her first cruise to the South Sea—the reason for her rebuilding by Master Commandant Gregory in New York—had been cancelled.

She sailed in company with her new squadron's flagship, the 8-gun sloop of war USS *Vincennes*, and the other four ships of the United States Exploring and Surveying Expedition on the mission outlined in Secretary of the Navy James Paulding's week-old sailing instructions.

"At 3 o'clock P.M., on the 18th, the signal for sailing was made, and we got under weigh with an ebb tide, and a light air from the southwest," began the six-volume history of the expedition published beginning in 1845 by its commander, Lt. Charles Wilkes, USN, riding in *Vincennes*. "At 5 P.M. we anchored at the Horseshoe, in consequence of its falling calm and of the tide making against us; but at 9 P.M. the wind freshened, when we tripped and stood down the bay. At 4 A.M. on the 19th, we passed Cape Henry light; at 9 A.M. discharged the pilot and took our departure. . . . The day was beautiful, the sea smooth, the wind light."

With that, the squadron was off for Rio de Janeiro, via Madeira and the Cape Verde Islands, where the last of its ships, USS *Relief*, finally arrived November 26, 1838, after a record slow passage on a direct track. All stayed there until January 6, when the squadron—*Peacock* now really ready for sea—sailed for Patagonia's Rio Negro estuary to survey the bar.

The squadron would be at sea through all of James Paulding's remaining time as secretary of the navy; through the six-month term during 1841 of his short-service successor, George Badger of North Carolina; and into the term of Abel Upshur of New York. It would eventually fall to Upshur to deal with the fallout of its return, including the court-martial of the squadron commander, before he moved on to become President Tyler's secretary of state in July 1843.

Lieutenant Wilkes was an odd, even bizarre, choice for command of a squadron of six ships and more than three hundred officers and men that was to spend four years at sea in distant waters. He would prove himself to be a superb navigator and surveyor but a terrible commander of men at sea. The United States Exploring and Surveying Expedition's brilliant achievements—sailing along many hundreds of miles of the coast of Antarctica, surveying dozens of uncharted islands, preparing nearly two hundred new charts, and collecting the thousands of specimens and artifacts that formed the basis of the Smithsonian Institution's incomparable collection—are testimony to his technical skill. The furious wardroom infighting and miserable morale of the squadron's officers, and the flurry of trials on arrival home, including his own on five charges, testify to his many leadership failures.

As a junior officer, Wilkes had cruised in USS *Guerrière* in the Baltic and Mediterranean Seas, in USS *Franklin* off South America, and as a lieutenant in USS *Boston* and USS *Fairfield*, again in the Mediterranean. All together, a modest amount of time at sea under way for an officer with twenty years in uniform. Fortunately, technical skills and not expertise as an officer of the deck lay at the core of his new squadron's mission.

Not quite in the upper third of the Navy's 279 lieutenants, Wilkes had commanded the nearly new USS *Porpoise* on surveying duty his last time afloat, doing nothing that prepared him to lead a squadron, which in any case was a captain's assignment not a lieutenant's. Among the nearly two hundred officers senior to him—fifty captains, fifty commanders, and ninety-four lieutenants—a quarter were already in command of something, but nearly half were home, awaiting orders. Every one of these men, presumably, might have expected preference over Wilkes. One who did, in writing to both the secretary and the president, was Lt. Cornelius Stribling, the former "acting commanding officer" of USS *Peacock*. Stribling, now assigned to the Navy rendezvous (recruiting station) in Norfolk—and seventy-two numbers senior to Wilkes—had reason to brood about how selection for command at sea actually worked in the Navy Secretariat.

Odder still than Wilkes' deep selection for command is the fact that he was chosen by the secretary of the army, Joel Poinsett. Dismayed by the lack of progress under Navy management in the months since the enabling legislation had been passed by Congress in the spring of 1836, President Van Buren put Poinsett in charge, an appointment that reflected the turmoil and politicization that had marked everything associated with the expedition since it had first been conceived ten years earlier.

The decade of delay between initiative and execution had several sources. One was in Congress. Spending public money for science was always a hard sell on Capitol Hill, where even improving ports and roads found scant support in the federal budget, especially from southerners. (Ten years later, in 1848, then-secretary of the navy John Mason felt compelled to mask an exploration of the Dead Sea as a mission to resupply the Mediterranean Squadron to avoid a battle in Congress over funding what looked like idle curiosity about its elevation.) Eventually, however, vigorous lobbying succeeded in making an economic case for the adventure. A thirty-seven to five majority in the Senate and a vote of ninety-two to sixty-eight in the House passed the 1836 Naval Service Bill, which contained $150,000 in new money to pay for the expedition and permitted the expenditure of a matching sum from other sources. President Jackson signed it into law a few days later.

Another cause of delay was internal to the Navy, where among senior officers suspicion grew that the cruise of the squadron—grown since 1828 from three ships to five, a frigate and four others—would be led by its scientists and not them. Delay was a force in the Navy Secretariat, too, where Secretary Dickerson dragged his feet and made elaborate excuses for the expedition's slow progress in his department's 1836 and 1837 annual reports to the president.

But powered by vocal export and trade interests in New England, by support from former secretary of the navy Southard, now head of the Senate's Committee on Naval Affairs, and by the tireless advocacy of Jeremiah Reynolds, once funding was in hand, planning limped forward. Even as the economy sank in the Panic of 1837, details began to be extruded from the Navy.

In the 1838 edition of the *Biennial Register of All Officers and Agents in the Service of the United States* (Blair & Rives, 1838), Thomas ap Catesby Jones, twenty-ninth on the lineal list of Navy captains and the same officer who in 1826 had sailed into Honolulu with the Pacific Squadron, appears as "Comd'g Exploring Expedition." His expedition was to include the frigate USS *Macedonian*, the stores ship USS *Relief*, the barks USS *Pioneer* and USS *Consort*, and the schooner USS *Pilot* (later USS *Clara* instead), every one hand-selected by him.

The navy secretary's visible lack of interest, slow recruiting (fully 85 officers and 518 men were required to crew these five ships), squabbles about mission, schedule and cost, uncertainties about the ships' material condition, and Jones' own declining health led to his surprise resignation from command at the end of November 1837. The commodore surrendered his post a month or so after he'd published "General Order No. 1," suggesting wrongly that the squadron would soon—finally—sail from New York, and only days after he'd received Dickerson's sailing instructions.

By then even small problems—among them unhappiness with the new design, anthracite coal-burning galley stoves—as well as large began to get a lot of attention. The stoves were prominently mentioned in the secretary's annual report to the president, further illustrating why getting the expedition to sea was so difficult.

Jones gone, now followed a small procession of potential successors to the retiring commodore, among them Capt. William Shubrick, Capt. Lawrence Kearney, and Capt. Matthew Perry (yes, that Perry), each of whom upon being offered the expedition's command by Secretary Dickerson declined the honor. Frustrated, President Van Buren turned to Poinsett for help, and after tenders to Capt. Joseph Smith and Cdr. Francis Gregory (the same officer who ten years before had supervised the keel-up rebuilding of *Peacock*) were both rejected, Poinsett resorted to Wilkes.

47

Paulding (1778–1860), Dickerson's recent replacement in President Van Buren's cabinet, was much better known in his day as an author of fiction and playwright than as a civil servant. His thirteen-hundred-word obituary in the April 6, 1860, issue of the *New York Times* mentioned eighteen of his titles by name and then disposed of his service as secretary to the Board of Naval Commissioners, as navy agent in New York, and as secretary of the navy in three short sentences. But Paulding brought to Van Buren's cabinet more than twenty years of experience in naval affairs and more enthusiasm for a chesty navy in general and for this cruise in particular than former Secretary Dickerson had ever exhibited.*

The new secretary's instructions began by relating the work of the expedition directly to America's business interests. "The Congress of the United States," he wrote, "having in view the important interests of our commerce embarked in the whale-fisheries, and other adventures in the great Southern ocean, by an Act of the 18th of May, 1836, authorized an Expedition to be fitted out for the purpose of exploring and surveying that sea, as well to determine the existence of all doubtful islands and shoals, as to discover and accurately fix the position of those which lie in or near the track of our vessels in that quarter, and may have escaped the observation of scientific navigators." The instructions also provided: "Although the primary object of the Expedition is the promotion of the great interests of commerce and navigation, yet you will take all occasions, not incompatible with the great purposes of your undertaking, to extend the bounds of science, and promote the acquisition of knowledge." For this purpose nine "scientific gentlemen" were to be embarked, down from the nearly two dozen academics that had congested the planning process earlier.

In between references to commerce and science, Paulding outlined in detail the "long and devious voyages" the expedition was to follow around the world, from Norfolk to Rio de Janeiro to resupply, then continuing on to

- a survey of the Rio Negro in Patagonia;
- an exploration of the southern Antarctic by *Porpoise*, *Sea-Gull*, and *Flying-Fish*, "endeavouring to reach a high southern latitude" while the larger ships remained in Tierra del Fuego supporting scientific investigations on shore;

---

* In *Sea of Glory* (Viking, 2003), Nathaniel Philbrick described Secretary Dickerson as the expedition's "principal detractor, applying what little reserves of energy he possessed in deploying strategies to delay its departure." The judgment of Dickerson's contemporaries was no more generous. Through late summer 1837 and over the following winter, the *New York Times* and the *New York Courier and Enquirer* published a lengthy exchange of anonymous letters between Jeremiah Reynolds ("Citizen") and Secretary Dickerson ("a Friend to the Navy") in which Reynolds repeatedly accused Dickerson of deliberately obstructing the expedition and Dickerson defended himself against the charges. Their published correspondence is on the Internet at https://archive.org/stream/exploringexpedit00reynrich#page/n1/mode/2up.

In mid-December 1837, Lt. John "Mad Jack" Percival wrote the secretary to tell him that a "very general belief exists here [Boston] that you have a personal hostility to the Expedition, and an unconquerable repugnance to its late commander and that your wishes are for its being broken up that any new modification which may be proposed is only the precursor to its final abandonment." After leaving the cabinet, Dickerson was again offered the post of U.S. minister in a foreign capital. Brussels, Madrid, and Naples were mentioned, but he declined them all and returned home to manage his estate and wealth (from iron mining), and recover his health. He later became a district judge.

- an excursion southwest toward Captain James Cook's "ne plus ultra" (his farthest south, 71° south, 107° west) followed by resupply in Valparaiso in March 1839;
- a survey of the Navigator Islands (Samoa) and then to the Feejee Islands ("which you will examine with particular attention, with the view to the selection of a safe harbor, ease of access, and in every respect adapted to the reception of vessels of the United States engaged in whale-fishery, and the general commerce of these seas");
- Sydney, for a second penetration of the Antarctic, this one south of Van Diemen's Land, a rendezvous at the "Isle of Desolation" at the western entrance to the Strait of Magellan, and on to the Sandwich Islands for resupply in April 1840;
- the northwest coast of America ("making such surveys and examinations, first of the territory of the United states on the sea-board, and of the Columbia River, and afterwards along the coast of California");
- the Sea of Japan, followed by the Sea of Sooloo or Mindoro (to "ascertain whether there is any safe route through it, which will shorten the passage of our vessels to and from China . . . pay very particular attention to this object");
- Singapore, where yet another stores ship would be standing by in early April 1841; and
- finally home via the Straits of Billiton, the Sunda Strait, and the Cape of Good Hope.[5]

Its actual track was close to that prescribed by the secretary's instructions, but the expedition never entered the Sea of Japan. Not exactly on Paulding's track, and not on his schedule either. Not until May 8, 1841, did *Peacock* and *Flying-Fish* leave the Gilbert Islands for the mouth of the Columbia River, forcing a very late start of the strategically important survey of Oregon, and adding an extra year to what was to have been a three-year cruise. This extended time deployed explains what appears to be extraordinary turnover in ships' crews.

The expedition shed men like chaff: 524 names are attached to the original 346 crew positions. In addition to the familiar causes for loss—desertions, deaths (two dozen or so), and a few trips home on sick tickets—the enlisted crews' terms of enlistment expired along the way, beginning with those who had long ago signed on to sail in *Macedonian*. Some men volunteered to extend their enlistments, but others did not and had to be replaced by recruits picked up at ports along the way. And not just men. Ships too.

Of the six ships that sailed out of the Chesapeake Bay in August 1838, only *Vincennes* and the *Dolphin*-class gun brig USS *Porpoise* completed the around-the-world voyage to come. Among those first six, next in size behind the two sloops of war was Catesby Jones' nominee to be the expedition's stores ship, the 6-gun USS *Relief*, 468 tons and 109 feet long, the only one of his personal choices that actually sailed with the expedition. Built in 1835–36 at Philadelphia to a merchant ship design, beamy *Relief* (she was nearly a third as broad as she was long) could never keep up with the squadron. She was unloaded at Callao in 1839 and sent home via the Sandwich Islands and Sydney, reaching New York on March 18, 1840. *Relief* went to sea off and on for the next twenty-plus years. She was sold in 1877, after spending her last six years as the receiving ship at Washington.

Neither of the two schooners, USS *Sea-Gull* (110 tons, ex–*New Jersey*) and the slightly smaller USS *Flying-Fish* (96 tons, ex-*Independence*) made it back to the U.S. East Coast. Both were former New York pilot boats hastily converted by Webb and Allen in New York to something like a Navy specification to serve as tenders with the expedition. So small that they were steered by a tiller, not a wheel, each was under the command of a passed midshipman. *Sea-Gull* had fifteen in her crew. *Flying-Fish* only a dozen. The pair's very shallow draft, ideal for surveying in coastal and inshore waters, explains their presence in the squadron.

Tiny, pretty *Sea-Gull* was the first expedition ship lost. She disappeared in bad weather with all hands sometime in early May 1839 after having left Orange Bay, the first harbor west of Cape Horn, that February for distant Valparaiso in company with USS *Flying-Fish*. *Flying-Fish* entered port in Chile May 19 alone and went on to accompany *Peacock* during her two Antarctic investigations in 1839–40. The two were together later, on a 228-day, two-ship survey of several mid-Pacific island groups that after a quick stop in Honolulu for provisions and water ended off the mouth of the Columbia River on July 17, 1841.

A few months later Wilkes sent his ninety-second numbered report to the secretary of the navy, written in San Francisco on October 30. Foreshadowing bad news, his letter began, "I have now to report what I have expected long since might occur to one of us from the dangerous nature of the service committed to the squadron under my command the loss of the United States Ship Peacock on the 18th of July on the bar of the Columbia river in attempting to enter it." The letter, containing a copy of Capt. William Hudson's report to Wilkes on the loss of his ship, was *Peacock*'s obituary.

A little after noon on July 18, Captain Hudson started *Peacock* toward the channel and its known dangers, in his hands sailing directions and a chart provided by Capt. Josiah Spaulding of *Lausanne*, out of Salem, who'd been in and out of the river recently. (Later, but apparently not then, Wilkes expressed some skepticism about Captain Spaulding's directions, commenting that the bearings offered referenced magnetic headings, and such were "generally of little value.") After an unsuccessful first approach, *Peacock* "again stood in, and in less than five minutes the ship touched, the helm was immediately put a lee, and every effort made to bring her by the wind and haul off, but thump after thump, and the heave of the sea forced her on end and made her unmanageable."

Five years later, in a letter to Senator James Pearce, Wilkes tried to put what faced *Peacock* at the start of the survey into context a landsman would understand. "To add force to my own opinion," to wrote Pearce, "I might here appeal to the account of all voyagers who have, from time to time, visited the Columbia since its first discovery":[6]

> They all, without exception, clothe it with dangers; and none have had the hardihood to attempt its entrance except under the most favorable circumstances; and almost every vessel that has attempted a passage, in or out, has met with some disaster more or less serious: even those who have been deemed the most expert navigators, and, we have reason to believe, had the best information respecting it, have not escaped uninjured. Indeed, all the information the officers and myself received from the masters of the [Hudson Bay] company's vessels . . . was indicative of the dangers and perils they were surrounded with in entering and departing from the Columbia at all seasons of the year.

Sarah Josepha Hale's poem, quoted in the epigraph, says nothing at all about the crew's brave response to the sudden threat to their ship, a response very like that at Masirah. Launching boats to find the nearest deeper water and to help *Peacock* kedge off from the shoal. Lightening ship to reduce her draft, including heaving shot over the stern, emptying drinking water over the side, and taking down everything heavy from the tops. Manning the pumps when the hull opened up. All the familiar, desperate evolutions that experience had taught might save a sailing ship in extremis.

USS *Peacock* had survived the reef at Masirah, but here, in hail and fog and at ebb tide, she didn't survive grounding a second time. "At 11:30 P.M. it was high water," Hudson described to Wilkes when they met later,

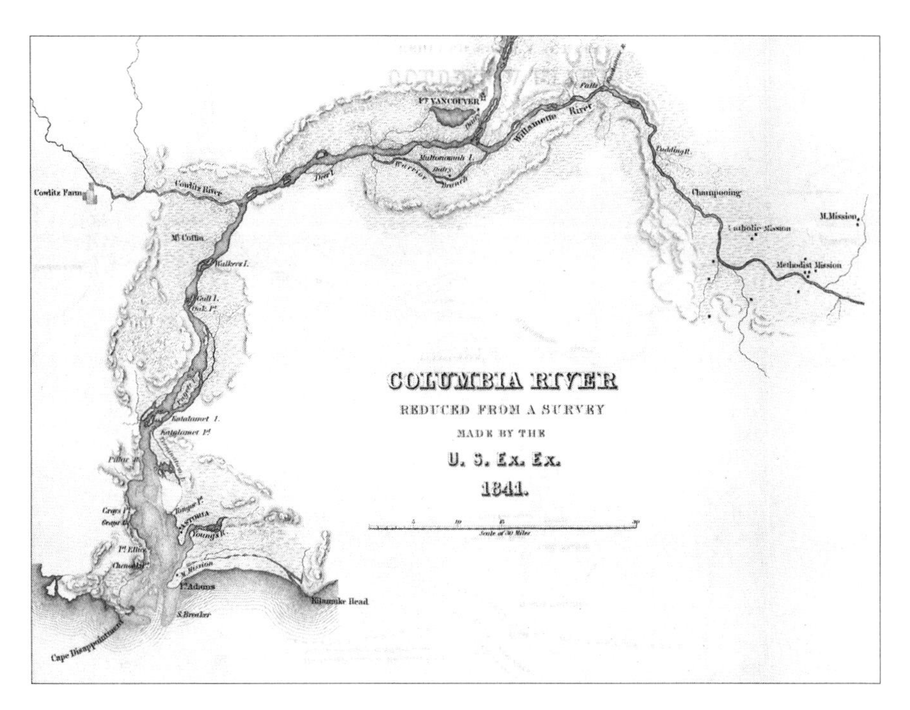

Map 3. "The Mouth of the Columbia River from Kilamuke Head to Cape Disappointment." USS *Peacock* went aground and was destroyed on the North Breaker, near the tip of Cape Disappointment shown in this detail from the "Columbia River, Reduced from a Survey Made by the U.S. Ex. Ex. 1844."

Sarah Hale's sappy poem "The Wreck of the Peacock," quoted in part in the epilogue's epigraph, appeared in the May 1842 issue of the enormously popular *Godey's Lady's Book and Ladies' American Magazine* (published in Philadelphia between 1830 and 1898). Hale, the author of "Mary Had a Little Lamb" and a giant figure in women's literature of the era, was the magazine's editor for four decades. She was also the mother of Horatio Hale, the linguist from Harvard who was one of the expedition's "scientific gentlemen." He rode *Peacock* out of Norfolk, joined *Vincennes* in New Zealand, transferred back to *Peacock* in Honolulu, and returned home after her wreck overland from Astoria in time to publish in 1846 the expedition's first scientific report, *Ethnography and Philology*.
Atlas of the Narrative of the U.S. Exploring Expedition.
LIBRARY OF CONGRESS, G4240 CT 000908

sea somewhat abated, ship still striking and occasionally with a very heavy thump . . . anticipating as the tide runs out with *great force* we should again be subject to a heavy combing sea. At 1 A.M. the sea was rapidly increasing & at 2, ship striking very heavily, the sea occasionally combing in over the larboard bow &c. along the waist, which stove in the larboard bulwarks & flooded the spar deck. . . . The ship at this time striking so heavily that I had little hopes of her holding together until daylight, and should have cut away her masts to ease her, but that would have left us without the means of getting out our

"The Wreck of the Peacock." Drawn by Alfred Agate, engraved by T. House. Sailing up the North Channel toward Bakers Bay behind Cape Disappointment on July 18, 1841, USS *Peacock* ran aground on the North Breakers, a shallows of the Columbia River bar, where she was beaten apart by the surf. In this illustration from Lieutenant Wilkes' *Narrative*, the schooner USS *Flying Fish*, under the command of Passed Midshipman Knox, stands seaward of the bar, watching one of *Peacock*'s boats capsize in the surf after it has returned to the wreck of her stranded mother ship to rescue the last of the survivors. All others of the sloop's crew have already been put ashore at Bakers Bay. A signal from the wreck delayed further dangerous attempts at rescuing these last few, among them Captain Hudson. Later Hudson would be criticized for not sending the shallow draft schooner ahead of his sloop to test the depth of water across the bar.

Peacock's substitute became the brig USS *Oregon*, until recently the trader *Thomas H. Perkins*, bought at Astoria for nine thousand dollars then emptied of her load of salted salmon and rerigged. A few years later, in 1845, *Oregon* was sold out of the Navy.
WILKES, *NARRATIVE OF THE U.S. EXPLORING EXPEDITION* 4:493

boats, should the occasion offer. At 7 A.M. of the 19th the first opportunity which occurred when a boat could be ventured over the side to reach the shore, Lt Perry was dispatched with the charts papers and everything connected with the surveys of the present cruise, Purser Speiden with his books and accounts—The launch and three boats hoisted out, some trifling provisions put in the former, and all the boats of the ship successfully filled with the crew, officers, and scientific gentlemen, the Marines only taking their arms and accoutrements, and no one allowed to take any clothing but what they stood in, to prevent the lumbering and swamping the boats; three or four of the boats succeeded in making a second trip, after which it became improbable from the violence of the sea, and force of the current for a boat to get off or live anywhere near the ship.

Peacock's boats returned to the wreck midafternoon on July 19 to rescue the last of the survivors, Hudson and a handful of others who included the boatswain and the carpenter. All were successfully brought safely ashore at around sunset. Ultimately the completed survey, under Wilkes' close supervision after August 7, extended upriver 125 miles.

From San Francisco out of Hawaii in November 1841 for the third time, *Vincennes* and her three remaining escorts sailed almost due west, pausing to survey some of the island groups on the way. The four were making for the Bashi Channel and Manila, then across the South China Sea to Singapore, and finally around the Cape of Good Hope to home, still 22,000 miles away.

But in Singapore, "various reports were made to me of defects in the tender Flying-Fish," Wilkes explained in his *Narrative*. "I felt a natural desire to carry her home with us. . . . But the idea of risking the lives of her officers and crew, after the disaster that had already befallen her sister craft, was not to be endured; and I saw it was necessary to have a thorough examination of her."

The judgment of this second inspection of the vessel (one had been done in Honolulu) was that "long and hard service" had "weakened her frame" and repairs would be long and costly. With the assistance of Consul Balestier, Wilkes' host during the squadron's call at Singapore, *Flying-Fish* was sold there for thirty-seven hundred dollars leaving only the sloop of war *Vincennes* and the brigs *Porpoise* and *Oregon* to sail for home.

NOTES

Chapter 1. President Jackson, Secretary Woodbury, and Mister Roberts

1. My thanks to Betty Jean Lofland for this insight.
2. Remarks by U.S. Consul General Stephen Young on October 17, 2012, to the American Chamber of Commerce, Macao, http://hongkong.usconsulate.gov/cg_sy2012101701.html.
3. William Samuel Waithman Ruschenberger, *Narrative of a Voyage round the World, During the Years 1835, 36, and 37; Including a Narrative of the Embassy to the Sultan of Muscat and the King of Siam*, 2 vols. (London: Richard Bentley, 1838), 11. Ruschenberger says the two, Roberts and Woodbury, were friends, but it was rumored that they were "kinsmen by marriage."
4. Entry 34, Instructions to Special Agents 1823–1906, Vol. 1, General Records of the Department of State, NARA, College Park, MD.
5. John M. Belohlavek, *Let the Eagle Soar! The Foreign Policy of Andrew Jackson* (Lincoln: University of Nebraska Press, 1985), 31.
6. Roger Knight, *Britain Against Napoleon: The Organization of Victory, 1793–1815* (London: Penguin, 2013), 447.
7. Edmund Roberts Papers, New Hampshire Historical Society, Concord (hereafter cited as Roberts Papers, New Hampshire).
8. Capt. William Stevens of the brig *Mary Ann*, quoted in the *New York Spectator*, May 6, 1828.
9. Jon Meacham, *American Lion: Andrew Jackson in the White House* (New York: Random House, 2008), 175.
10. *North American Review*, October 1838, 66.
11. Sharom Ahmat, "Joseph B. Balestier: The First American Consul in Singapore, 1833–1852," *Journal of the Malaysian Branch of the Royal Asiatic Society* 39, no. 2 (December 1966): 116.
12. Francis L. Hawks with M. C. Perry, *Narrative of the Expedition of an American Squadron to the China Seas and Japan Performed in the Years 1852, 1853, and 1854, under the Command of Commodore M. C. Perry, United States Navy, by order of the Government of the United States* (Washington, DC: A. O. P. Nicholson, 1856), 115–116.
13. J. Smith Homans, *An Historical and Statistical Account of the Foreign Commerce of the United States, 1820–1856* (New York: G. P. Putnam, 1857), 113.
14. Nan Powell Hodges, *The Voyage of the Peacock: A Journal by Benajah Ticknor, Naval Surgeon* (Ann Arbor: University of Michigan Press, 1991), 269.
15. Brent to Shillaber, December 13, 1830, quoted in Richard Hopkins Miller, *The United States and Vietnam, 1787–1941* (Washington, DC: National Defense University Press, 1990), 17–18.

Chapter 2. The Frigate USS *Potomac* at Kuala Batee

1. J. N. Reynolds, *Voyage of the United States Frigate Potomac, Under the Command of Commodore John Downes, During the Circumnavigation of the Globe, in the Years 1831, 1832, 1833, and 1844* (New York: Harper and Brothers, 1835), 528–529.
2. "Battle of the Potomac with the Malays," Folder 20, Portfolio 55, Printed Ephemera Collection, Library of Congress, Washington, DC.
3. Hodges, *Voyage of the Peacock*, 191–192.
4. *Niles' Register* 42 (July 14, 1832): 354–355. The paper returned to the subject twice that summer, in its issues of July 21 and September 8.
5. Quotations from Reynolds, Downes, and Woodbury are from the searchable, digital text of Reynolds' book on the website of the Hathi Trust, http://babel.hathitrust.org/cgi/pt?id=hvd.32044082185729;view=1up;seq=13.

Chapter 3. Master Commandant Geisinger, Chargé d'Affaires Baylies, and Surgeon Ticknor

1. 1832 fleet statistics from "The Naval Register for 1833," 22nd Cong., 2nd sess., No. 491, January 2, 1833.
2. About which see Nathaniel Philbrick, *Sea of Glory: America's Voyage of Discovery: The U.S. Exploring Expedition, 1838–1842* (New York: Viking-Penguin, 2003). USS *Vincennes*, the sloop of war that beat USS *Peacock* by several years to the distinction of being the first U.S. Navy ship around the world, was Commodore Wilkes' flagship.
3. Quoted from a caption on one of thirty watercolors of the War of 1812 by an unknown nineteenth-century English artist, part of the Beverley R. Robinson Collection of the U.S. Naval Academy Museum, Preble Hall, U.S. Naval Academy, Annapolis, MD, Cat. No. USNA 1951.007.0494(11).
4. N. A. M. Roger, *The Command of the Ocean: A Naval History of Britain, 1649–1815* (New York: W. W. Norton, 2005), 568.
5. *Niles' Weekly Register* 35 (November 8, 1828): 162–163.
6. Geisinger to Dickerson, April 21, 1836, David Geisinger Papers, MS 1283, Maryland Historical Society, Baltimore.
7. Hodges, *Voyage of the Peacock*.
8. Quotations from Baylies' official and family correspondence are taken from the holdings of the Old Colony Historical Society, Taunton, MA.
9. William Dusenberry, "Juan Manuel de Rosas as Viewed by Contemporary American Diplomats," *Hispanic American Historical Review*, November 1961, 499. This USS *Warren* (commissioned in 1827, sold in 1863) was the fourth of five U.S. Navy ships of that name.
10. Charles Francis Adams, ed., *Memoirs of John Quincy Adams*, 12 vols. (Philadelphia: J. B. Lippincott, 1874–77), 9:446–447.

Chapter 4. Monte Video to Manila

1. Log book entries in the 1830s followed one of two formats fairly rigidly: one reported a ship's progress at sea; the other described the passage of time in port. Entries for ships under way described the weather (cloud cover, precipitation, sea state, and the strength and direction of the wind), included an inventory of sails aloft, and recorded

crew drills, all in a single, short paragraph covering each two- or four-hour watch and signed by the officer of the deck. The bottom of every daily page contained a table showing the ship's estimated position in latitude and longitude, one or the other often unknown and therefore disconcertingly left blank, sometimes for days.

In port, the officer of the deck reported the depth of water and the scope of anchor cable paid out, the movement of ship's boats, the employment of the enlisted crew, the nationality and rig of other vessels in the anchorage, the receipt of water, foodstuffs, and other material from shore, and occasionally but not always the movements of the captain, the departure and return of junior officers, and the presence of distinguished guests. Food surveyed (inspected) and condemned (thrown over the side as spoiled and inedible), the gallons of drinking water consumed that day and the total gallons remaining in casks below, and the number of men being carried by the surgeon on that day's sick list were recorded both under way and in port.

Other than the log's first-page crew roster, punishment inflicted on members of the crew and their deaths on board were the only times the name of an enlisted sailor appeared in the log, in the first instance with the infraction committed and the number of lashes inflicted and in the second with the disposition of the body.

Chapter 5. China, Cochin China, and Siam

1. Ruschenberger, *Narrative of a Voyage*, 386.
2. The full text of Captain Porter's letter to President Madison is available at the Founders Online website of the National Archives, http://founders.archives.gov/?q=%20Author%3A%22Porter%2C%20David%22%20Recipient%3A%22Madison%2C%20James%22&s=1111311111&sa=Porter&r=2&sr=.
3. Pierre Poivre, *Voyages d'un Philosophe; ou, Observations sur les moeurs & les arts des peoples de L'Afrique, L'Asia & et de L'Amérique* (Maastricht: Jean-Edme Dufour & Philippe Roux, 1779). Poivre's chief efforts focused not on rice but on breaking for France the eighteenth-century Dutch monopoly of trade in nutmeg and cloves.
4. "From Thomas Jefferson to William Drayton, 30 July 1787," Founders Online, National Archives, http://founders.archives.gov/documents/Jefferson/01-11-02-0568; see also *The Papers of Thomas Jefferson*, vol. 11, *1 January–6 August 1787*, ed. Julian P. Boyd (Princeton: Princeton University Press, 1955), 644–650.
5. *North American Review* 18, no. 24 (January 1824): 140–157. White's book was also reviewed generously in the *Asiatic Journal and Monthly Register for British India and Its Dependencies* 18, no. 106 (October 1824): 377–385, and in the *Oriental Herald and Colonial Review*, early 1825.
6. Lt. John White, *History of a Voyage to the China Sea* (Boston: Wells and Lilly, 1823), 182.
7. See Susan Kepner, "Anna (and Margaret) and the King of Siam," *Crossroads* 10, no. 2 (1996): 1–32, and Susan Morgan, *Bombay Anna: The Real Story and Remarkable Adventures of the King and I Governess* (Berkeley and Los Angeles: University of California Press, 2008).
8. Balestier's embassy is described in the thirty-nine papers contained in "Message from the President of the United States [Fillmore] . . . information relating to the mission of Mr. Joseph Balestier . . . to Eastern Asia," Senate Ex. Doc. No. 38, 33rd Cong., 1st sess.

Chapter 6. Oman, Mozambique, Cape Town, Rio de Janeiro, and New York

1. Selected documents from the Reynolds Family Papers, from which this description is quoted, are held in Archives and Special Collections, Franklin and Marshall College, Lancaster, PA. The papers include William's letters to his father and his siblings written on board USS *Columbus*, USS *Boxer*, USS *Peacock*, USS *Vermont*, and USS *Tennessee*. Midshipman Reynolds (1815–1879) was transferred from *Boxer* to *Peacock* at his request in July 1833 before departing Angier.
2. Quoted in *Niles' Weekly Register* 51, no. 1,317 (December 24, 1836): 258.

Chapter 7. Commodore Kennedy, Captain Stribling, Lieutenant Commanding Campbell, and Surgeon Ruschenberger

1. Dickerson to Kennedy, April 2, 1835, M-149, Roll 23, NARA, College Park, MD.
2. Dickerson to Kennedy, April 2, 1835, Reel 2, Edmund Roberts Papers, Manuscript Division, Library of Congress, Washington, DC (hereafter cited as Roberts Papers, LOC).
3. C. U. Aitchison, ed., *A Collection of Treaties, Engagements and Sunnuds Relating to India and Neighboring Countries*, vol. 7 (Calcutta: O. T. Cutter Military Orphan Press, 1865), 210–211.
4. *Asiatic Journal and Monthly Register for British and Foreign India, China and Australasia* 15 (September–December 1834): pt. 2, 165.
5. Hermann Frederick Eilts, *Early American Diplomacy in the Near and Far East* (Washington, DC: New Academia, 2012), chap. 8. Ambassador Eilts (1922–2006), a retired officer of the U.S. Foreign Service, was director of Boston University's Center for International Relations when he researched and wrote this book.
6. Ibid., 167.
7. Gilbert Wesley, "Our Man in Zanzibar: Richard Waters, American Consul (1837–1845)," unpublished master's thesis, 2.

Chapter 8. Grounded!

1. Kennedy to Dickerson, Bombay, December 1, 1835, M125, Roll 212, Captains' Letters, 12/1–31, 1835, NARA, College Park, MD.
2. Roberts to his children from Bombay, October 22, 1835. Quoted with the kind permission of the Vaughan Homestead Foundation, Hallowell, Maine.
3. Kennedy to Dickerson, September 30, 1836, M147, Roll 21, Captains' Letters, RG 45, NARA, College Park, MD.
4. Low, *History of the Indian Navy (1613–1863)*, 2 vols. (London: Richard Bentley and Son, 1877), 5.

Chapter 9. Colombo, Batavia, and Bangkok

1. Ruschenberger, *Narrative of a Voyage Round the World*, 248.
2. Ibid., 347.

Chapter 10. Cochin China and Macao

1. Ruschenberger, *Narrative of a Voyage Round the World*, 340.
2. This and the following quotation are from W. Everett Scotten, "Sire, Their Nation Is Very Cunning . . . ," *American Foreign Service Journal* 12, no. 1 (January 1935): 45.
3. File no. 1939.004, Roberts Papers, New Hampshire.
4. No. MSS37960, Roberts Papers, LOC.
5. This was William Shepard Wetmore (1801–1862), the Vermont-born China trade merchant who three years earlier had established Wetmore and Company, eventually to become one of the largest trading houses in the East Indies.
6. Roberts Papers, New Hampshire.

Chapter 11. The Voyages Home

1. A good, short history of this remarkable antimissionary, antigovernment, and pro-Catholic newspaper is in Helen P. Hoyt, "Hawaii's First English Newspaper and Its Editor," *Annual Report of the Hawaii Historical Society*, 1955, 519.
2. George Tays, "Commodore Edmund B. Kennedy, U.S.N. vs. Governor Nicholas Gutierrez: An Incident of 1836," *California Historical Society Quarterly* 12, no. 2 (June 1933): 137–146.
3. See Lawrence A. Clayton, "Private Matters: The Origins and Nature of United States-Peruvian Relations, 1820–1850," *Americas* 42, no. 4 (April 1986): 377–417 for the history.

Epilogue

1. Charles I. Bevans, ed., *Treaties and Other International Agreements of the United States of American, 1776–1949*, Department of State Publication 8615 (Washington, DC: GPO, 1972), 1291–1293.
2. And possibly escorting two European women, hitchhiking from East of Suez to London on what would have been a one cushion bank shot. Fitchett, "Embassy Ahoy," 2–3. No documentation substantiates the presence of any women on board.
3. Rawson, *Life of Admiral Sir Harry Rawson*, 98.
4. Ibid., 105.
5. Wilkes' introduction to the first volume of his *Narrative of the United States Exploring Expedition* quotes Secretary Paulding's instructions in full, xxv–xxxii.
6. Statement of Charles Wilkes, 29th Cong., 1st sess., Document No. 475, August 5, 1846, 475–476.

SELECTED BIBLIOGRAPHY

PRIMARY SOURCES

NARA, RG 24. Records of the Bureau of Naval Personnel:
Logs of U.S. Naval Ships and Stations, 1801–1915. USS *Peacock*, 1832–37; USS *Boxer*, 1832–34; USS *Enterprise*, 1834–39.

NARA, RG 45. Records of the Naval Records Collection of the Office of Naval Records and Library:
Letters Received by the Secretary of the Navy from Commanders 1804–1886. NARA Microfilm Publication M147, Rolls 17–21, March 1832–December 1837.
Letters Sent by the Secretary of the Navy to Officers, 1798–1868. NARA Microfilm Publication M149, Rolls 20–27, August 1831–December 1837.
Registers of Letters Received, 1823–1886, April 1835–November 1837.
Entry 502, Box 206, MA 1836, and Box 418, OM 1836.

NARA, RG 52. Records of the Bureau of Medicine and Surgery:
Medical Journals of Ships, 1813–1910. USS *Peacock* Hospital Daily Journal, April 17, 1835–May 27, 1836; USS *Peacock* Medical Journal, April 17, 1835–August 29, 1836.

NARA, RG 59.2.1. General Records of the Department of State, Diplomatic Correspondence:
Records of and Relating to Special Agents, Missions, and Commissions, including Instructions, Dispatches, and Correspondence, 1794–1906.

Baylies, Francis. Papers. MSS12096. Manuscript Division, Library of Congress, Washington, DC. Baylies' diary is held by the Old Colony Historical Society, Taunton, MA.

Cadwalder, Henry [Midn.]. "Private Journal of a Cruze in the U.S. Schooner Enterprise, Lt. A. S. Campbell Esq. Commanding in the East Indias & China Seas." Unpublished ms., 1836.

Craven, Thomas T. [Lt.] "Journal of a Cruise on Board the U.S. Ship Peacock & Schooner Boxer." Unpublished ms., 1834.

Geisinger, David. Papers. MS 1283. Maryland Historical Society, Baltimore. The papers include Geisinger's handwritten journal, "Notes of a Cruise on board the United States Ship Peacock."

Reynolds Family Papers. MS6. Series II and V. Archives and Special Collections, Franklin and Marshall College, Lancaster, PA. The papers include Midn. William Reynolds' letters to his father while on board USS *Boxer* and USS *Peacock*.

Roberts, Edmund. Papers. MSS37960. Manuscript Division, Library of Congress, Washington, DC.

Ruschenberger, William S. W. Papers. 1826–1887. MS 629. East Carolina Manuscript Collection, J. Y. Joyner Library, East Carolina University, Greenville, NC.

Ticknor, Benajah. Papers. MS 495. Manuscripts and Archives, Yale University Library.

Woodbury, Levi. Family Papers. MSS 46326. Manuscript Division, Library of Congress, Washington, DC.

PERIOD SECONDARY SOURCES

Sources marked with an asterisk are available online in searchable form. Quotations not cited in the notes can be searched for in the parent digital text.

*Aitcheson, C. U., ed. *A Collection of Treaties, Engagements and Sunnuds Relating to India and Neighboring Countries*. Vol. 7. Calcutta: O. T. Cutter Military Orphan Press, 1865.

*Bate, R[obert] B[rettell]. *Admiralty Catalogue of Charts, Plans, Views and Sailing Directions, &c. Constructed Under the Orders of the Lords Commissioners of the Admiralty, for the Use of His Majesty's Navy*. Westminster, England: G. Hayden, 1830.

*A Citizen of the United States. *Symmes's Theory of Concentric Spheres: Demonstrating that the Earth Is Hollow, Habitable Within, and Widely Open about the Poles*. Cincinnati: Morgan, Lodge and Fisher, 1826.

*Cosenza, Mario Emilio, ed. *The Complete Journal of Townsend Harris*. New York: Doubleday, Doran, 1930.

Cotheal, Alexander I. "Treaty between the United States of America and the Sultân of Maskat: the Arabic Text." *Journal of the American Oriental Society* 4 (1854): 341, 343–356.

*Crawfurd, John. *Journal of an Embassy from the Governor-General of India to the Courts of Siam and Cochin China*. London: Henry Colburn, 1828.

*Downing, C. Toogood. *The Fan-Qui in China in 1836–7*. 3 vols. London: Henry Colburn, 1838.

*Earl, George Windsor. *Eastern Seas, or Voyages and Adventures in the Indian Archipelago in 1832–33–34 . . .* London: Wm. H. Allen, 1837.

*Ellis, Henry. *Journal of the Proceedings of the Late Embassy to China*. London: John Murray, 1817.

*Ellms, Charles, and Samuel N. Dickinson. *The Pirates Own Book; or, Authentic Narratives of the Lives, Exploits, and Executions of the Most Celebrated Sea Robbers: With Historical Sketches of the Joassamee, Spanish, Ladrone, West India, Malay, and Algerine Pirates*. Portland, ME: Sanborn & Carter, 1837.

*Force, Peter. *The National Calendar, and Annals of the United States for MDCCCXXXV*. Washington, DC: Fishey Thompson and Franck Taylor, 1835.

Gillis, James D. *Sailing Directions for the Pepper Ports of the West Coast of Sumatra, North of Anabaloo: To Accompany a Chart of That Coast*. Salem, MA: John M. Ives, 1834.

*Hawks, Francis L., with M. C. Perry. *Narrative of the Expedition of an American Squadron to the China Seas and Japan Performed in the Years 1852, 1853, and 1854, under the Command of Commodore M. C. Perry, United States Navy, by order of the Government of the United States*. 3 vols. Washington, DC: A. O. P. Nicholson, 1856.

*Hillard, Katharine, ed. *My Mother's Journal, a Young Lady's Diary of the Years Spent in Manila, Macao, and the Cape of Good Hope*. Boston: George H. Ellis, 1900.

*His Widow [Eliza Morrison], ed. *Memoirs of the Life and Labours of Robert Morrison, D.D.* 2 vols. London: Longman, Orme, Brown, Green, and Longmans, 1839.

*Homans, J. Smith, ed. *An Historical and Statistical Account of the Foreign Commerce of the United States, 1820–1856*. New York: G. P. Putnam, 1857.

*Horner, G. R. B. *Diseases and Injuries of Seamen, with Remarks on their Enlistment, Naval Hygiene, and the Duties of Medical Officers*. Philadelphia: Lippincott, Grambo, 1854.

*Horsburgh, James. *Horsburgh's East-India Pilot*. London: Kingsbury, Parbury, and Allen, 1824.

*[Hunter, William C.] An Old Resident. *The "Fan Kwae" at Canton Before Treaty Days, 1825–1844*. Reprint, Shanghai: Oriental Affairs, 1938.

**The India Directory; or, Directions for Sailing to and from the East Indies, China, Australia, and the Interjacent Ports of Africa and South America . . .* 5th ed. London: Wm. H. Allen, 1841.

*Low, Charles Rathbone. *History of the Indian Navy (1613–1863)*. 2 vols. London: Richard Bentley and Son, 1877.

*Luce, S. B. *Seamanship: Compiled from Various Authorities, for the Use of the U.S. Naval Academy*. New York: D. Van Nostrand, 1877.

*Malcom, Howard. *Travels in South-Eastern Asia, Embracing Hindustan, Malaya, Siam, and China, with Notices of Numerous Missionary Stations, and a Full Account of the Burman Empire, with Dissertations, Tables, etc.* 2 vols., 2nd ed. Boston: Gould, Kendall, and Lincoln, 1839.

*McLeod, John. "Narrative of a Voyage . . ." *Edinburgh Review, or Critical Journal: for October, 1838 . . . January, 1839* 68:46–75. Edinburgh: Ballantyne and Hughes, 1839.

———. *Narrative of a Voyage in His Majesty's Late Ship Alceste . . . with an Account of Her Shipwreck in the Straits of Gaspar.* Philadelphia: M. Cary and Son, 1818.

[National Medical Convention.] *The Pharmacopoeia of the United States of America*. Philadelphia: John Grigg, 1831.

*Naval Register for 1832. 22nd Cong., 1st sess. Document No. 461, December 28, 1831.

*Naval Register for 1833. 22nd Cong., 2nd sess. Document No. 461, January 2, 1832.

Noland, Edward J. "A Biographical Notice of W. S. W. Ruschenberger, M.D." *Proceedings of the Academy of Natural Sciences of Philadelphia* 47 (1985): 452–462.

*Owen, Capt. W. F. W., RN. *Narrative of Voyages to Explore the Shores of Africa, Arabia and Madagascar.* 2 vols. London: Richard Bentley, 1833.

Paine, Ralph D. "How Sumatra Pirates Took the 'Friendship.' " *Outing Magazine* 53 (October 1908–March 1909): 413–425.

**Register of All Officers and Agents, Civil, Military and Naval in the Service of the United States on the Thirtieth September 1835 . . .* Washington, DC: Blair & Rives, 1835.

*Reynolds, J. N. *Voyage of the United States Frigate Potomac, Under the Command of Commodore John Downes, During the Circumnavigation of the Globe, in the Years 1831, 1832, 1833, and 1844*. New York: Harper and Brothers, 1835.

*Roberts, Edmund. *Embassy to the Eastern Courts of Cochin-China, Siam, and Muscat; in the U.S. Sloop-of-War Peacock, David Geisinger, Commander, During the Years 1832–3–4*. New York: Harper & Brothers, 1837.

*Ruschenberger, William Samuel Waithman. *Narrative of a Voyage Round the World, During the Years 1835, 36, and 37; Including a Narrative of the Embassy to the Sultan of Muscat and the King of Siam*. 2 vols. London: Richard Bentley, 1838.

*Stewart, C. S. *A Visit to the South Seas in the U.S. Ship Vincennes, during the years 1829 and 1830; with scenes in Brazil, Peru, Manila, the Cape of*

Good Hope, and St. Helena. 2 vols. London: Henry Colburn and Richard Bentley, 1832.

U.S. Congress. "The Rules and Regulations . . . for the Government of the Navy of the United States." 23rd Cong., 1st sess. Document No. 20, December 23, 1833.

*———. "Statement of Charles Wilkes, a Commander in the U.S. Navy." 29th Cong., 1st sess. Document No. 475, August 5, 1846.

*Warriner, Francis. *Cruise of the United States Frigate Potomac Round the World During the Years 1831–1834*. New York: Leavitt, Lord, 1835.

*Wilkes, Charles, USN. *Narrative of the United States Exploring Expedition during the Years 1838, 1839, 1840, 1841, 1842*. 6 vols. Philadelphia: Lea and Blanchard, 1845–49.

*Wines, E. C. [Enoch Cobb]. *Two Years and a Half in the American Navy Comprising a Journal of a Cruise . . . on Board the U.S. Frigate Constellation, in the Years 1829, 1830, and 1831*. 2 vols. London: Richard Bentley, 1833.

*Wood, William Maxwell, USN. *Fankwei; or, the San Jacinto in the Seas of India, China, and Japan*. New York: Harper Brothers, 1859.

MODERN SECONDARY SOURCES

Ahmat, Sharom. "Joseph B. Balestier: The First American Consul in Singapore, 1833–1852." *Journal of the Malaysian Branch of the Royal Asiatic Society* 39, no. 2 (December 1966): 108–122.

Backhouse, E[dmund], and J[ohn] O. P. Band. *Annals and Memoirs of the Court of Peking*. Boston: Houghton Mifflin, 1914.

Belohlavek, John M. *"Let the Eagle Soar! The Foreign Policy of Andrew Jackson*. Lincoln: University of Nebraska Press, 1985.

Bennett, Norman R., and George E. Brooks Jr., eds. *New England Merchants in Africa*. Boston: Boston University Press, 1965.

Bernstein, William J. *A Splendid Exchange: How Trade Shaped the World*. New York: Atlantic Monthly Press, 2008.

Bevans, Charles I., ed. *Treaties and Other International Agreements of the United States of America, 1776–1949*. Department of State Publication 8615. Washington, DC: GPO, 1972.

Bickers, Robert A., ed. *Ritual and Diplomacy: The Macartney Mission to China, 1792–1794*. London: Wellsweep Press, 1993.

Bowers, Q. David. *The Rare Silver Dollars Dated 1804 and the Exciting Adventures of Edmund Roberts*. Wolfeboro, NH: Bowers and Medina Galleries, 1999.

Brooks, George E., Jr. *Yankee Traders Old Coasters and African Middlemen*. Boston: Boston University Press, 1970.

Cleaver, Anne Hoffman, and E. Jeffrey Stann, eds. *Voyage to the Southern Ocean: The Letters of Lieutenant William Reynolds*. Annapolis: Naval Institute Press, 1988.

Cole, Allan B. "Plans of Edmund Roberts for Negotiations in Nippon." *Monumenta Nipponica* 4, no. 2 (July 1941): 497–513.

Collis, Maurice. *Foreign Mud, Being an Account of the Opium Imbroglio at Canton in the 1830s and the Anglo-Chinese War that Followed*. London: Faber and Faber, 1946.

Dennett, Tyler. *Americans in Eastern Asia*. New York: Barnes & Noble, 1922.

Dolin, Eric Jay. *When America First Met China: An Exotic History of Tea, Drugs, and Money in the Age of Sail*. New York: Liveright, 2012.

Eilts, Hermann Francis. "Ahmad Bin Na'aman's Mission to the United States in 1840, the Voyage of Al-Sultanah to New York City." *Essex Institute Historical Collections* 98, no. 4 (October 1962): 219–277.

———. *Early American Diplomacy in the Near and Far East: The Diplomatic and Personal History of Edmund Q. Roberts (1784–1836)*. Washington, DC: New Academia, 2013.

———. *A Friendship Two Centuries Old: The United States and the Sultanate of Oman*. Washington, DC: Middle East Institute Center, 1990.

Fitchett, Joseph. "Embassy Ahoy." *Saudi Aramco World* 26, no. 5 (September/October 1975): 2–3.

Gilbert, Wesley. "Our Man in Zanzibar: Richard Waters, American Consul (1837–1845)." Unpublished master's thesis.

Goodrich-Hedrick, Karen, and John D. Hedrick. "Cruise of the United States Frigate Potomac." *Expedition* 14, no. 2 (1972): 27–33.

Hillard, Katharine, ed. *My Mother's Journal: A Young Lady's Diary of Five Years Spent in Manila, Macao, and the Cape of Good Hope*. Boston: George H. Ellis, 1900.

Hodges, Nan Powell. *Voyage of the Peacock: A Journal by Benajah Ticknor, Naval Surgeon*. Ann Arbor: University of Michigan Press, 1991.

Johnson, Robert Erwin. *Far China Station: The U.S. Navy in Asian Waters 1800–1898*. Annapolis: Naval Institute Press, 1979.

Keliher, Macabe. "Anglo-American Rivalry and the Origins of U.S. China Policy." *Diplomatic History* 31, no. 2 (April 2007): 227–257.

Lamas, Rosemarie W. N. *Everything in Style: Harriett Low's Macao*. Hong Kong: Hong Kong University Press, 2006.

Langley, Harold D. *A History of Medicine in the Early U.S. Navy*. Baltimore: Johns Hopkins University Press, 1995.

Livermore, Seward W. "Early Commercial and Consular Relations with the East Indies." *Pacific Historical Review* 15, no. 1 (March 1946): 31–58.

Long, David F. *Gold Braid and Foreign Relations: Diplomatic Activities of U.S. Naval Officers, 1798–1883*. Annapolis: Naval Institute Press, 1988.

Manning, William R., ed. *Diplomatic Correspondence of the United States, Inter American Affairs 1831–1860*. Washington, DC: Carnegie Endowment for International Peace, 1932.

McHale, Thomas R., and Mary C., eds. *Early American-Philippine Trade: The Journal of Nathaniel Bowditch in Manila, 1796*. New Haven: Yale University Press, 1962.

Meacham, Jon. *American Lion: Andrew Jackson in the White House*. New York: Random House, 2008.

Miller, Richard Hopkins. *The United States and Vietnam, 1787–1941*. Washington, DC: National Defense University Press, 1990.

Paullin, Charles Oscar. *Diplomatic Negotiations of American Naval Officers, 1778–1883*. Baltimore: Johns Hopkins Press, 1912.

———. "Early Naval Voyages to the Orient." *Proceedings* 37 (March–June): 239–275, 387–417. Annapolis: Naval Institute Press, 1911.

Peterson, Harold F. *Argentina and the United States, 1810–1960*. New York: State University of New York, 1964.

Philbrick, Nathaniel. *Sea of Glory: America's Voyage of Discovery: The U.S. Exploring Expedition, 1838–1842*. New York: Viking-Penguin, 2003.

Phillips, James Duncan. *Salem and the Indies*. Boston: Houghton Mifflin, 1947.

Rawson, Geoffrey. *Life of Admiral Sir Harry Rawson*. London: Edward Arnold, 1914.

Ride, Lindsay, and May Ride. *An East India Company Cemetery: Protestant Burials in Macao*. Hong Kong: Hong Kong University Press, 1996.

Schroeder, John H. *Shaping a Maritime Empire: The Commercial and Diplomatic Role of the American Navy, 1829–1861*. Westport, CT: Greenwood Press, 1985.

Smith, Gene A. *Thomas ap Catesby Jones: Commodore of Manifest Destiny*. Annapolis: Naval Institute Press, 2000.

Strauss, W. Patrick. "Preparing the Wilkes Expedition: A Study in Disorganization." *Pacific Historical Review* 28, no. 3 (August 1959): 221–232.

Van Dyke, Paul A., ed. *Americans and Macao, Trade, Smuggling, and Diplomacy*. Hong Kong: Hong Kong University Press, 2012.

CHARTS AND MAPS

Ackerman, Benjamin. "Plan of Portsmouth, N.H. Lithographed for the Directory." Portsmouth, NH: Joseph M. Edmonds, 1839.

Arrowsmith, John. "The World on Mercator's Projection." London: J. Arrowsmith, 1835. 1:70,000,000.

Aschemore, Samuel. "Carte de principales Rades & Marchés à poivre dans le partie Nord de la Côte Ouest de Sumatra." 1821 manuscript map of the pepper ports of western Sumatra between Analabou and Singkil by Samuel Ashmore, in French.

Berghaus, Heinrich. "Die Chinesische Küste: Der Provinz Kuang-tung, zu beiden Seiten des Meridians von Macao." In *Atlas von Asia*. Gotha: Justus Perthes, 1832–34. 1:460,000.

Boynton, G. W. "Boston." In *An Illustrated Atlas, Geographical, Statistical, and Historical of the United States and Adjacent Countries*. Boston: Thomas G. Bradford, 1838.

Disturnell, John, J. Calvin Smith, and T. R. Tanner. *Guide to the City of New York*. New York: Tanner & Disturnell, 1840.

Lambert, Samuel. "A New Chart of the West Coast of Sumatra from Analabo to Bankolle Drawn from the Latest Authority." Salem, MA: James R. Buffum, 1827.

Norie, John. *The Country Trade, or Free Mariner's Pilot Being a Set of New and Accurate, General and Particular, Charts . . .* London: J. W. Norie, 1833.

———. "Indian Ocean Ceylon South Coast." Admiralty Chart No. 813. London: Hydrographic Office, January 1858.

———. "India West Coast Bombay Harbour." Admiralty Chart No. 2621. London: Hydrographic Office, September 1858. 1:48,000.

———. "Map of the City of Portsmouth from Original Surveys under the Direction of H. F. Walling, Civil Engineer." [Philadelphia]: C. W. Brewster, 1850. 1:3,960.

INDEX

Page references in italics indicate illustrative material and material in captions.

ABOUT THE AUTHOR

Andrew Jampoler lives in the Lost Corner of Loudoun County, Virginia with his wife, Susan, a geographer and cartographer. He is an alumnus of Columbia College and the School of International and Public Affairs, both of Columbia University, in New York City, and of the U.S. State Department Foreign Service Institute's School of Language Study.

During nearly twenty-five years on active duty in the U.S. Navy, Jampoler served on the personal staffs of the chief of naval operations, the secretary of defense, and the commander in chief of the Pacific Fleet. He also commanded a land-based maritime patrol aircraft squadron and an air station. Later he was a senior sales and marketing executive with German and American aerospace companies.

Jampoler has been researching and writing non-fiction for fifteen years. His first book, *Adak: The Rescue of Alfa Foxtrot 586*, was the story of a navy patrol aircraft ditching off Soviet Kamchatka in October 1978. A review in the *Wall Street Journal* described the book as "an adventure story to rival the best you've ever read." *Adak* later won Jampoler recognition as the Naval Institute Press' author of the year. His sixth book, *Congo: The Miserable Expeditions and Dreadful Death of Lt. Emory Taunt*, told the story of the United States and the Congo in the late nineteenth century through the biography of the first resident American diplomat in West Africa, a deeply troubled former navy officer. This book is his seventh.

Jampoler has given illustrated presentations on the subjects of his books, articles, and research to audiences at the Library of Congress, the National Archives, at the Smithsonian Institution and other museums in the United States and abroad, at embassies and academic symposia, in book stores, and on board cruise ships sailing the oceans of the world.

He can be reached through his website, www.jampoler.com.

The Naval Institute Press is the book-publishing arm of the U.S. Naval Institute, a private, nonprofit, membership society for sea service professionals and others who share an interest in naval and maritime affairs. Established in 1873 at the U.S. Naval Academy in Annapolis, Maryland, where its offices remain today, the Naval Institute has members worldwide.

Members of the Naval Institute support the education programs of the society and receive the influential monthly magazine *Proceedings* or the colorful bimonthly magazine *Naval History* and discounts on fine nautical prints and on ship and aircraft photos. They also have access to the transcripts of the Institute's Oral History Program and get discounted admission to any of the Institute-sponsored seminars offered around the country.

The Naval Institute's book-publishing program, begun in 1898 with basic guides to naval practices, has broadened its scope to include books of more general interest. Now the Naval Institute Press publishes about seventy titles each year, ranging from how-to books on boating and navigation to battle histories, biographies, ship and aircraft guides, and novels. Institute members receive significant discounts on the Press's more than eight hundred books in print.

Full-time students are eligible for special half-price membership rates. Life memberships are also available.

For a free catalog describing Naval Institute Press books currently available, and for further information about joining the U.S. Naval Institute, please write to:

Member Services
U.S. Naval Institute
291 Wood Road
Annapolis, MD 21402-5034
Telephone: (800) 233-8764
Fax: (410) 571-1703
Web address: www.usni.org

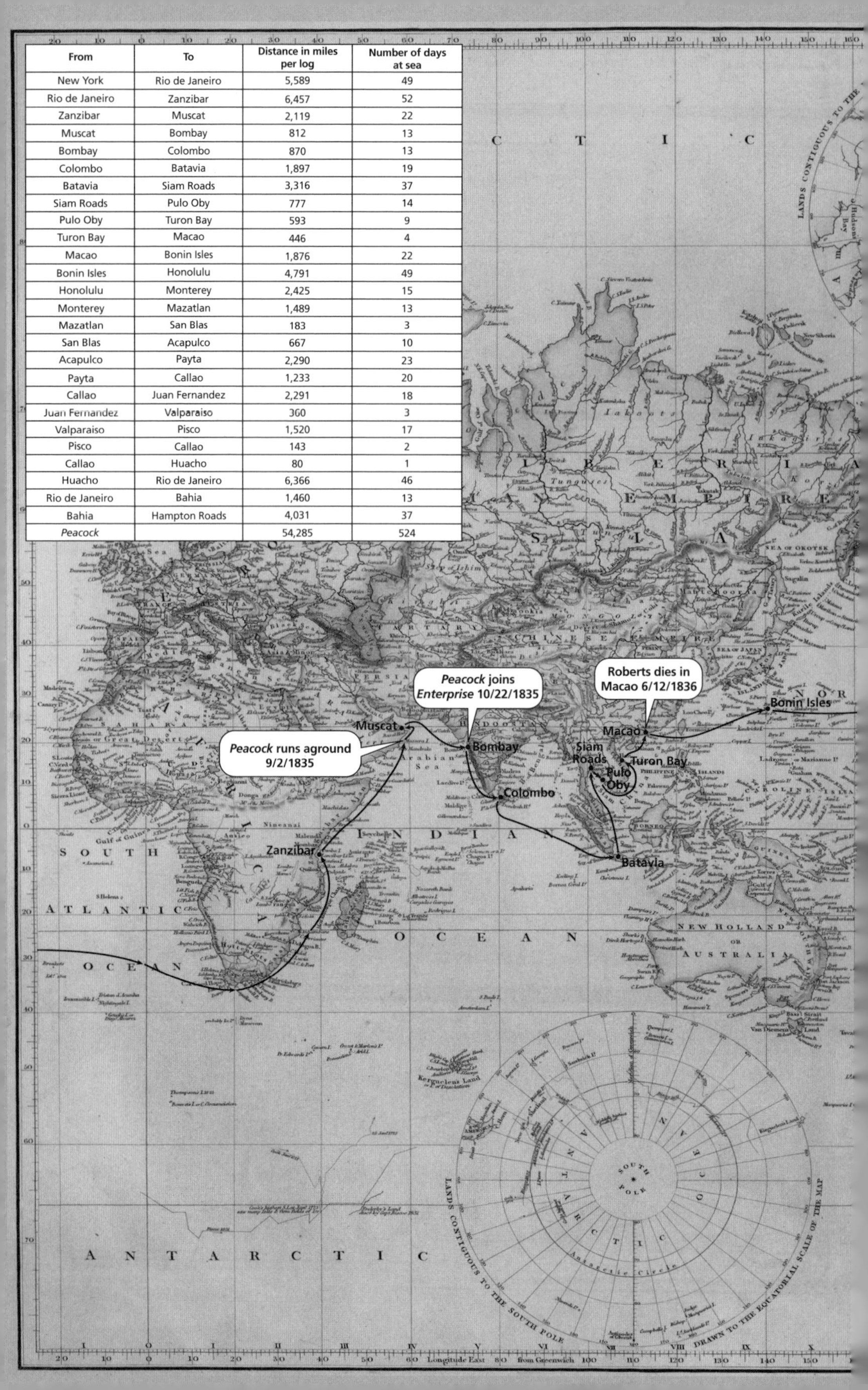

From	To	Distance in miles per log	Number of days at sea
New York	Rio de Janeiro	5,589	49
Rio de Janeiro	Zanzibar	6,457	52
Zanzibar	Muscat	2,119	22
Muscat	Bombay	812	13
Bombay	Colombo	870	13
Colombo	Batavia	1,897	19
Batavia	Siam Roads	3,316	37
Siam Roads	Pulo Oby	777	14
Pulo Oby	Turon Bay	593	9
Turon Bay	Macao	446	4
Macao	Bonin Isles	1,876	22
Bonin Isles	Honolulu	4,791	49
Honolulu	Monterey	2,425	15
Monterey	Mazatlan	1,489	13
Mazatlan	San Blas	183	3
San Blas	Acapulco	667	10
Acapulco	Payta	2,290	23
Payta	Callao	1,233	20
Callao	Juan Fernandez	2,291	18
Juan Fernandez	Valparaiso	360	3
Valparaiso	Pisco	1,520	17
Pisco	Callao	143	2
Callao	Huacho	80	1
Huacho	Rio de Janeiro	6,366	46
Rio de Janeiro	Bahia	1,460	13
Bahia	Hampton Roads	4,031	37
Peacock		54,285	524